She Can Coach!

Cecile Reynaud, PhD

Editor

HUMAN KINETICS

Library of Congress Cataloging-in-Publication Data

She can coach! / Cecile Reynaud, editor.
    p.   cm.
  Includes index.
  ISBN 0-7360-5232-1 (soft cover)
  1. Coaching (Athletics)   I. Reynaud, Cecile, 1953-
  GV711.S53   2005
  796'.07'7--dc22

                                        2004018975

ISBN: 0-7360-5232-1

The Web addresses cited in this text were current as of October 2004, unless otherwise noted.

Acquisitions Editor: Jana Hunter; **Developmental Editor:** Susanna Blalock; **Assistant Editor:** Cory Weber; **Copyeditor:** Cheryl Ossola; **Indexer:** Bobbi Swanson; **Graphic Designer:** Robert Reuther; **Graphic Artist:** Sandra Meier; **Photo Manager:** Dan Wendt; **Cover Designer:** Keith Blomberg; **Photographers (cover):** Photo of Pat Summitt courtesy of the University of Tennessee, photo of Mary Wise courtesy of the University of Florida, photo of Margie Wright courtesy of Fresno State University; **Printer:** Versa Press

Human Kinetics books are available at special discounts for bulk purchase. Special editions or book excerpts can also be created to specification. For details, contact the Special Sales Manager at Human Kinetics.

Printed in the United States of America

10   9   8   7   6   5   4   3   2   1

Human Kinetics
Web site: www.HumanKinetics.com

United States: Human Kinetics
P.O. Box 5076
Champaign, IL 61825-5076
800-747-4457
e-mail: humank@hkusa.com

Canada: Human Kinetics
475 Devonshire Road Unit 100
Windsor, ON N8Y 2L5
800-465-7301 (in Canada only)
e-mail: orders@hkcanada.com

Europe: Human Kinetics
107 Bradford Road
Stanningley
Leeds LS28 6AT, United Kingdom
+44 (0) 113 255 5665
e-mail: hk@hkeurope.com

Australia: Human Kinetics
57A Price Avenue
Lower Mitcham, South Australia 5062
08 8277 1555
e-mail: liaw@hkaustralia.com

New Zealand: Human Kinetics
Division of Sports Distributors NZ Ltd.
P.O. Box 300 226 Albany
North Shore City
Auckland
0064 9 448 1207
e-mail: blairc@hknewz.com

She
Can
Coach!

Contents

Preface **vii**

PART I   Professional Foundation and Conduct *1*

Chapter 1   Coaching Philosophy **3**
Beth Anders

Chapter 2   Ethics **13**
JoAnne Graf

Chapter 3   Professionalism **27**
Margie Wright

Chapter 4   Leadership **37**
Marcia McDermott

Chapter 5   Competitiveness **51**
Mary Wise

PART II   Personal Investment and Self-Direction *61*

Chapter 6   Motivation **63**
Nell Fortner

Chapter 7   Decision Making **73**
Jan Harville

Chapter 8   Self-Discipline **87**
Mary Jo Peppler

Chapter 9   Focus **101**
Lorene Ramsey

Chapter 10   Stress Management **113**
Jill Sterkel

PART III   *Program Implementation and Management* *123*

Chapter 11   Organizational Skills **125**
Diane Davey

Chapter 12   Staff Management and Mentoring .**137**
Pat Summitt

Chapter 13   The Assistant Coach's Role **155**
Lele Forood

Chapter 14   Team Management **165**
Dorothy Gaters

Chapter 15   Athlete Recruitment **177**
Terry Crawford

PART IV   *Relationship Building and Promotional Activities* ... *189*

Chapter 16   Coach–Athlete Relations **191**
Kim Kincer

Chapter 17   Team Cohesion **203**
Sharon Pfluger

Chapter 18   Parent Relations **217**
Joan Powell

Chapter 19   Marketing and Media **231**
Sarah Patterson

Chapter 20   Networking **245**
Amy Ruley

Index **253**   •   About the Editor **259**
About the Contributors **261**

Preface

My obsession with sports first began in elementary school, and it *really* came to light in junior high. I played every sport available, and I knew I wanted sports to be a fixture in my life. After a high school career filled with basketball and field hockey, softball and volleyball, I continued my sports-minded education at Southwest Missouri State—before Title IX and scholarships for women—where I studied physical education while playing field hockey and volleyball.

My involvement and growth in athletics can be traced to three women. First, there is my mom. Her support was unwavering, and it encouraged me to fully pursue my dreams. Second and third are my former college volleyball coaches, Mary Jo Wynn and Linda Dollar, who were the best possible role models as I prepared to enter the profession. They were highly competitive and well respected around the country, and they taught me that working hard would pay off, but that it was important to also have fun doing it. All three women were instrumental in my development as a coach.

Throughout my coaching career, which includes one year at the high school level and 26 years as head volleyball coach at Florida State University, I searched for information and ideas I thought would help me become a more successful coach. I gradually began to realize that although there were plenty of female mentors who were happy to share their knowledge and wisdom in person, almost all coaching books were authored by men with backgrounds in football or basketball. Although their written advice and insights were useful, they didn't speak directly to the experiences I faced as a female coach coaching female athletes.

That void in literature became even more evident a few years ago. While teaching a class titled "Principles and Problems in Coaching," I gave an assignment to read a book written by a coach. When no one in the class of more than 60 students came up with a book written by a female coach, the idea for this project came to mind.

She Can Coach! is a long-overdue book for female coaches of all sports, for women who are preparing to coach, for women considering the profession, and even for male coaches, who can also benefit from such expertise and perspective. Girls' participation in high school athletics has increased by 800 percent since 1970, and participation by females at the college level has quadrupled during that time. However, the percentage of female teams coached by women has dropped from 90 percent in 1972 to 44 percent in 2000.

Our society encourages girls and women to compete in athletics and provides enlightening messages to help them experience the joys, benefits, rewards, and challenges that come with competition; now we need to do the same for females who are in, entering, or considering the coaching profession so that they are better prepared to lead future athletes. Understanding the profession from the successful female coach's point of view can only help further those efforts.

She Can Coach! does just that. This resource—the only of its kind—features the knowledge, experience, and approaches of many of the top female coaches in a variety of sports. These highly successful women share how they have grown into their roles and learned to handle them with proficiency. Their insight relates uniquely to all female coaches at all levels of all sports.

Rather than focusing on techniques, tactics, drills, and conditioning, *She Can Coach!* covers subjects that relate to professional foundation and conduct, personal investment and growth, program implementation and management, and relationship building and salesmanship. The skills and topics in these 20 chapters lay the foundation for achieving long-term success and having a positive influence.

Some of the topics in this book deal with challenges that face both women coaches and their male colleagues—challenges such as self-discipline, motivation, and recruiting—but there are also issues addressed that specifically face women in coaching. You will find the methods these top women have used can be implemented in your own programs, increasing your opportunity to become even more successful as a coach while your athletes enjoy the process.

The dynamic list of contributors represents 13 sports of various levels of competition and different regions of the country. Their accomplishments could fill an entire book, but their reason for contributing to this project is to help promote the coaching profession as a positive career choice for women and girls and to emphasize the right way to coach. Their willingness to share their wisdom is but one way they are role models for us all.

My goal in collecting this wisdom is to empower women who already coach and those who are entering the field to be more confident in their pursuit of greatness. The profession needs not only more female coaches—we need more and *better* female coaches who can excel in their roles and encourage other women to follow in their footsteps.

If you already are coaching and mentoring, congratulations and thank you. Glean from this book a pointer or two that will help you be an even better coach next season. If you are deciding whether to continue coaching or begin coaching, this book might just give you the perspective and motivation you need to become the enthusiastic and effective coach so many athletes need and deserve. Either way, please enjoy reading the pages that follow and gaining great ideas from some of our country's most successful female coaches.

Professional Foundation and Conduct

1

Coaching Philosophy

Define an approach to your sport
that you can believe in,
with an emphasis on athlete development

Beth Anders

I have always loved sports. When I was growing up I loved to play anything that involved a ball. It didn't matter what it was—tennis, basketball, or golf. Then, in college, I played field hockey, basketball, lacrosse, softball, and squash and coached during the summers.

I started developing my coaching philosophy in my first full-time coaching position at Perkiomen Valley in Collegeville, Pennsylvania, where I went from coaching junior high to coaching high school. Then in 1980 the U.S. field hockey team, which I was on, qualified for the Olympic Games. I was preparing to go to Moscow as a player on the national team before the U.S. boycott of the Olympics came through. My superintendent told me that I had to choose between playing in the Olympics and teaching, because the team was going to miss the last two weeks of school. It was an easy decision for me: I was going to play.

Later, a field hockey head coach position opened at Old Dominion University; when I interviewed for it I said that it was very important to me to continue to play as well as coach. They didn't have a problem with that; in fact, since I began coaching there in August 1980, the administration has also allowed me to take sabbaticals in order to coach the national team.

Purpose of a Coaching Philosophy

A coaching philosophy consists of beliefs or principles that guide a coach's actions. Those fundamental values function as the base of the philosophy, and they should guide the coach every day, in every decision she makes. A coach's philosophy is more apparent through her actions than through her words. You cannot fake your philosophy; what you consider most important will eventually become evident through your behavior, regardless of your stated philosophy, goals, or priorities. Daily actions and behaviors will betray you if you claim to espouse one set of beliefs yet clearly hold others more important.

The three cornerstones of my coaching philosophy are to be consistent in what I expect of my players, to be as prepared as possible so that I can perform as well as possible, and to continue to learn as much as I can about the players and the game. If, instead, I were to send mixed messages to my players, fail to organize and ready myself and my team to meet future challenges, and disengage myself emotionally from my players' lives and mentally from gaining new knowledge about the game, I would lose the respect of anyone paying attention.

A coaching philosophy provides perspective by helping coaches identify and remember what is important to them. Keeping that philosophy intact is as important during the good times as it is during the bad times. It may seem like it would be easy to remember it during the good times, when things go smoothly. But after tasting success, a coach may become intoxicated with the high that comes with victory and accomplishment and thus be tempted to break from any part of her philosophy that she perceives is holding the team back. In bad times, the same may happen—the lack of success or presence of challenges may cause coaches to rationalize behavior that isn't consistent with their values. Either way, through good times and bad, sticking to your philosophy allows you to keep balance in your life.

> The three cornerstones of my coaching philosophy are to be consistent in what I expect of my players, to be as prepared as possible so that I can perform as well as possible, and to continue to learn as much as I can about the players and the game.

During my first year of coaching, my basketball team at Perkiomen Valley High School struggled through a losing season. One response to our lack of success could have been to berate the players and focus on winning games. But we kept working on the fundamentals and concentrating on doing our best. The next year we had a winning season and continued on to the state playoffs.

A sound coaching philosophy helps a coach formulate a strategy. Without one, she may feel uncertain about her course of action; that lack of conviction will lead to inconsistent behavior, which in turn will result in chaotic conditions or a lack of direction for the team or program. Having an established philosophy removes any doubt about decisions regarding training rules, style of play, discipline, codes of conduct, competitive outlook, or short- and long-term objectives.

Finally, a philosophy helps a coach develop a plan or process by which to run her program, which is necessary for success. Not only does she need to have a plan, but the people involved in her program—the athletes, assistants, and other staff—need to recognize, understand, and buy into it. Their acceptance enables the coach to build consistently on the plan, allowing for growth of the individuals, team, and program.

More important than simply providing a clear picture of the process, the plan demonstrates that you, the coach, have a vision. You have to articulate that vision until everyone understands your mission, goals, and expectations. Writing down the plan or process is important; everyone needs to look in the same direction and see the same big picture. They must see it not only on paper but also in their minds so that they understand it. Ideally, it is also in their hearts!

Developing a Coaching Philosophy

Without question, I believe that a person's parents or guardians give them a foundation for how they coach. Most of my philosophy comes from my parents. Their motto was "Always do the best you can!" They also gave me good morals and ethics. They taught me that there is a right way and a wrong way, which is an important concept to remember as you coach athletes.

Throughout your life, your coaches influence you and help in the development of your coaching philosophy in some way. For example, my high school field hockey and lacrosse coach, Elizabeth (Libby) Williams, had a tremendous sense of humor but was very demanding. She cared about her players, and although she didn't show it that much, we knew it. Libby taught me how to be demanding and still keep my sense of humor, that being demanding was a way of showing that you care about your players. My college field hockey, basketball, and softball coach was Eleanor Snell. She let us make our own decisions while she guided us and allowed us to be our own person. I try to use that method with my teams. Marge Watson, my lacrosse coach in college, showed me how important it was to believe in somebody. I could fail big time and she would still believe in me; she stayed with us through the good and bad times.

If you ever want to get a room of coaches quiet, ask them, "What is your coaching philosophy?" When you discuss your philosophy you reveal your beliefs, values, and outlook. To develop a philosophy, you need to know yourself as well as your values and beliefs. Most people can gain this understanding by looking at their life experiences and seeing what was consistently important to them and what they stand for. The foundation of a coaching philosophy stays the same over time, but each year's players and unique situations lead you to tweak it a little bit. My players have made me a better coach, and I have learned a great deal from them over the years.

Although coaches constantly modify the process of handling athletes, one thing remains constant: the foundation of their philosophy. As a longtime coach, I must change with the times. A philosophy is an ongoing, lifelong process, but my basic values will not change. My coaching philosophy can be summed up with the following formula:

Why + How = Journey or process

Two short words—"why" and "how"—are important to me. *Why* do you do something? Because you love it and believe in what you are doing. You have genuine enthusiasm or passion for the game. There is no false behavior! *How* do you do something? You attack a situation and always give the best you are capable of performing. You accept challenges, respect others, and are prepared.

In my role as a coach, I like to refer to several quotes:

- "Do what is right, do the best you can, and treat others like you want to be treated."—Lou Holtz
- "First we will be best, then we will be first."—Lou Holtz
- "You win not by chance, but by preparation."—Roger Maris

Define an approach to your sport that you believe in, with emphasis on athlete development.

- "The will to win is not nearly as important as the will to prepare to win."—Bobby Knight
- "The heart does not know skill, does not know technique; nor does it know systems. The heart does know how to play. The heart will *win*."—Anson Dorrance, women's soccer coach, University of North Carolina

I will always be a teacher who demands the best of the *why* and *how* from each player, but I will also make sure that the demands are realistic. I push my players to do their best, but I would never ask them to do something they are physically unable to do. Players usually do not realize what they are capable of achieving. As a coach, you must be aware of their abilities and limitations.

Another facet of my coaching philosophy is that pride is very important. Fight and find a way! When you play with me you learn to never give up. You will fight for and earn everything you get. Players should focus on performance and on becoming the best person and the best athlete they can be. They need to get better one step at a time. The end result will come on its own, just as winning and losing will occur on their own. I focus on performance. I teach information, knowledge, and understanding so that players can make decisions that enhance performance.

Player Behaviors

All groups have leaders and followers. In sports, the coach is the first leader. Players must believe in the direction of the program and be excellent followers. In time, others will develop as leaders and followers; some need to excel as leaders and others need to be good followers.

Leaders should have ambition, confidence, courage, intelligence, responsibility, creativity, and empathy. They must be trustworthy and demonstrate selflessness; that is, they must be above personal gains and considerations. Leaders place the team and organization first, ahead of their personal goals and needs, at all times, not merely when it is convenient or when they think it will make them look good. Leaders also follow rules and standards. Leadership is a process; its essence is motivating people toward achievement of shared goals.

Four important markers characterize followers. First, they are good listeners. Second, they are self-motivated and have a sense of purpose and self-worth. For them, the job well done is its own reward; they do not look for shortcuts or blame someone else. If they feel there is a point of discussion that could benefit the group, they bring it forward. Third, they must have a sense of belonging to a group, a feeling that makes each individual and thus the team stronger. In a sense, they must surrender and commit to practicing the values of the team or group. Finally, good followers understand the importance of self-discipline and time-management skills.

I have identified eight specific player behaviors or actions that work within my philosophy and demonstrate what I stand for. They are what make the formula of "why + how = journey" work.

Part of any coaching philosophy encompasses preparing the team for the season, which takes hard work and direction. All eight of these player behaviors are important to my coaching philosophy, so coaching the players to succeed in these areas is essential:

1. Accept responsibility and be accountable for your actions and learning. All players have responsibilities, and they are expected to recognize and meet the responsibilities of their role by being prepared. Responsibility and accountability mean that each of us takes the first step. Start being responsible for yourself, and take quiet pride in what you and your teammates do. You must pull your own weight because no one is more important than anyone else. Players must learn to be responsible and accountable for themselves.

2. Respect other players and expect respect in return. Respect the efforts and thoughts of others, and accept them for who they are and the effort they give. Learn to demand respect from yourself and others.

3. Demonstrate trust, honesty, and loyalty. These three characteristics require unconditional giving. Saying what you feel is being honest and trusting so that all can come together for the good of the team.

4. Contribute to an atmosphere with shared purpose. No one is more important than someone else. Everyone has a responsibility to the team and a role on the team. With the group, individuals develop purpose and objectives. Everyone shares the purpose.

5. Engage in healthy competition. Go hard and challenge every situation you encounter, without breaking rules or cheating. You have a right to earn whatever you get or else there is no reason to go after something. You want to earn everything that you achieve.

6. Keep things in perspective! *We can do this.* This game is fun and the challenges are great! We must not blow things out of perspective. People are the most important factor, therefore enjoying what you do and the people with whom you choose to accomplish your goals is most important.

7. Try to control only those things you can control. Do what you are capable of doing, and play within your abilities. *Be yourself.*

8. Take care of yourself, both mentally and physically. Physically, do the basics with regard to proper nutrition and enough water, rest, and exercise. Mentally, strive for balance. Give yourself a rest. Pay attention to your feelings, and deal with them. Keep things in perspective. *Have fun.*

Teaching Through Organization and Understanding

When organizing themselves to teach a game, coaches must enable their players to understand it. I suggest including the following four important components in your daily plans.

Develop a common language. A uniform method of communication (verbal and nonverbal) is important since you must play as a team with a common language. Clear communication enhances learning. To perform well, players must communicate with each other and with the coach. This is possible with a common language. Thinking and performing together results in a team achievement of fun! Communication is the key to successful coach–athlete and teammate interaction.

Teach decision making and problem solving. Players need the ability to make decisions or problem solve, and they must all do so with the same knowledge or information. Decisions are made not only individually but also with others. The acquisition of decision-making skills is vital to any learning process. In order for players to make good decisions, they must be exposed to the information that will justify those decisions. Problem solving is a decision-making system in which people can grow only if given the opportunity. The more they do it, the more they learn. Therefore players need to have roles or responsibilities and be given experiences to practice problem solving. I teach field hockey knowledge by emphasizing players' responsibilities and roles in practice settings first.

Simplify situations. Coaches need to simplify understanding of the game or approach different situations with a similar understanding. For example, action equals reaction in a game; hopefully this concept creates better understanding by simplifying a game that is ever-changing . People in every role need to know all the information so that everyone can be thinking together.

Have fun. Enjoy the game—it's fun! Teach in an enjoyable manner and get the players to believe in themselves, each other, and the coaches. Making decisions is fun for the players, and it becomes even more fun when they share that belief.

Applying Your Philosophy

In 1992 I had a dominating field hockey team at Old Dominion University that had won more than 60 games in a row. We were going to be in the national championship game on a field that was definitely an equalizer—it was bumpy and in poor shape. The other team had as good a chance of winning as we did because of the terrible field conditions.

At a meeting the night before the game, the team appeared ready to go. I couldn't tell these players one more thing; the only thing left to do was to get them on the field to play. At this point they probably could make better decisions than I could because they were playing the game. So I thought, "What do I say and do?" I went right back to my philosophy because I could see that they were nervous and scared—they were just kids. So I looked at them and said, "What happens tomorrow won't make a difference in your lives. But what will make a difference in your lives is *how* you play this game and *why*. That will make a difference forever!"

Those two words—"how" and "why"—are the key of my philosophy. I don't believe a win or loss will make or break your life, but I do believe that *how you play* and *why you play* will. Our team dominated the other team and won the national championship , and it was exciting for me to watch. I appreciated and respected what they did and *how* and *why* they played so hard.

Although I have always stressed the importance of having fun to my teams, sometimes even I have to be reminded. In 2000, the Old Dominion University field hockey team had not won a national championship in a few years, so there was some pressure to win. I wanted to see these special people win.

A couple of weeks before the NCAA championship, the team captains came to me asking to talk. They said they needed to have fun; when I asked them what they meant, they stated that I had been pushing them too hard. They said they needed to have fun at practice and laugh once in a while, and they were right. I wanted so much for them to win a national championship that I had forgotten about the fun part. So for the next two weeks we laughed and had a good time, but we still got everything done that we had to do to prepare to be successful. They won, and the credit went to those captains for coming forward and reminding me of the importance of fun!

> I don't believe a win or loss will make or break your life, but I do believe that *how you play* and *why you play* will.

Coaches' hearts are in the right place, because they try to do right by their players. But a common mistake is getting too focused and forgetting what is important. You have to have a passion for the game and enjoy it. You need a staff and good team captains who will help you remember to have fun.

When I coached the national field hockey team in 1993 the team had not qualified for the top competition for several years, so I focused on getting them back in it. We were trying to earn a berth to qualify for the World Cup. I prepared and prepared and prepared them—and then the last three days before we played I sent the team up to the Pocono Mountains with our manager to relax. My staff and I stayed at the qualifying tournament to watch all the teams play. I even watched them practice and scrimmage, taking extensive notes. I knew exactly what each player was going to do in every situation.

Winning that game was all about preparation. The tied game to qualify for the World Cup came down to strokes. I had watched the other team a few times, so I told the goalkeeper where each player would shoot. Their two players both took the shots I had told our goalkeeper to anticipate. One of the lessons I learned from my parents was that you never quit; you just keep preparing. It is always up to the coach to put her players in a place to win—then they have to win it for themselves.

I have often told my teams to prepare with a passion—then believe in this anonymous quote: "When you come to the edge of all the light you know and are about to step off into the darkness, the unknown, faith is believing that one of two things will happen: There will be something solid to stand on, or you will be taught how to fly."

2

Ethics

*Act virtuously, operating within
both the letter and spirit of the rules*

JoAnne Graf

If there is a buzzword in intercollegiate athletics at the present time, it is "ethics." The National Collegiate Athletic Association (NCAA) president, Myles Brand, made it clear soon after his appointment in 2003 that reform would be integral to his tenure. Concern over a lack of ethical behavior by the NCAA men's basketball coaches reached such a high level that the National Association of Basketball Coaches (NABC) called a mandatory meeting prior to the 2003-04 season to discuss the problem. A rash of recent incidents involving coaches, players, athletic administrators, and university presidents makes it clear that unethical behavior—ranging from academic fraud to improper gifts to questionable personal behavior—is on the rise, placing sports in a bad light.

I have been fortunate to work with ethical people for most of my college and professional life. During my junior year at Florida State University I decided that marine biology consisted of more lab work than I desired. I enjoyed sports and working with people, so coaching seemed to be a natural fit. I also considered it a plus to be able to work outside and wear shorts and warm-ups to work as opposed to dresses and heels. After graduating with a marine biology major and minors in criminology and coaching, I worked for the Department of Corrections to earn money for graduate school.

I was accepted to graduate school at the University of North Carolina at Greensboro and became the head men's and women's swimming and diving coach and the assistant softball coach. The wonderful faculty and athletes provided me with positive experiences that fueled my desire to continue coaching. After earning a master's degree in sports psychology, I was hired as the first full-time softball coach at Florida State University. Coming back to my alma mater was exciting, and I have been there ever since, adding to my credentials a doctorate degree in athletic administration in the '90s.

Is a Lack of Ethics the New Norm?

Unethical behavior certainly is not restricted to athletics, as the numerous examples of alleged financial impropriety by CEOs of major companies in the business world prove. In fact, it is becoming the norm rather than the exception.

Today's society seems to value winning over the teaching and use of ethical standards. Players who violate team rules are often handed minor punishments rather than game suspensions. Coaches have bonuses for winning (but not for teaching positive behavior) built into their contracts, making it potentially harmful to them to suspend a player from competing. (Do administrators have a code of ethics? If a coach suspends her best player because of team-rule violations, does she then get fired if her team doesn't win a certain number of games, or does the administration back her stand?) I have always believed that ethics starts from the top. Good coaches, often with a one-year contract, frequently aren't backed up when they try to discipline players. Coaches are asked to keep a certain number of players on the roster to satisfy gender-equity numbers even though some players really aren't a part of the program. That sends a message to the coach that ethics are not the administration's top priority.

Make sure you know whom you are working for and what their values are. Your superiors may say they want you to produce quality people, but you had better do your homework to find out if in truth they only want you to win. Also, if your organization hires a new president, athletic director, assistant coach, or a principal, you need to be prepared for the ideals and goals they bring to the position.

Understanding Ethics

To begin a discussion on ethics, we must first define it. For the purposes of this chapter, we define ethics as "that which determines proper and improper conduct." Each person's ethical standards are determined by their value system. In their book *Ethics in Sport Management,* Joy Theresa DeSensi and Danny Rosenberg (1996) state that "ethical decisions may relate to a person's conduct in terms of what an individual should or should not do, or to something that is either valued or not valued."

Any organized group—from college athletics to businesses to community associations—determines the level of ethical standards that it will follow, whether its members realize it or not. Some spell it out clearly; for others it is unwritten. Some groups abide by very high ethical standards; others seem to have no regard for them.

In his book *There's No Such Thing As "Business" Ethics* (2003), John C. Maxwell proposes that two important points in achieving ethical behavior are the presence of a standard and the will to follow that standard. An ethical outlook is developed over one's lifetime. Parents influence the ethical value systems their children develop. Children refine this development through contact with their peers and teachers. In athletics, coaches and administrators are important role models in the development of ethical standards. The resolve to behave ethically is reinforced through both positive and negative behavior. However, even ethical people can blur the lines when their environment supports and encourages unethical behavior. Maintaining ethical standards in such an environment is a challenge that many people in athletics face today.

Rules and Standards

Within a collegiate athletic department, employees have personal ethical standards that affect their decision making. The department itself has an organizational ethical standard that can also affect its employees' actions. This organizational culture is set by the standards of those at the top. However, if

Code of Ethics for Coaches

Most sport governing bodies have a code of ethics for coaches that can be found on their organization's Web site. For instance, the code of ethics for the American Football Coaches Association (AFCA) is as follows:

The ultimate success of the principles and standards of this Code depends on those for whom it has been established—the football coaches. The welfare of the game depends on how the coaches live up to the spirit and letter of ethical conduct and how the coaches remain ever mindful of the high trust and confidence placed in them by their players. The Code of Ethics has been developed to protect and promote the best interests of the game and the coaching profession. Its primary purpose is to clarify and distinguish ethical and approved professional practices from those considered detrimental to the public.

The United States Olympic Committee (USOC) goes into great detail in its published Coaching Code of Ethics:

This Code is intended to provide both the general principles and the decision rules to cover most situations encountered by coaches. It has as its primary goal the welfare and protection of the individual and groups with whom coaches work. This Code also provides a common set of values upon which coaches build their professional work. It is the individual responsibility of each coach to aspire to the highest possible standards of conduct. Coaches respect and protect human and civil rights, and do not knowingly participate in or condone unfair discriminatory practices.

Having a code of ethics in place and visible is an excellent start for any organization; it makes clear which behaviors, standards, and principles are considered most important. However, the true test of an organization's ethics is not in the drafting of a code of ethics but in the enforcement of it. Only then does the group demonstrate its level of commitment to running a clean ship.

these standards are lower than those of the individual employee, conflict will arise. In a club situation, the responsibility rests on the director of the club as well as the coaches. Coaching younger children can bring different ethical challenges, even in a junior high, high school, or club situation where there is no compliance office. For example, club coaches should show interest in having their players recruited by all schools, not only those they favor. Another ethical responsibility for high school and club coaches is to refuse to work with college coaches who intentionally violate recruiting rules.

Having a code of ethics in place and visible is an excellent start for any organization; it makes clear which behaviors, standards, and principles are considered most important. However, the true test of an organization's ethics is not in the drafting of a code of ethics but in the enforcement of it. Only then does the group demonstrate its level of commitment to running a clean ship.

The NCAA also has a set code of rules and ethics by which member institutions must abide. Among those regulations is one that states that all employees must report any suspected violations to the university's compliance office. However, employees who report violations and are reprimanded or ignored may tend to think twice about reporting the next violation they observe. If the compliance office acts on the report, the employee will be encouraged to continue to report suspected violations. It is a coach's responsibility to ensure that her assistants, staff, and players have a forum for reporting inappropriate behavior. If a rule interpretation is vague, a coach should seek clarification before taking action instead of possibly committing a violation and risking an unnecessary penalty. A no-tolerance atmosphere encourages people to follow the rules, which in effect protects a university from being investigated by the NCAA. Schools that break the rules and are caught can suffer severe damages, such as the loss of TV revenues, staff resignations, negative public relations, and revoking of championships. But avoiding sanctions should not be the reason why schools follow the rules. They should follow them because it is the right thing to do.

Those who follow not only the "letter of the law" but also the "spirit of the law" demonstrate the highest ethical standards. An example of this occurs with the NCAA 20-hour-per-week rule, which says that athletes can be "required" to work out with coaches and strength coaches for only 20 hours per week during the declared team-practice period. Some coaches follow the letter of the law by having the weight-room requirements declared "voluntary"—but is that ethical, since the athletes know that they are still expected to be at weights? This scenario does not follow the spirit of the rule, which is to limit the amount of time student-athletes are required to practice. Ethical coaches will fight the temptation to bend the rules; others will try to find the loopholes.

Ethical Concerns

Discussions of ethical behavior should include not only the simple right and wrong answers but also gray, or less clearly defined areas, where the answers are not so simple.

College Recruiting. Unethical behavior seems to occur frequently in recruiting. Often coaches say, "Some of these rules are ridiculous and we aren't going to follow them!" Such an attitude reflects situational ethics, in which a coach behaves ethically only in certain situations. A better alternative to breaking a rule you feel is unfair is to work to change it.

Unethical recruiting is also unprofessional, and it often occurs because coaches feel the pressure to win. Competition for recruits who can ensure a winning season can be intense. Negative recruiting is a sign of desperation in coaches who believe that they must demean another program in order to make theirs sound better. I have found that most recruits are wise to this tactic and do not respond well to negative recruiting. Coaches should concentrate on building up their own programs and let the recruits do their homework on the weaknesses of other programs. If you do know something negative about another school, simply suggest that the recruit check out each program thoroughly. Starting or spreading rumors is not fair to other coaches. Negative recruiting will come back to haunt you because players don't want to go where it's practiced.

Courtesy of JoAnne Graf

Ethically recruiting quality student-athletes ensures a successful program for many years.

Another type of questionable behavior occurs when coaches tell recruits what they want to hear even if it is not the truth. A common promise made in recruiting is that a player will automatically become a starter as soon as she joins the team. Another is promising recruits a scholarship after the first year if they walk on, with no intention of doing so. Although honesty may hurt you in the short term, in the long run the players you do recruit will trust you for telling the truth.

The most common illegal booster activity is giving money or expensive gifts to prospective student-athletes whom coaches believe will be impact players who will help the team win. The players know this behavior is wrong, but adults are telling them that it is OK to break the rules. This behavior may be more widespread than we know due to the unspoken code of silence among athletes.

Many coaches who observe a colleague doing something they consider to be unethical in recruiting do not have a clear idea of how to handle the situation because they feel uncomfortable. The first step is to determine whether the behavior is unethical according to the observer's standards or if a conference, NCAA, high school federation, or club rule has been violated.

If you consider a behavior unethical but it does not break a specific rule, the best approach is to talk with that coach to determine why she feels that what she is doing is acceptable. If she respects your opinion, a friendly debate may help her to change her behavior. It could also help you understand why that behavior might not be as unethical as you think.

Actions that violate stated rules require a different type of response. If you observe someone breaking the recruiting rules, try to determine whether that person is aware of the rule. By approaching her at the time, you can inform her of the rule and how she is violating it. If she believes she is following the rule, I tell her that I will request that my compliance office contact her university to get a clarification.

Sometimes your interpretation of a rule may not be correct. For example, I read in a newspaper article that the mother of a collegiate women's basketball coach had eaten dinner with a recruit and the recruit's mother. I knew that a representative of athletic interest, such as a booster or alumnus (in this case the coach's mother), could not eat with a recruit, so I asked our compliance office to check on it. The compliance office at that coach's institution said that the coach's mother lived with him, and therefore she could attend the meal because it was at his house. Now I know that a meal at a coach's house can include any of its occupants, even if they are not coaches. I learned something new, but only because I asked.

If a coach breaks an obvious rule, such as talking to a recruit during a tournament, you may choose to talk with her or you may report her to the compliance office at your school. Your compliance office should then contact the other school's compliance office. If that does not solve the problem, you should ask the compliance office to contact the offending school's conference office. The university compliance office should report serious violations to the NCAA. Serious violations often require personal interviews and on-site investigations by the NCAA compliance and enforcement staff. Every sport governing body, whether for international, collegiate, interscholastic, or club teams, has a person who is responsible for monitoring player eligibility and recruiting violations. A variety of penalties can be invoked, including loss of eligibility for that player or forfeiting contests, depending on the rules of that organization.

If you hear about a coach breaking a rule but don't observe it, you may need to call that coach to inform her of the accusation and get her side of the story. If she did break a rule but denies it, at least she is aware that others know about it, which may encourage her to refrain from doing it again. If coaches do not report rule violations, non-ethical coaches will continue their behavior. This is damaging to the entire coaching profession because fans may come to believe that everyone cheats.

Rules must be strictly enforced. My feeling is that the NCAA does not punish coaches severely enough. At the present time the rewards that come from violating the rules far outweigh the punishments. The opposite should be true; the punishment should be so dire that it is not worth breaking the rule.

High School Recruitment of Student-Athletes. Transfer and recruiting issues in high schools exist in every sport. Schools will talk to players about transferring or suggest to parents they may want to consider buying a condominium in their school district so that the athlete can attend their school. Some parents want to move so that their child can play for a certain coach and that's fine, as long as the coach doesn't initiate it.

Parents As Coaches. A parent who coaches her own child presents an interesting issue. Are you going to give your daughter more playing time because she is your daughter, or is she really the best player? Even if she is the best player, that may not be the perception of other players and parents. If she is not the best player, yet is getting more playing time to gain more exposure to college coaches, you are only causing team problems. Sometimes the reverse happens: Parent-coaches are harder on their children. This is a delicate situation. Coaches need to monitor their own behavior and separate the family issue in order to be fair to all players. They can prevent this problem by having their children play for other coaches or by keeping statistics during practice.

Unethical Game Coaching. Some coaches teach their players to play illegally by doing something they can get away with, such as setting up in front of the catcher as they try to make a throw to second base or sliding with their cleats up high. I don't know if these situations are unethical or simply bad coaching. If your opposition coaches in this manner, point out your concerns to the officials calling the game. By being informed they will be on the lookout for this type of behavior. Once coaches receive negative feedback in the form of penalties, these behaviors no longer help the team and the coaches might change their approach.

Team Rosters. Playing illegal or ineligible players is getting harder to do, but sometimes coaches do it and hope they don't get caught. Unfortunately these coaches will do whatever it takes to win in the short term. At no level are coaches allowed to sign off on eligibility forms; such infractions are frequently caught and reported by the institution.

Sexual Harassment. A coach's personal involvement with a player crosses ethical and moral boundaries. Coaches who have an intimate relationship with a player create problems for everyone—the team, the player, and the coach's family. Using your position of power as a coach to take advantage of an athlete is wrong and should never be allowed to happen on any level. Never put yourself in a position where this could happen or even let it appear that anything has happened. When meeting with a player in your office, always leave the door open. If having the door closed is necessary, include a staff member or another adult to witness the meeting. I recommend not meeting with individual players privately at other locations, such as hotel rooms on a team trip or in your home. In high school or club programs, use caution in giving individual players a ride home after a game or practice. Remember, accusations can arise even when no inappropriate behavior occurs.

Promises, Promises. In summer softball programs, sometimes coaches promise an athlete more than they can deliver. They tell them that if they play on their team they will get a scholarship or get recruited more readily than they would if they were on another team. In effect, they promise them something they have no control over. A player's ability determines whether she gets recruited or not. Although it may not be illegal to recruit off another summer team, it is definitely a gray area. Players make a commitment to one program. However, those who look at other teams because they are not happy and aren't getting what they were promised present a very different scenario than when a coach tells a player, "You are never going to get seen if you play with that coach," or "That coach is not very good. I know all the college coaches!"

If a coach sees that someone on another team is unhappy, she should remember that the coach may be limiting that player's playing time or putting her in a less desirable position because of a bad attitude or because of the player's ability. If you recruit from another team, you may get someone who is as malcontent and disruptive on your team as she was on the other.

Overselling. Boosting a student-athlete's statistics to get her recruited only harms her in the long run. High school and club coaches and parents must understand the importance of being honest and knowledgeable about the level of each program they are considering for a player. If a high school, club, or even junior college coach is not realistic and honest enough about a player's ability, she will soon lose all credibility with college coaches. The overselling of players seems to stem from the coaches' need to satisfy their egos instead of doing what is best for their student-athletes, who need to attend schools where they will enjoy living, play for coaches they will work well with, and have teammates they enjoy being around.

Ethics Within the Team

The head coach directs the ethical expectations of a staff, which in turn affects the development of a value system for the student-athletes. On our staff, we try to bring up situations as they occur around the country, such as a player who receives extra money from a booster and becomes ineligible. I do this for both ethical and normal behavior. In an effort to teach my players that short-term gain does not equal long-term gain, I describe the situations to them and explain what was gained and what was lost. When the players complain about students who cheat in class or athletes who don't attend class, we try to help them understand that those players are only cheating themselves.

The prospective players know the rules; if you break the rules to sign them, they will have that over you forever. Once they are in your program, if you try to discipline them or if they don't want to do something you've asked them to do, they can threaten to go to the press or report you to the administration for breaking the rules when you recruited them. We've seen that happen in several sports. Athletes become unhappy and transfer to another school, where they describe what was done for them at the previous program. They like to brag about it. It is also impossible for coaches to preach to players about following rules if the players know that the coaches are violating them.

Discussions should occur when a situation is not clear. A high school coach needs to check with her athletic director and maybe even her state high school athletic association. A college coach can receive guidance from her compliance office as to whether a behavior is allowed by NCAA rules. Interpretations by the NCAA staff can vary from year to year depending on which staff member is doing them. However, the NCAA standard is the minimum that coaches must follow. Do you follow the letter of the law or the spirit of the law as well? These standards determine the level of ethical behavior of the staff, which then will filter down to the players.

Universities have an ethical standard that states that you should report people who break rules. The NCAA depends on people monitoring each other to comply with the rules. The NCAA compliance office meets monthly with our coaching staff to go over new rules and any changes. Every coach should go to her sport's convention and participate in discussions regarding the NCAA rules. You can get around a rule, but are you breaking the spirit of it? The rulebook is so thick because coaches try to figure out a way around the rules.

Make sure your standards are clear to your staff and players. If an assistant coach wants to break a rule, don't let her, even if she tells you everyone else does it. You tell her that you do not coach like that. I tell our assistant coaches, "Before you do something and then find out it was wrong, you should check with our compliance office first if you have any questions." I also ask them to read the *NCAA News* infraction section so that they can see which kinds of rules are being broken and how schools are being penalized. They need to understand that you might get away with something for a while, but you're not going to get away with it for a long time. Again, a short-term gain is not necessarily a long-term gain. If you illegally recruit someone by calling her three times a week instead of the once a week that is allowed, you might sign that player, but you might get turned in for illegal recruiting. You could lose your job and you might not even get the recruit.

The ethical behavior of assistant coaches is up to the head coach. If she asks an assistant to do something unethical, the assistant will know she is not ethical and won't listen to her on that topic again. Ethics play into a coach's relationship with her assistants—she depends on having her loyalty and ethical standards emulated by her assistants. However, if the assistants don't agree with her and do something that is not ethical, like going to see a player during a dead period, she should crack down on it right away.

Most assistant coaches hope to move up to a head coaching position. Whichever path they decide to take in looking for another job, failing to inform their head coach or supervisor of their intentions is a major mistake. Communication and honesty about professional dealings are important because most head coaches want to help their assistants. Those are long-term relationships in which they work and recruit together, so they need to respect one another. When the assistants do go to another program, they may even end up coaching against their former bosses as their careers go on.

Head coaches should emphasize to assistant coaches that they should not talk about things that the players don't need to know. Sometimes assistants cross the line by being involved with the players socially so that they will like them—but once you decide to become a coach, you need to be a coach. If your head coach tells you not to do something, then don't do it. If you disagree with her, then you need to work for another coach. If you work for a head coach who does something you consider improper, you don't have to be involved. Assistant coaches need to steer clear of such behavior since they are establishing their own coaching reputation. Sometimes it's better to change jobs if you're not comfortable.

All coaches set the standards and ethics by which their teams and coaching staffs operate. If a coach makes a team rule that is not enforced, it should not be a rule. It is a coach's responsibility to clearly spell out not only the written rule but also the spirit of the rule. Let the team and staff—all those who are expected to abide by the rules—bring up questions so that misconceptions can be cleared up immediately. For example, if you establish a rule that the athletes may not drink alcohol, you need to clarify whether you mean they should not drink at all, not drink during the season, or not drink before a game. Can those players who are over the legal drinking age drink in the fall when your season is in the spring? If your rules are vague, the players and staff will interpret them in a way that suits their purpose.

I suggest having specific rules, but a few general ones regarding behavior, like stating that you will treat your players as adults as long as they act like adults, are also helpful. They enable you to discipline players who do something inappropriate or unethical that you have not specifically addressed. An example of such behavior might be talking back to a coach. You would probably not include this in a list of team rules because it seems to be common sense, yet you won't want to tolerate it. If you are too specific with your rules, players will argue that their negative behavior is not on your list.

In the following list of team rules used for the Florida State softball program, you'll see a mix of both specific and vague rules. This system has worked very well for me during my many years of coaching. Some coaches have more extensive lists and some have shorter ones. You need to have as many as you feel comfortable enforcing and which fit your situation. For example, a younger team may need more stringent rules than a veteran team.

Florida State softball team rules:

1. Be on time for all required sessions.
2. Report all illnesses to the athletic trainer by 11:00 a.m.
3. You must not miss practice unless excused by a trainer or coach.
4. Use of illegal drugs or prohibited supplements is not allowed.
5. Use of alcohol on road trips or the night before a home game is prohibited.
6. Act like adults and you will be treated as such.
7. Do not do anything that would embarrass you, the coaching staff, your family, or Florida State University.
8. You must follow all rules and regulations of the NCAA, ACC, and FSU.

Many options are available to coaches for disciplining a player who breaks a team rule. There must be some type of consequence for inappropriate behavior or else it will probably continue. Players will test a coach to see how far "over the line" she will let them go. It is up to you to set that standard and send a message to all players who may consider going against team rules that you will not look the other way. If you list a specific consequence for a rule violation, then you must abide by that preset punishment. An example could be that if a player skips a class, she has to run three sets of stadium steps. If you find out that a player skipped a class, you must make her run the required number of stadium steps. I find it helpful to announce who broke which rule and let the team know that the punishment will take place. Remember, part of your goal is to deter further negative behavior.

If you do not list specific consequences for a violation, you have the flexibility to vary the punishment based on the level of the action and the player involved. In such cases, some might accuse a coach of not treating every player the same, and that is somewhat true. In fact, most coaches do not treat every player exactly the same. No two situations or players are exactly alike. If a student-athlete with a 4.0 grade point average asks to be allowed to miss a class, you might decide to give her permission—but you might deny that permission to one with a 2.0 grade point average. You might also be more lenient on a first-time offender than a repeat offender.

> There must be some type of consequence for inappropriate behavior or else it will probably continue. Players will test a coach to see how far "over the line" she will let them go. It is up to you to set that standard and send a message to all players who may consider going against team rules that you will not look the other way.

Explaining to the student-athlete why her behavior was inappropriate is important. Education is as important than the punishment—or even more so. If she does not understand the reason or disagrees that her behavior was inappropriate, you must continue the discussion until you reach agreement. Again, the goal is to create a change in behavior from the negative to the positive.

The punishment should fit the crime. You are trying not to hurt a player but to make sure she won't do it again. The most effective type of punishment I have found is to have the player miss practice. All players want to be in practice because playing the sport is what they enjoy doing. If they are starters, they do not want to lose their starting spot. If a player misses study hall, having her go to study hall during practice is more effective than having her run sprints. Make sure the study-hall coordinator lets you know about infractions instantly so that the punishment is immediate. This strategy has proven to be very effective; repeat behavior is almost nonexistent. Other examples of punishment are running sprints, running stadium steps, cleaning out the equipment shed, picking up trash around the facility, pulling weeds from around the field, extra study time, extra weights, game suspension, season suspension, and the worst-case scenario: team dismissal.

I have found that when I discipline a player for a rule violation, other players step up their level of play because they know the suspended player made the wrong decision. They respect the coach because they are following the rules and feel others should as well. Players are responsible to each other and understand that team discipline comes before winning. I will not hesitate to suspend a player if she breaks a team rule. The choice to break a rule is the player's, and so is the resulting suspension. The coach is merely carrying out the consequence of the player's decision. Again, I always tell my athletes that I will treat them as adults if they behave as adults.

Several people are responsible for discipline when rules are not followed. The head coach is ultimately responsible; however, if she has given that responsibility to another staff member, she must support that person in the punishment she wants to hand out.

For example, the strength coach may be authorized to supervise the punishment for a player who constantly comes late to weights, but the head coach should follow up to make sure the punishment was doled out and that the player understood why she was being punished. If a player violates a university rule, the school might dictate the type of punishment. Although it might be up to the coach to enforce it, the type of punishment will be determined by school policy, and the coach should make it clear that she supports it.

Some punishments hurt the whole team rather than only the player involved, but the athletes should understand that their decision to break a rule has consequences—their decisions, not the policy, hurt the team. Drug-rule violations are usually governed by athletic-department policies rather than individual sport coaches. Sometimes head coaches have stricter policies than the athletic department or school, but they are never allowed to have more lenient policies. Criminal behavior is always governed by university policy. Regardless of who handles discipline, ultimately the head coach is responsible for the team's behavior. The team is a reflection of her standard of behavior. The buck stops with the head coach.

One of the benefits of participating in athletics is learning ethical behavior. Coaches should be role models for young people in that regard. The impact coaches have on forming behavioral patterns for their student-athletes is profound. Although the majority of coaches do an excellent job, too many do a poor job.

Schools contribute to poor behavior by coaches with the overemphasis on winning that we see today. A football coach at a university in the Midwest recently was fired because his 9-3 record playing one of the toughest schedules in the country was not considered good enough. Can you win with high ethical standards? Many coaches (including those in this book) have proven that you can. Abiding by high standards may seem to hurt in the short run, but inevitably it results in a stronger program in the long term. As John Maxwell states in *There's No Such Thing As "Business" Ethics,* "Ethics + Competence is a winning equation." Unethical behavior may benefit a program temporarily, but you can't sustain that success. The Josephson Institute of Ethics sums this chapter up well in its article "What Is Ethics Anyway?" at www.josephsoninstitute.org: "Ethics is about how we meet the challenge of doing the right thing when that will cost more than we want to pay."

3

Professionalism

Embrace the role and reflect
full preparation and class in all facets

Margie Wright

Thirty years of coaching softball is a long time. During those years I have seen many changes—in rules, style, strategy, equipment, and certainly in the athletes and parents. Coaches also have changed. Their philosophies, backgrounds, experiences, salaries, and the expectation to win have all made a difference in the sport of softball. Some say these changes are for the better—and in most cases, they are. But the area that has been challenged the most is that of professionalism.

When I graduated from college in 1974, I never would have believed that I would have such a fulfilling career. I have been fortunate to coach some of the best young female athletes ever to play softball. They have allowed me to fulfill every goal a coach could have. Sometimes I feel like I'm dreaming when I think about the accomplishments these young women have allowed me: gold medals in the Pan-American Games, junior world championships, world championships, and Olympic Games, and an NCAA national championship—and recently I have become the softball coach with the most wins in NCAA history. These achievements simply mean that I have had great athletes and my coaching philosophy has been validated.

What Is a Professional?

Professionalism by definition means that an individual is well trained, good at her job, and dependable, but there's one additional component. It might be easy to do a particular job, but doing it from your heart is also an essential part of professionalism. Twenty to thirty years ago, good coaches put their heart and soul into their work. The salary was meager, but we chose coaching because of our love for the game.

After college I wanted to become a teacher and a coach who would make the same kind of positive difference in young athletes that my coaches had made in me. My first job was at a high school, coaching five sports, but I was never compensated for all the extra hours. I thought I was making progress the next year when I got an additional 1 percent each for coaching bowling and track, 2 percent for volleyball, and 3 percent each for basketball and softball. What more could I ask for, right? But I wanted some sort of promotion, so when I was offered a coaching position at a university, I was ecstatic, even though it meant a $3,000 cut in salary. Coaches have come a long way since then. In those days, most of us chose coaching not to become wealthy but because it was an avenue to make someone else's life better and it allowed us to continue to compete. Being professional in our jobs was expected by everyone involved in sport, including ourselves.

Some of today's younger coaches might find it difficult to understand why working so hard to fulfill our dreams and goals as coaches could mean so much when we were being paid "peanuts." The reality was that we didn't have high school sports to play before Title IX and we paid our way through college playing multiple sports, so we were ready and willing to become a professional doing what we loved. In those times, professionalism was a way of life; without it, there was much less success. Times have changed.

Over the past few years the importance of professionalism in coaching has been overlooked because all of the changes taking place in softball and other sports. Changes in attitudes sometimes alter our views of what coaching as a professional means. We may forget that we are regarded as role models by those we coach, our peers, and society in general.

Recruiting Professionally

Recruitment has become one of the biggest challenges in coaching. Professionalism in recruiting begins with following the rules. Being able to hang on to your soul without feeling you must sell it to recruits, coaches, or parents is essential to professionalism, along with being honest and respectful to opposing coaches and to the athlete you are recruiting. When we allow junior coaches, athletes, or parents of athletes to take control of the recruiting process, we are not being true to our profession. Being a professional in the recruiting process means the coach does her own planning, decision making, and communicating, and she stands up for what is right for her program and the recruits. It also means being ethical, realistic, fair, and honest despite feeling that you have to be unprofessional in order to survive.

In recruiting, as in many other areas of coaching, taking the easy way is becoming the choice of many coaches. They force 17-year-olds to make decisions without having all the information they need by threatening to pull their scholarship offers off the table. Whatever happened to letting recruits visit the campus and make informed decisions? A professional coach can sell her program and believe she can get the recruit while still showing respect to a young woman who is making the biggest decision of her life. Coaches don't need to sacrifice their professionalism by talking negatively or starting rumors about the programs they recruit against. Being a pro means that you sell your program and let others do the same with respect and honesty.

> Being a professional in the recruiting process means the coach does her own planning, decision making, and communicating, and she stands up for what is right for her program and the recruits. It also means being ethical, realistic, fair, and honest despite feeling that you have to be unprofessional in order to survive.

Our program has always had the reputation of being intense, and the players are held accountable for their actions on the field and in the classroom. I have established parameters because I care about the athletes and I want them to make good choices as they make their way into adulthood. Parents used to appreciate that someone was looking out for their daughters while they were away from home. But these days, doing what we think is right provides other coaches with a way to be negative about our program.

Here's an example: We were recruiting a player from California who asked our players if the program was as bad as her coach and one from another top collegiate program had said. When my players asked her what she was referring to, she said those coaches had told her that I follow my players through the grocery store to see if they were following the nutrition plan, and that I had taken a team poster to every fast-food restaurant in Fresno and told the managers not to serve anyone on that poster. Obviously, her two informants were unaware of the number of grocery stores and fast-food restaurants in a city of a half-million people. Another recent rumor was that we don't allow non-starters to speak to starters, which would only undermine team spirit and cohesiveness. Perhaps this rumor arose from the fact that during practice I send the players who are not playing defense to the batting cages to hit. Hopefully, recruits are able to realize that rumors are simply a way to paint a negative picture of a program.

Softball coaches behave unprofessionally when they pass on misinformation to others in the guise of "helping" someone in the recruiting process. We hear rumors all the time, but we can respond to them in the professional manner that should be a part of the sport. When I hear my players talking negatively about another program, I stop them immediately and remind them of what gossip has done to us at times and how they don't like it when others spread false information about us. That usually takes care of it.

Players need to learn how to defend and support their programs, so I often speak to them about professionalism in the hope that they will become role models for their parents and other adults who find satisfaction in gossip. I also hope that coaches will recruit by emphasizing the positive aspects of their own program rather than creating negative images of their colleagues.

Developing professionalism in recruiting is simple: We must plan for our needs and seek out the athletes who fulfill those needs. We must visit them, watch them play, put them together with the current team, and decide if they fit into the program. Being professional means being clear in communicating with recruits and their parents and showing respect for the competing programs throughout the process. If we keep the NCAA recruiting rules and regulations in mind at all times, professionalism will be a given.

Promoting Your Program

Another area of professionalism that is key to coaching is how we show and promote our programs. Most of what we convey comes from the way

Courtesy of Margie Wright

Never forget that you are looked upon as a role model by those you coach, as well as your peers and society in general.

we present ourselves. I use this scenario as a measure of positive presentation: If a family with two young daughters who play softball walks into a roomful of coaches, I would want the parents to see the coaches and feel excited that their daughters chose softball. The parents' first impressions of the people in that room should reinforce their wish for their daughters to continue in softball. When we coaches lead by example, we put our personal philosophies on display. When parents see us as a positive, they will consider keeping softball in the lives of their daughters for the future.

Professionalism through appearance and presentation should also include acceptance of others and their choices. We must realize that coaches are all different, and presentation may or may not be a priority for them. If we intend to be taken seriously, we should consider the importance of making a professional impression on potential recruits, fans, sponsors, and society. I have never believed that anyone should be judged by appearance, but the reality is that we are. Coaches of women's sports, particularly the female ones, have to make twice the impression on someone in order to be taken as seriously as their male counterparts.

Many people scrutinize how professional we are; because they all judge coaches in different ways, other factors are as important as presentation. Time-management and follow-through skills and even a sense of humor can make a lasting impression on those watching. An ability to prioritize is essential to show the highest level of professionalism possible. Dressing for success, being nonjudgmental, on time, and organized, and having the ability to laugh at ourselves and with others give us an edge.

Professionalism also has a huge effect on the promotion of a sport. Sponsors and the media sometimes need to be impressed in order to get on board, and the head coach must impress them. Our softball program at Fresno State has led the nation in attendance in 16 of the last 18 years. I believe our approach to the community and our sponsors has made that difference. When I decided to accept the challenge of building a stadium, developing a large booster club, and gaining fan support, I had to find a way to be taken as seriously as football and basketball were in our community—and run with it.

First, because I had to sell my players and philosophy to special-interest groups and corporate leaders who might donate large sums of cash to our program, I purchased a businesslike wardrobe that allowed them to take me seriously on first impression. I had to "walk the walk," and the team had to be successful on the field and in the classroom—that was our selling point. We gave the appearance of a type of professionalism these people would be familiar with—major league baseball—and incorporated all types of marketing tricks to entertain our fans. We showed a level of professionalism that others wanted to be a part of, and our efforts have worked. Our team has the top attendance record and largest booster club in the nation; all games are broadcast on radio and cable television; season-ticket sales number more than 2,000; and the team has nearly a 100 percent graduation rate. This kind of support does not come without the kind of professionalism that sponsors and fans want to be a part of. It is hard work and you end up living in a fishbowl, but your athletes get to feel like pros and our fans get to be in a professional and entertaining environment.

Professionalism cannot be displayed without being honest and respectful to others. That respect should be reciprocated, but even when it isn't, true professionals continue to show that trait and know they are doing the right thing. The first place I start is with my athletes. There are several areas to consider in teaching honesty and respect to these young people. We all have challenges, but if we want to show professionalism we must face them.

Player Professionalism

It is getting tougher and tougher to hold players accountable for their actions. I blame part of this challenge on our society, but coaches still have the responsibility to help them be accountable and become responsible adults. We can allow for their independence and individuality but still make sure they understand that the time will come when they will have to conform to a boss or a job. If today's athletes want to pierce their noses to show individuality, that's fine—but they should realize that jewelry is not allowed on the playing field. Personal choices have a time and a place, and it is the coach's job to teach her players to understand the difference. That understanding is essential if we hope to teach young women how to win in every part of their lives.

A coach's goal is to hold these women accountable and have the blessing of their parents so that the team has the best chance possible to succeed. As professionals, coaches must see all sides of every issue and be fair in all decision making. Double standards can destroy individuals and the team, so we must make hard and fair choices in order to send the right message. We must also be consistent in those decisions, thus creating mutual respect and trust.

Accountability and leadership are also essential for player professionalism. Leadership, although difficult to find these days, is necessary in order for athletes to be professional in performance and in their actions on and off the field. Leadership from an athlete supports a coach's decisions that hold players to a standard of accountability needed for team success. This trait appears to be missing in sports that compete in specific age groups. For example, is a 14-year-old athlete going to hold another 14-year-old accountable, or even know how to confront a peer at that age? Probably not. I was fortunate to grow up competing at a time when there were no age groups. At 14, I was playing with and being led by players who were 5 to 10 years older than I was, and I either matured and held myself accountable or I didn't play. Players who compete in age groups are now held accountable only (and seldom) by coaches or parents, which does not allow for the development of leadership skills. Players who lead their peers and make good decisions regarding their teammates' accountability support their coach's efforts instill the accountability needed to portray professionalism in all athletes. Athletes may not like being held accountable, but they will realize the consistency and fairness of the decision. One day they will realize that they have been given a gift of personal responsibility that they will have for the rest of their lives.

> Leadership is necessary in order for athletes to be professional in performance and in their actions on and off the field. Leadership from an athlete supports a coach's decisions that hold players to a standard of accountability needed for team success.

Staff, Administration, and Coaches

Coaches must also treat assistant coaches, secretaries, trainers, equipment managers, and all staff members who contribute to the success of the program as professionals. I usually have a meeting with my coaches, trainers, weight coach, and academic adviser in the fall to discuss my philosophy, and I open the floor for their questions. I believe that the only way our softball program can succeed is for all involved to walk the same professional line and do whatever they can in their role to help us achieve our goals. The expectation of common sense and courtesy are key to the professionalism of this extended staff.

A professional relationship with co-workers and administrators is also a key factor for success. Challenges concerning budgets and equity are common at most institutions, so this relationship must be a priority. A coach must be able to push for what is necessary in the program in a professional way and must show that her requests are justified. When we are honest, respectful, and knowledgeable about our needs as coaches, the administration and others we work with will take us seriously. We must use good problem-solving skills and sell the ideas we seek support for.

When administrators do not support us, we have to decide what to do next. So many coaches sit back and accept not getting the help they need because they think they are being professional. I disagree. If I have been professional in all areas of my program and the administrator does not make what I think is a correct decision, the professional thing for me to do is to stand behind my request. I believe it is my professional duty to fight for what is right; if I want to teach my athletes to do the right thing, I would be remiss if I didn't fight for the betterment of my program. I would make a presentation that my administrator would have to consider, and I would continue to present it until my request was granted or a compromise was reached.

Several years ago, when I made the decision to get a new stadium, I went to the president to ask for his support in my fund-raising efforts and was denied several times. It would have been easy for me to accept those decisions, but I believed we deserved a stadium and continued to push for it. I had formed a committee of business people who met every Friday morning for two years to get our plan ready to implement once the university and athletic department gave us their support. It took the Office of Civil Rights to get us that support from the campus, but we now have a $5 million stadium. We have had to raise money to repay the construction loan, but we have the stadium and our athletes get to feel like professionals playing there in front of large crowds. I could have settled for something less, but I felt that we deserved the best—and that effort made the difference.

The relationships within our own small circle of softball coaches must also be very professional. Although we all have different philosophies and opinions, personal feelings must be put aside for the good of the sport. We cannot allow power struggles to take place, and we must listen to every voice. Just because a coach works at a wealthy school or coaches in a particular conference does not mean she has all the answers and that her way should be followed by all others. Everyone who works with athletes has opinions, and those opinions should carry the same weight when a group makes decisions that will affect all programs. Not every college or university has the same resources; if those who have more are allowed to make decisions based on their resources without listening to others who have less, professional decisions that would have a positive affect on all programs involved cannot be made.

Professionalism in coaching can help level the playing field because all opinions are heard and respected, and a compromise can usually be made. Then the outcome is decided on the field or court in a professional, healthy competition instead of by strong opinions that do not have the success of the sport in mind. We must try to see both sides. Our circle of coaches, which includes novices and 30-year veterans, becomes much more professional when we accept help from others, offer help to others, and regard each others' successes and failures as experiences to learn from. Discovering that we have much more in common than we thought is a sure way to allow respect and professionalism to carry our sport to a higher level.

Media

Finally, professionalism dictates that coaches and players maintain their dignified and respectful behavior in front of the media representatives. In the information age, with multiple news-gathering agencies and television cameras broadcasting our games to thousands of homes, everyone involved in our sport must remember that someone is watching every move we make and listening to every word we say. Players and coaches should always remember that the microphones set up to record the games are always "hot" and the far-away cameras may be zoomed in. This level of scrutiny dictates the utmost professional behavior on and off the field.

Further, coaches must realize that what they say on or off the record, within earshot of reporters, camera crews, or people looking for a negative story, can be broadcast completely out of context. Some people may report their perception of what was said and spread it all over the Internet. A sure way to destroy professionalism in any sport is to encourage these Webmasters and provide misinformation that can be destructive to coaches, players, or programs. Coaches may visit chat rooms and give opinions that spew negative and incorrect information—unprofessional behavior that can have a negative affect on many people. Therefore, coaches, athletes, and parents must always be aware of what they say and how they say it. Allegations, rumors, personal attacks, or generalized logic are bound to be taken out of context or revived months or years later by the media. Remembering that cameras, microphones, and negative people may always be present is a sure way to keep coaches and athletes behaving like disciplined professionals all the time.

To instill professionalism in ourselves and in our programs requires integrity and the ability to maintain it throughout our careers. We must honestly represent our sport with competency, consistency, and commitment. Our honesty must remain above question according to the governing rules of the NCAA. We must honor our contracts with our employers and athletes and keep an open line of communication with all involved. We should be inclusive of others who share our profession and realize that simply doing a job for a long time doesn't make that person a professional. However, doing a job "right" for a long time usually does. If we are good planners, make good decisions, communicate, and do what is right, we can call ourselves professionals.

Leadership

*Take the initiative, set an example, and be
accountable for words and actions*

Marcia McDermott

I never intended to be a soccer coach. I loved playing it, and I loved being a college athlete, but I had no intention of coaching or making a career in sports. When I graduated from the University of North Carolina in 1987 with a degree in English, after having played soccer there for four years, I had no idea what I would do for a living. So naturally I said yes to the first job that was offered. Luckily for me that was a graduate assistant position with the newly created soccer team at the University of North Carolina at Greensboro, where I quickly fell in love with coaching. I went on to an 11-year career as a college head coach, with my last and longest stint at Northwestern University. After seven years there, I accepted a position as head coach of the Carolina Courage, a professional team in the newly created Women's United Soccer Association (WUSA). For the first two years I was the only female head coach in WUSA. In my second year as coach of the Courage, we won the regular season championship and the postseason trophy, the Founder's Cup.

What Is Leadership?

Leadership is difficult to define—even a leadership scholar as notable as Warren Bennis concedes this point in his book *On Becoming a Leader:* "The study of leadership isn't as exact as, say, the study of chemistry. . . . So I have been forced again and again to qualify my answers. People wanted The Truth and I was giving them opinions. To an extent, leadership is like beauty: It's hard to define, but you know it when you see it." Michael Useem comes closer to defining it in a manner useful for a soccer coach in his wonderful book *The Leadership Moment,* but he, too, is unwilling to commit: "A precise definition is not essential here; indeed it may be impossible to arrive at one. But I take leadership to signify the act of making a difference. Leadership entails changing a failed strategy or revamping a languishing organization. It requires us to make an active choice among plausible alternatives, and it depends on bringing others along, on mobilizing them to get the job done."

So is leadership an art? A science? Can it be taught? Are we born to lead? The answer to these questions is yes. If we consider leadership a skill, we can approach it as we do any other skill: as a set of proficiencies that can be learned, developed, and maximized. Yet at the same time we can acknowledge that some individuals, born with an extraordinary talent for leading, are skilled at the subtle art of managing people, crises, and situations.

For the rest of us, leadership is a responsibility and a requirement for effective coaching. This is the heart of the matter. When you agree to coach a team, you agree to lead the team. You are responsible not simply for the team's results but also for its quality. You do not have a choice in this matter. The job becomes intolerable when you allow yourself to adhere to or accept other people's standards. Presumably you want the job of coach in order to achieve something: to win games, develop great players, or be an educator. Leading your program is the only way to achieve those goals.

> If we consider leadership a skill, we can approach it as we do any other skill: as a set of proficiencies that can be learned, developed, and maximized. Yet at the same time we can acknowledge that some individuals, born with an extraordinary talent for leading, are skilled at the subtle art of managing people, crises, and situations.

I learned about leadership the hard way. After my first season with the Courage, we found ourselves marooned in a tie for last place with the Washington Freedom. I had arrived at professional soccer assuming incorrectly that what I knew about soccer was more important than what I knew about leadership. I was too tolerant of the "good enough" mentality that plagues us all from time to time. Taking responsibility is a very powerful thing. The truth is you cannot change anything you are not willing to take responsibility for—so if you want to change your organization, or grow it, or take it to the next level, you have to be willing to accept responsibility for where you are today. If what needs changing is always somebody else's fault, then it will be somebody else's to change, somebody else's to lead.

Vision

The coach is responsible for the vision of her team or program. A vision is more than a destination; it's an inspiration, a motivator, and a rallying point for a team. Results matter, but they are often the by-products of an effectively created and communicated vision. Everybody who competes wants to win, but not everybody can. By the very nature of sport each game has a loser. If you build your foundation on standards, expectations of excellence, and performance you will win games; but more important, you will give your team a reason to compete and play even when a win is not immediately possible.

My first season at Northwestern was also the program's first season. Obviously that made the job a big challenge but also a tremendous opportunity. The first coach could be the architect of the traditions that would define Northwestern soccer. I had taken the job because I had tremendous respect for the athletic department and its approach to college sports. I wanted to be a part of that, and build a soccer program that fit the institution. My vision for that first program was simple: Create a program where athletes know they will develop to their potential as soccer players and as people, and where participation on the soccer team will enhance and inform their education. Make a program where we work hard so that we could play the game hard. Speak often of commitment, integrity, excellence, and success. Instill a sense of belonging and loyalty in the student-athletes and give them a desire to remain connected to the program and the people long after their playing days are done.

This vision made it clear to the athletes on the team that the coaching staff was committed to their development; it created a larger context for measuring ourselves. At the same time, we all wanted to win. In only our third season as a program we earned a bid to the NCAA tournament. I am proud of that accomplishment, but I am more proud of the fact that so many contributing players were members of our team from that first year—when their record was 3-13-1 and they struggled to maintain possession of the ball, much less score many goals. Those players had risen to the challenge.

At the Carolina Courage, where we had far more resources, this vision would have been too limiting. Those at the professional level have a different expectation. Although the coach must create an atmosphere in which people are playing for more than wins and losses, everybody involved knows that winning matters deeply.

After evaluating the first season with our staff I knew where we should go. I wanted the Courage to represent the highest standard of professionalism in women's soccer, and I wanted a culture in which people were willing to accept responsibility for their play and the overall quality of the team. This ambitious vision was motivating to everybody involved. If you achieve that high a standard of professionalism, positive results, including championships, are likely to follow.

After a couple of months on the job, I realized that being a great professional soccer player had as much to do with being a great "pro" as it did with being a great player. The pro understands that she needs to prioritize the requirements of her sport; she takes care of herself physically and accepts responsibility for working on the deficiencies of her game. She comes to work every day understanding her responsibility to the team and the organization. In rare instances these qualities come naturally to a player, but usually they need to be taught, nurtured, demanded, and rewarded.

We had some tremendous professionals on our team that first year, players like former U.S. national team captain Carla Overbeck and the 1995 FIFA Women's Player of the Year, Hege Riise, who had played and led at the highest levels of our sport. But we also had too many players who assumed they knew the requirements of professionalism—I assumed it too. The lack of professionalism I tolerated during our inaugural season detracted considerably from the harmony of our team. And, more important, it had a negative effect on our ability to win.

When the first season ended I immediately began selling the new vision within our organization and to the team, not only with words but with the consistency of my behavior and the standards I set and maintained. Character would now matter as much as talent. I wanted the team to *see* that things would be different, not just *hear* it. Bill Walsh writes in his great book on coaching, *Finding the Winning Edge*: "Handling a team that had a poor season the previous year also places particular demands on a head coach. In responding to these demands, you must resist the inevitable tendency to simply make bold proclamations or grandiose statements on how things are going to be different. Your players will be looking for tangible evidence that next season will be different."

The staff and I crisscrossed the country in search of players while carefully preparing for the draft. We thoroughly researched international selections, recognizing that this would be the best and quickest avenue to elevate our talent and professionalism. The staff had to model the changes in professionalism and the new standard through commitment, attire, work ethic, and sacrifice. In my opinion the best way we could give them tangible evidence of our new priorities was to change the quality of players on the roster, not only by acquiring more talent but by placing a higher value on character and, at the same time, demonstrating through our own actions and behaviors that the professionalism of the Carolina Courage would be at the highest level. A leader may set different visions at different levels of her profession, but she knows that she is responsible for defining the context for her team. Where do you want to lead your team? A bold vision, effectively communicated, is critical from the youth coach through the professional.

The Plan

As the leader of the team, the coach cannot simply throw out a lofty vision without also providing a plan, or series of plans, for getting there. At Northwestern we knew that the first season would be hard. I had to take this into account while establishing the plan. We were clear that we would not spend our scholarship money early to get a player who could not grow with the program. We would rather have a walk-on who might play only one year but wouldn't cost us four years' worth of money. The plan I established for that team was straightforward: We would improve every season (and from fall to spring as well) at every position on the team, as we steadily became a nationally competitive program. We would do this by developing the athletes currently on the team and by recruiting. I also believed that a particular type of player would thrive at Northwestern: talented athletes and students, who were versatile, adaptable, and willing to play a role. We put our focus on finding the Northwestern type.

In that first season I had asked the coaching staff that they be positive with the team. They could use constructive criticism as a teaching tool, but they also had to have the discipline to maintain a positive approach to each athlete's and the team's development. If a different message needed to be sent, it would come from me, and it would be well thought out and well placed. I knew that first team would struggle; beating them up verbally about it would be both cruel and counterproductive. Our plan, which expanded as our ambition did, was a very disciplined approach to building the program systematically, with an emphasis on recruiting the right type of player and developing those who did commit to Northwestern.

At the Courage we were able to be more immediately ambitious, which required a different (but still disciplined) focus. Our plan centered around our need for more cohesion on the field, which we felt was more important than simply acquiring more talented players. Therefore, the plan dictated that we would build our team around our world-class center midfielder, Hege Riise. It also stated that we would use all the avenues available to us to improve the roster—trades, waivers, free agency, the international discovery process, and the draft. We could not acquire all the players we identified, so flexibility was required, but we still held each potential player up to the standard—would she fit Hege's style of play? Rather than pursue a great player who did not fit our plan, we continued the search for a very good one that would.

This approach to building a roster requires a coach to make tough decisions to waive or trade a player or opt not to pick up an outstanding player who was not the right fit for her team. I found this to be true when I was a college coach as well. My teams at Northwestern were better when I stuck to the right fit than when we were able to attract a more talented player who had different standards or priorities than our teams. Although talent matters (a lot!), a cohesive team is more effective than one built solely around talent.

Our plan with the Courage also called for us to develop the core of our current team. We identified those players we felt were central to our success, focused on their development and, although it was difficult, waived everybody else. In the first year I never had a deep enough commitment to the players, in part because I had not known them well enough and in part because I did not know yet the value of such a commitment. Too often I behaved as though I were stuck with the roster instead of in charge of it. This changed before we were halfway through the first season when I waived a very good player who did not fit our team. We also executed the first trade in the history of the league. The trade was a risk—it was unpopular with fans and the media—but it was the right move to make our team better immediately and in the long run. It also established that I was willing to risk derision and maybe even my job in pursuit of my vision and plan for the team.

You must commit to your plan, but you also have to be smart enough to change it when necessary. You cannot predict how circumstances may change—due to an injury or eligibility or the acquisition of a great player in the middle of a season—so you have to be prepared to continue improving your team while adhering to the principles on which you are building.

Committing to the Players' Greatness

Committing to each player's potential is the core responsibility for any coach who is interested in leadership. Our job is to create an environment in which our athletes and coaches can thrive. In his book *The 21 Irrefutable Laws of Leadership*, John Maxwell defines what he calls "The Law of the Lid": "Leadership ability is the lid that determines the person's level of effectiveness. The lower an individual's ability to lead, the lower the lid on his potential. The higher the leadership, the greater the effectiveness."

I would take this a step further. I believe a coach's leadership ability is also "the lid" on the team and the athletes. If you can view yourself as the lid on the jar of everybody around you, then you can understand the importance of committing to each person's greatness. This does not mean simply being positive, but rather that you also are willing to have the hard conversations necessary for each player's development. You must challenge them to reach their potential. Leading is not about you the leader; it is about the people you work with on the team.

> Committing to each player's potential is the core responsibility for any coach who is interested in leadership. Our job is to create an environment in which our athletes and coaches can thrive.

Between my first and second seasons with the Courage, the staff and I spent a lot of time considering each player and where they would fit. We wrote a job description of each position and then decided if a player could fill the bill. If so, the information would serve as an important guide in her preparation. The players with whom we did this were thrilled to have received the knowledge they needed in order to contribute. Players who were obviously hungry for the challenge inundated us with questions about job descriptions, the system, and their own development. They wanted to be a part of the plan. Each player rose to the challenge and worked hard to prepare, but no one grew more than Tiffany Roberts.

Tiffany, or T.R. as we called her, was one of the "founding players." She had been on the winning Women's World Cup team in 1999, so she was one of the three players who had been assigned to the Courage before any players were drafted. T.R. was widely regarded for her tenacity, heart, and individual defending skills, but rarely had she ever asked to have a larger role on any team. In fairness, her teams had not needed her to be more than a defensive specialist. Great players had surrounded her, and the role she played was essential to those teams' success. After the 1999 Women's World Cup, she was cut from the national team by the new coaching staff. She was supposed to be one of the elite players on the Courage, one of our most talented pieces.

She played well the first year, routinely defending our opponents' best players and working hard as a defensive midfielder, but she also gave up possession too easily and too often. Our midfield was predictable in the attack because only Hege Riise could consistently contribute creative attacking soccer. We had allowed T.R. to settle into her normal role as a great defensive presence in the midfield.

Courtesy of Northwestern University Media Services

The coach's job is to create an environment in which athletes can thrive.

She and I scheduled a meeting in the off-season. T.R. was easy to speak with because she always took responsibility for her actions and was respectful. The first question she asked set the stage for her future and for ours as a team. She asked, "What do I need to do to make sure that we are a winning team next season?" What a great question! It demonstrated that her motivation and commitment was for the good of the team. She would be willing to do what was necessary for us to get better. She was willing to take responsibility.

I told her that rather than accepting her role as a defensive midfielder on the team, she needed to elevate her game to a much higher level. We could not have one of our most expensive players and one of our founders play such a limited role. If we were going to be great, then she had to be great. Instead of working all the time on her fitness, which came easily to her, she needed to spend time every day on her skills. It would be frustrating and it wouldn't be fun, but it was necessary. She needed to be a player we could trust with the ball, not merely a role player who expected the Courage to win. We laid out a plan; she accepted it, left my office, and went to work on her game.

T.R. took to the challenge, and when the next season started, the change was evident in both her play and demeanor. She no longer viewed herself as a defensive specialist but rather as a soccer player. It required relentless commitment and tireless training, but T.R. liked the vision for herself as well as the team, believed in the plan, and made the transition from role player to leader. At the same time, her confidence soared. It was as if someone had taken the lid off her jar and allowed her to jump as high as she could. The good news for T.R. was that her hard work led her back to the U.S. national team; in fact, only one year after our conversation she was the Courage's captain, a WUSA all-star, a league champion, and a Founder's Cup champion.

As leaders, whether we coach youth, high school, or a professional team, we create the space in which the players on our roster can expand their potential. Sometimes in our reluctance to have a difficult conversation with a player, or when we set the bar too low for her, we limit that player's growth. Every athlete I had challenged to become better responded positively. Those for whom I had abdicated my responsibility as coach were often the ones who did not improve with the Courage, or quit, or were traded or waived. I know that for each player who did not develop with the Courage or thrive in our culture, I share responsibility.

My commitment to T.R. yielded another benefit. Because I had challenged her in an appropriate fashion, she committed to my leadership on a deeper level. She became a locker room leader. I could trust T.R. to reflect the vision to the team and support my decisions. She would also challenge me when she thought I was wrong and always gave me a chance to explain myself before judging. She was at the center of the team socially, a founder who had worked hard to improve her game without ego, and a tireless worker in every game. Now she was also tireless in her commitment to our vision and plan. The team trusted T.R., and she had become a loyal advocate in the locker room.

Your Inner Circle

If you want to be a successful leader, surround yourself with leaders. John Maxwell uses the term "inner circle," and I think it's a good one. Your inner circle begins with your staff—if you have the luxury of a staff—and extends out to include administrators, players (to a certain extent), and in some cases, parents. At the Courage I had the luxury of a fairly large and extremely talented staff working with me daily. Of course, simply having that talent on your staff or team is not enough—you must communicate effectively with them and consistently be conscious of your role as the leader.

In the Courage's first season I often made decisions without fully explaining them to the staff. By leaving them to guess what I was thinking, I reduced their effectiveness dramatically. Between seasons I corrected this with detailed meetings in which I laid out my philosophy, standards, expectations, and views of professionalism. I also asked a lot of questions and listened intently to my staff's ideas and opinions. We set goals together—things we wanted this team to achieve. The team later set goals as well, but the staff goals allowed us to consider individual players and their value to the team. For instance, we knew that Kristen Luckenbill, our young goalkeeper, would be important to our success, so we quantified what that meant to us in those meetings. We decided that for us to achieve our other goals she had to be all-star caliber. This deepened our commitment to her and required us to consider her strengths and weaknesses while refining our defensive philosophy and teaching. At the end of the season Kristen was not only an all-star, she was also voted WUSA Goalkeeper of the Year. Anyone who saw our first and last games of the season knows that she was a critical factor in our success. Keep in mind that all the credit for that achievement goes to Kristen. She has one of the strongest mentalities of any goalkeeper that I have seen. And, by the way, we never shared that staff goal with her because it was outside of her control and therefore not of much value to her. The goals she and I set were more valuable to her because they were achievable without being at the mercy of other people's opinions or votes.

As part of my stepped-up efforts to improve communication, the staff spent more time together on the road and ate lunch together the day before each home game. We understood each other better—the staff comprehended my thought process better, and they kept me more informed about the team. Together we were able to solve problems; by this point, they could handle many things that I never had to deal with. They had the freedom and power to work harder, make more decisions, and solve more problems; as a result, we were able to enact the vision and the plan.

My inner circle extended to members of our front office, who became much more invested in providing insight into salary caps, international opportunities, and potential trades during the off-season and into the new season. I worked hard in the second season to develop relationships with people who provided me with valuable ideas and information. I know we would not have won a championship without everybody's contributions. The coaching staff, trainers, managers, and front-office people were essential to our success.

Developing Leaders

In order to enact your vision you need strong leadership on your team. Locker room leaders who support the vision and are willing to speak honestly are very valuable. This requires courage on their part. You also need players who are willing to tell you the truth and confront you directly when they disagree. A thousand conversations go on around a team. This is natural. Players may be concerned with playing time or their role or they may have issues with the length of practice—to name just a few. The more effective you have been in creating leaders on your team, the more effectively your team will handle these complaints, remain cohesive, and work together to succeed.

You can develop leaders in a variety of ways, but I also have been mindful to recruit, draft, or select leaders onto my teams. During the recruiting process I would pay close attention to an athlete's leadership skills on her team: Did she respond well to pressure? Was she generally positive when she spoke of her experience? Did she blame others or make excuses? Each coach can develop a list of things that she considers important in terms of leadership or team dynamics. I also liked to do an in-home visit to see how the player interacted with her family, which can indicate how independent she will be in college. And, of course, athletes would visit our campus, which gave us a good sense of how they would fit in academically and with the team. Still, despite the best attempts to evaluate such things, you will make mistakes when trying to recruit leaders.

Coaches also have a responsibility to develop leadership in athletes. At Northwestern I would often let athletes know my vision for them as leaders in their freshman season, to get them thinking about it before it was actually their turn to lead. I hoped this would prepare them for the future and also make them good followers of the current leaders. Throughout the athletes' careers I had individual conversations with them in which I made note of their leadership contributions or challenged them to solve leadership problems. I would ask them how they would handle certain situations and why. When you get athletes to commit to doing the right thing, you will find that they want to honor their word. They have a harder time going along with the crowd and are less careless about what they commit to.

In the spring of one class's junior year we set up a seminar to prepare them for their leadership roles as seniors. Not every senior can be the team captain, but all have an important leadership role to play. The younger players look up to them and gauge proper behavior by what the seniors do. A negative senior who pouts when things do not go her way provides space for the freshmen to follow her lead. Why not prepare your rising seniors for the variety of leadership challenges that will be present during their last and very important season?

We also had team conversations at Northwestern in which we tackled difficult topics together. Powerful examples of leadership would arise from these discussions. Early in my career at Northwestern, I did not think the team was committed enough to fitness. Many of the athletes had a "good enough" mentality and had not yet made the connection between fitness and confidence and success. We were trying to get them to make this leap. One of our players was extraordinarily fit. During the conversation the team was complimentary about her abilities and accomplishments but had not yet made their own commitment to improving the team's fitness level. She could have accepted their words simply as the compliment they were and felt special, or she could have resented her teammates who were not working as hard as she was. Instead she chose to demonstrate a powerful commitment to the team by challenging her peers to match her accomplishment. I do not remember her exact words, but she said essentially, "You all want to say that the reason I am fit is because I'm a freak of nature or talented, but the truth is I just work really hard at it. If you all would work really hard you could be fit too. And we would be a better team. You just aren't working hard enough." Wow—that's leadership! The team responded because her words were honest and came from her commitment to the team. I know it was hard for her to say; it takes courage to buck the team. But it was one of the reasons that the team improved so much so quickly. There was nothing my staff or I needed to say; the message was far more powerful coming from a member of the team. My only job was to acknowledge her leadership contribution and encourage more people to follow that kind of example.

Different athletes will make different leadership contributions, and you need to acknowledge the wide range because all of them will matter at some point. Plus, acknowledging human contribution is one of the most powerful motivators a coach has at her disposal.

Communicate, Communicate, Communicate

Communication is the coach's tool of leadership. I do not mean only direct verbal communication to your team, although that is critical, but also your body language, demeanor, composure, use of humor and anger, written communication, and comments to the press and others, as well as your capacity for listening. Your players pay close attention to all of these things in judging your leadership skills.

I believe that a well-run meeting has its place. A team meeting at the beginning of the season is essential for laying out your expectations and standards. Once you narrow your team down to the core players, meet again and set collective goals and expectations. Keeping those goals in front of your athletes at all times is also important. We all have different resources, so at Northwestern I used a lot of photocopier paper, but at the Courage my staff created a very professional (in keeping with our vision) sign that we hung front and center in our locker room, which allowed us to track our goals throughout the season. It was a very effective piece of communication.

I made it a habit as a college coach to meet with each athlete three times during the season. At the beginning of the year we set individual goals; midseason we discussed where things were; at the end of the season we evaluated their performance and mine. These meetings were important in three ways: First, they provided a forum to discuss specific ways for a player to achieve her goals, both athletic and academic. Athletes crave information and it is our job as coaches to provide as much specific and applicable information as we can. Second, they provided an opportunity for players to express their concerns and fears and ask questions. Athletes appreciate knowing that they have the opportunity to tell you what they think. An open-door policy is important and many athletes will access it repeatedly, but others will not meet with you without a scheduled appointment. And, finally, these meetings allowed me to get to know the players better as human beings and learn about their academics and interests outside of soccer.

As a professional coach I also found video to be a useful communication and learning tool. My staff spent hours creating video that we watched as a team, in small groups, and with individuals in order to illustrate our points about performance. Video is also an effective motivator. We were more likely to show the team examples of them playing well, especially in difficult times during the season, than to show them endless loops of problems.

Sometimes you can make a point without speaking. Early in my tenure at Northwestern, a handful of athletes frequently arrived late to practice. Rather than punishing them or lecturing the team, I decided to make my point in a different way. One day I purposefully arrived at training 30 minutes late. The team was surprised; I was always early for everything. I asked them how it felt to be waiting for me. Did they have better things to do with their time? I never needed to address the matter again.

Once you've dealt with an issue, be fair to the team and let it go. Athletes will respect you for this, trust will grow, and they will respond positively in the future. Leaders who hold grudges do not help their teams. Once you've addressed a problem, it should be resolved, so if you find that it's not over for you or the athlete, then you probably did not address it thoroughly enough and may need to revisit it. However, do not let grudges linger or allow your decisions to be influenced in an unfair way.

Athletes pay attention to how fair they believe their coach is. They are sophisticated enough to recognize that you treat people differently because they *are* different, but they value each other as people as well as athletes and want you to do the same. Therefore you must treat all athletes fairly, committing yourself equally to the development of all and communicating effectively with each.

Finally, don't wait to deliver bad news. You may want to avoid some issues, but the longer you do, the greater the problem grows. Sometimes you create more problems by not communicating. If a player complains that she doesn't know her role, then you have to consider the possibility that you have not done your job well enough. If you choose to change someone's role—a position or a starting role—and you fail to address it in advance, you can be sure that an athlete will be upset. Minimally she'll have internal turmoil; in the worst case she'll do damage to the chemistry of your team. Remember, your number one leadership responsibility is to expand your players' abilities and achievements. Active, consistent, thoughtful communication is the most critical tool you have to achieve that goal.

We should actively educate ourselves—about leadership, our sport, the science of sport, and so on—with the hope of becoming more effective coaches. Countless resources exist that can teach us valuable insights, and we should search through them for answers. But part of the key to growth as an effective leader is to cull all that material and pull out the information and techniques that will enable *you* to succeed. What is right for one person will not be right for another. I know of extremely successful coaches who yell all the time. It works for them; it would not work for me. And I would not want to do it. Anger has its place, but I think it is limited. We have an obligation as coaches to learn about ourselves in order to be more effective as leaders.

I mentioned earlier that I used to run a leadership seminar with the juniors in our off-season. Often we read books together, and their favorite was Michael Useem's *Leadership Moment*. This book is a collection of nine stories in which individuals are called to rise to their "leadership moments," which he describes as "those fateful moments when our goals are at stake and it is uncertain if we will achieve them, and when the outcome depends upon mobilizing others to realize success." The players liked this book because it was practical and the stories were analogous to team situations. I think it helped each player to think in terms of preparing herself for her own leadership moment, whenever it arrives. As coaches we need to prepare ourselves as well. You do not get a day off from leadership. Decisions must be made, preparations must be underway, players must be acknowledged, challenged, or scolded on an ongoing basis. Anything you do not deal with today will be waiting tomorrow, only by then it might be a much bigger deal. Steady, consistent leadership will prepare you for those moments—the big ones—when your goals and dreams are on the line and the responsibility for success is yours.

5

Competitiveness

Exude a desire to excel and be the best, and instill this in others throughout the program

Mary Wise

When asked, "Why did you choose coaching?" my response has always been to say that coaching is teaching with a competitive twist. Since education was part of my upbringing—my parents and three of my siblings have all taught—it seemed a natural choice. I grew up with four older brothers who loved to pick on their sisters, so the competitive part came naturally as well—I had to compete or be squashed! We were constantly playing games with a "survival of the fittest" mentality. The neighborhood had lots of kids; you either competed or you didn't get to play.

Although I learned to compete at an early age and grew up in a household in which teaching was highly valued, I owe my entrance into this profession to three female coaches: Tannie Bragel, a junior high basketball coach; Alice Simpson, a teacher and coach at Evanston Township High School; and Carol Dewey, my college coach at Purdue. From each of these mentors, I learned that coaching isn't as much about the Xs and Os as it is about organization and dealing with people. During the spring semester of my senior year in college, Coach Dewey spent hours preparing me for my chosen field. We spent less time on how to defend the back-row attack and more time on how to get the best out of a player by instilling confidence.

After graduation I was offered the head coaching position at Iowa State at the ripe old age of 21. If you can believe the record books, that makes me the youngest coach in NCAA history. The good news is I turned 22 before our first match, so at least I was one year older than the seniors on the team. Looking back on that time, I'm grateful that the mistakes I made (and there were many) weren't bad enough to hurt a player or the program. Times have changed, and hiring a 21-year-old fresh out of college isn't going to happen these days. But at that time, Iowa State was willing to take a chance on me because of my time spent with Carol Dewey and their desire to "hire someone competitive." Experience I couldn't give them; competitiveness I could. After four years at Iowa State, my less-than-typical career path led me to the assistant coaching position at the University of Kentucky. Four years with Head Coach Kathy DeBoer taught me the definition of "competitive." After UK, it was on to the University of Florida as the head coach, this time older and wiser.

Wanted: Competitive Players

Our University of Florida volleyball team prides itself on its competitiveness. When we recruit, we look for players with an "eat nails" personality—those who are less concerned with how they look and more concerned with the score. They are the players who want the ball at crunch time and desire to win regardless of the game being played. Competitive players aren't necessarily the loudest on the court, nor the angriest; they are the players who will do anything—throw their bodies into the air, the bleachers, or onto the floor to help their team win.

We then work to enhance that attitude in practice every day. Even in warm-ups we will have some sort of competition where we keep score so that there is a winner and a loser. It may be as simple as ball-handling drills with a partner in which the first group to get a pass, set, and dig is the winner. Competitive players are important to teams because under stress, we all go back to our comfort zones. If a player's makeup is to always compete, then even when the team is far behind in the score, she will continue to compete. It's easy to play hard when you're winning, but the competitive ones will give you more when they are behind. That's the type of player we look for at Florida.

> Competitive players aren't necessarily the loudest on the court, nor the angriest; they are the players who will do anything—throw their bodies into the air, the bleachers, or onto the floor to help their team win.

A few years ago I was in the home of former Florida All-American Jenny Manz. When we walked in, I couldn't help but notice that in the dining room was a foosball table. No dining-room table, no hutch, no corner cabinets, just a foosball table. Jenny grew up with three brothers and no sisters. Besides her wicked arm swing, Jenny has a competitive spirit, which no doubt was enhanced by growing up with brothers in a house where foosball was a priority. Unfortunately, I haven't noticed a direct correlation between parents and players being competitive; in fact, sometimes an overly competitive father has a daughter who is just the opposite.

During the recruiting process, I ask parents to rate their daughters' competitiveness on a scale of 1 to 10. Many times they say, "She hates to lose." Who doesn't? I've never met a person who likes losing. What we look for are players who detest losing so much that they will give anything to win. Once we've identified those competitive types—along with the big-jumping, hard-hitting, players with long arms, quick feet, and big hands—we try to create an environment in which always competing becomes a part of the player's persona.

We have a manager who spends most of his time updating the scoreboard. We keep statistics during practice because we are trying to teach that, like effort, you don't turn competing on and off. You *always* compete. If a coach has a team made up of competitors, she has a chance of seeing her players win every night.

Great players such as Aury Cruz are statistically going to score well in everything they do. Young, inexperienced players who don't possess a high skill level can still compete just as hard. We can control our competitiveness much more easily than we can control skill acquisition. You should never have an off day on competitiveness. How would I rate my own competitiveness? If I told you, your response would probably be, "That woman needs therapy." I hate losing so much that I avoid card games—there's too much luck involved and not enough skill. Raising children has helped; I can now lose in Go Fish to my 9-year-old and not go into a deep depression.

Females and Competition

Just because females don't compete in the same manner as guys doesn't mean they are not competitive. Even research shows that women do compete; it just happens in different ways. Everything I have learned about competition came from my time with Kathy DeBoer. I had the privilege of working with her for five years in the late '80s when she was the head volleyball coach and senior women's administrator at the University of Kentucky and I was one of her assistants. She was one of the most competitive people I had ever met, and also one of the most well read.

Part of our daily routine was to run together, either first thing in the morning or following practice. I learned early on that if I could keep Kathy talking, I could keep up with her running pace. While my reading list mostly included *Sports Illustrated,* Kathy spent her spare time engrossed in social and psychological material. Each day during the run, she would explain in length (if I was lucky), what she had recently learned about the differences between men and women. From there, she would transfer that knowledge to coaching. My job was to respond, "Uh huh," and keep up with her. It wasn't until I took the job as head volleyball coach at Florida in '91 that I could a) bring my running pace back to a humane rate and b) transfer everything she taught me to our team.

As Kathy explained in her book, *Gender and Competition: How Men and Women Approach Work and Play Differently,* the differences in how men and women view the world and what they value manifest in the way each gender approaches competition:

> *Girls come to the gym seeking to bond as the means to success; boys battle to achieve the same thing. Women enter a workplace predisposed to connect to achieve goals; men compete to achieve goals. Both want to win and both want results, but they hold markedly different ideas on how to access their aspirations. . . . Another piece of the worldview puzzle has a major impact on behavioral differentiation. Males learn to view the world as a hierarchical social order. They highly value independence . . . By contrast, a web of relationships characterizes the female culture . . . Views of self link closely to the individual's place in that web. They highly value attachment as a defining element of femaleness. These disparate assumptions about the nature of reality lead to most of our common gender-related stereotypes. In sports, stereotypes perceive males as competitive, females as social; winning is critical to males, team chemistry to females.*

In other words, a female's source of self-esteem and belonging comes from being a part of a web of relationships; a male's comes from how high he ranks in the pecking order.

I learned much from my time spent with Kathy but perhaps nothing more important than the concept of the web. If you want women to compete and be successful, keep the web intact. Don't publicly single out a player as being the star, expecting more from her than from her teammates and expecting her teammates to put her on a pedestal. That works on men's teams, because males relate to each other linearly—who is on which rung of the ladder. But with women, neither the star player nor the team will thrive with that arrangement. Women are uncomfortable with that separation because their web has been broken.

Often in a time-out a coach will take a player aside to talk to her away from the team. My assistants and I do not do that with our team because we don't want her teammates spending all their energy worrying: "Is she in trouble?" "What are they saying to her?" If I took the setter aside, the one thing she would want would be to be back with her teammates. So when we address the team during time-outs we try to always keep the players together.

Courtesy of the University of Florida

Address players as a group during time-outs to keep the web intact.

One year we were playing in the NCAA regional finals at the University of Texas at Austin. Up 2-0 in games and dominating, we were about to head back onto the court. I reminded the team of the adjusted game plan that anticipated the changes Texas would make—and then I made one heck of a coaching blunder when I blurted out, "We have the best player on the court in Aycan Gokberk. All we need to do is keep giving her the ball." Two-time first-team All-American Aycan went white. As we headed out the door, she stayed back to get my attention. "Everyone is playing well, not just me," she said. I had made the mistake of separating her from the group by singling her out as the best player on the court. Not that it was a close race in terms of her talents versus others—it wasn't, but Aycan didn't want to be separated from the web. Fortunately, I kept my mouth shut, and after losing the next two games, we won the fifth game and advanced to the NCAA national semifinals.

Here's the tricky part about coaching women: Keeping Kathy's web theory in mind, we don't post players' point totals or conditioning results on the blackboard, yet we still create competition in practice by keeping score. The key is that we don't single out one winner—we keep the web (even a sub-web) intact. We will, however, post our game statistics along with other teams' in an attempt to create an "us versus them" mentality. We're trying to keep that web strong. Going into competition, we look not at where one player is ranked on our team but where the team is, compared to the opposition.

So how does a coach discipline a player using the web theory? The greatest motivation to improve behavior I have found in coaching women is to kick the player who needs discipline out of the gym. She does not want to be removed from the web. Women will go to great lengths to stay together. The stronger that web, the more successful female teams are. It's when you have somebody hanging out on the fringes that you have issues. Guys don't care. They just want to be better than the next guy.

My staff and I also try to instill the notion that competitiveness is not only essential, it's fun. If we're in the middle of a drill and it's a great rally and the players are busting their tails and yelling at each other over a call, we applaud that. That display of competitiveness is what we're looking for. Coaches need to bring a lot of energy to the practice, especially when it is time to keep score; we sell it to the players and ask them to buy into it. In the same vein, the matches should be fun. We've always believed that the practices belong to the coaches and the games belong to the players. As coaches, we control everything that goes on in a practice setting. We are training them to make the step to independent decision making in a game situation. I don't think coaches should ever be bigger than the game. The competition is for the players.

Teaching Players to Compete

Getting athletes to compete starts with DNA—some, like Jenny Manz, seem to be born with it, or they learn to compete in order to survive living with brothers. When a player competes we call attention to and encourage it. It is a minimum expectation of ours. You can compete at a high level before your skills are at a high level.

In our gym, we score almost every drill used in practice—there's always a winner. The last thing we want is to fill practice with repetitions of skills just for the sake of doing them.

Constant competition can be intimidating for the freshmen because if they are expected to compete at everything, then there would be no off time. But it is demanded of them by the upperclassmen. Watching a competitive practice during their official visit doesn't prepare them; they can get ready for it only once they are in that environment. They either learn to compete or they move on because they don't survive. If they will not compete, that may be a symptom of another problem. The other thing we do is embrace competition: The tougher the opponent, the more we relish the challenge. We talk about competing; we practice it; we believe in it.

> Our job as coaches is to enhance and encourage competitiveness. We want the players to better their skills and learn to compete at the same time because to win, you must work on both.

Developing a young team requires a different approach. At the middle school or high school level, where you can't recruit and fill your roster with players who already possess the competitive gene, the tactic changes a bit. When a coach demonstrates through words and actions her passion for winning while maintaining the integrity of the web and showing respect for her players, the young athletes feed on that.

Using competitive drills in practice—again, while keeping the atmosphere positive and team oriented—helps generate excitement about competition and learning to create a way to win. Scheduling successful opponents instead of only beatable teams is a must, but so is building up the excitement of the challenge: "We are going to play against the toughest competition we can find. It should be really fun because this other team is great. We are going to line it up and see how we do against them."

Players will push themselves out of their comfort zones and compete hard if they are playing with confidence. It's my job as the head coach to help instill that confidence. I'm with them, not against them. I don't ever want the players worrying about what I'm thinking; I want them to spend all their energy on beating the opponent.

How easy is it to instill confidence in every player? Not very. But as a coach, you *must* find something each player does well, and run with it. The better she feels about herself, the easier it is for her to compete. We always start our talks with the players on a positive note: "Here is something you do well, but you need to improve in this other area." "You are doing a really good job with your feet. Now let's work on your arm swing."

Every player must have a role on the team. They have to have some way of contributing, so in order for them to feel connected and part of the web, you as the coach must identify something they do well and applaud it. That's how you build self-confidence. You also have to remind them, "I am not criticizing you as a person; I'm trying to make your skills better."

Positive Talk for Players

Offer encouragement to individuals and the group when you tell them how to improve on skills. One way to do that is to always recognize effort. If you are coaching a young player, you can't wait until she executes a skill properly to give positive feedback. Applaud the effort, no matter what the outcome: "That's great effort, Sally. Now let's try this to serve the ball over." Even word choice is important. Try using the word "we" even when you are making skill adjustments: "That's the effort we're looking for, Sally—now we can work on the timing." By using the word "we," the coach draws a connection to the athlete, enhancing the web. Have you ever noticed how few male coaches allow their athletes to address them by their first name? For female coaches, it's not that unheard of. Our players call me "Mary" (of course, under their breath at certain times they probably call me names that can't be printed), but I don't insist that they call me "Coach." Why not? Because I don't need to be higher on the ladder, but I do need to connect with them. That's how I can motivate and bring out the best in each of them.

Dealing With Losing and Winning

Perhaps you wonder, since competing is such a big part of our makeup, how we handle losses. Over the years we have tried to schedule the toughest teams as possible, with the understanding that we are willing to risk failure in order to get better. I once read this quote: "Failure is not falling down, but rather, not getting up after the fall." If you truly love to compete, then you can't wait for the next match after the loss. As a team and a coaching staff, we've always improved more after a loss than we ever have after a win.

Our program has great athletes who train hard and work hard. Do we always have the most talent on the court? No. But if we compete with passion, we've got a chance to win against anybody. It works for us. Sometimes after a loss, I think I could use therapy. We know we can always get better from the losses, but as the head coach I have to be even better. The players don't need me as much when we're winning. Watch a coach's nonverbal behavior when her team is losing—she'll cross her arms or sit back in her chair. But I think that when your team is losing, you need to get even closer to them—I try to get as close as possible to the sidelines.

Unless you win it all and retire, which would be the best way to go out, there is always that next match. It's hard to enjoy the losses, but to last in this business you have to learn to enjoy the ride. Sure, I'm motivated by the fear of losing—how many coaches aren't? But the teaching aspect of coaching also motivates me. I get as much of a thrill from witnessing a player master a skill as from anything else. We learn more from a loss than we ever do from a win. It is my job to convince the team that we can fix it. Everything is about learning from past experience and using it to get better for the next game. Whether the game was a win or a loss, I always ask, "What did we learn from it?" and "How can we get better?"

Athletes and coaches may have lots of faults, but I don't think being too competitive is one of them. I have never coached a player who I thought was too competitive. Confidence and competitiveness are definitely intertwined; work hard to give your players confidence and they'll find the competitiveness within themselves! Once when I was recruiting, a father told me, "We heard your gym was so competitive that the players compete to get water at the fountain during practice." If that is what other coaches are saying about our program, we have arrived.

Personal Investment and Self-Direction

6

Motivation

*Aspire to achieve meaningful goals and
sustain that drive through each season*

Nell Fortner

I loved sports from the second I knew what a sport was. I was a tomboy, and I wanted to do everything my brothers did. Even though Title IX did not exist when I was growing up, and there were no sports for girls in Mississippi, all I did was play basketball in my backyard. I was in seventh grade when, after my brother got a football scholarship to Tulane, I said, "I'm going to get a scholarship to play basketball in college."

My family moved to Texas in 1974, and the combination of the emergence of Title IX along with the state being more advanced financially than Mississippi meant that my high school in New Braunfels offered several sports for girls. I played every one of them: basketball, volleyball, tennis, and track. I had always wanted to go to the University of Texas, and that desire intensified when I met the basketball coach, Jody Conradt. She was impressive: articulate, classy, and charismatic. I knew I wanted to play for her the moment I met her. She motivates all her players to play hard and perform what she asks them to do.

My motivation comes from passion. Passion drives me in whatever I'm doing, in my job or recreationally. I am a fairly flexible person and can usually change course mid-stream without a second thought. But when I am doing something I am passionate about, nothing can deter me. I have passion for basketball—I love the sport, the athletes, and the competition. I have passion for animals and jump into that full force sometimes. I am passionate about exercise; when I'm in that mode, nothing can deter me from my morning workouts. And I am passionate about speaking to groups, whether they're accountants, AAU players, or lawyers. I take seriously the fact that they want to learn something from me or be motivated by me.

Why Not Me?

When I was in college, I knew I wanted to be the Olympic basketball coach some day. When I worked at camps I would ask my campers, "Who is going to be the Olympic coach in 2008?" When they asked who, I would say, "I am!" They would all clap and congratulate me, and I would explain that I hadn't been named yet, but that was my goal. Then I'd ask, "Who are the Olympic basketball players going to be in 2008? Somebody in this room could play. I've got to have players!" and all their hands would shoot up. The crazy thing is that I believed I would be the Olympic coach one day—and it became reality!

Early on I remember thinking, "Somebody has to be the Olympic basketball coach in 2008, so why not me?" The concept of "Why not me?" stuck with me, and I started thinking in those terms about a lot of things. I wanted to be a college coach. Why not? Those words were motivating because they kept me moving forward. I knew that if I wanted to be the Olympic coach, or if I wanted to coach in college, I needed to do certain things to meet those goals.

Part of my drive to the goal was coaching in high school for three years and then for Gary Blair at Stephen F. Austin State University for four years before becoming Leon Barmore's assistant at Louisiana Tech. That was the best move in my career. Leon is a phenomenal coach, and I learned more about basketball from him than I have from anyone. Plus, it opened up the doors for me nationally because of his program's success.

In 1995, I learned that the national team was going to train year-round for the 1996 Olympics in Atlanta. Tara VanDerveer had already been chosen as head coach of the national and Olympic teams, and Ceal Berry and Nancy Darsch had been selected as the Olympic assistants. However, neither wanted to take a leave of absence from their programs to assist with the team for a year, and I knew assisting with the national team would help me meet my longtime dream of coaching in the Olympics. It was the most phenomenal experience I'd ever had.

A year later, after winning the Big Ten Conference and signing a good class of recruits at Purdue in my first season as a head coach, it happened. I got a call from Warren Brown, the executive director of USA Basketball, who asked me to make a three-year commitment to be the coach of the national and Olympic teams. I loved Purdue, but how do you turn down an offer to be the Olympic coach? This was my dream come true.

The goal of being the Olympic coach always kept me driven. If it happened, it happened, and if didn't, it didn't, but I always had that goal.

Makeup of a Motivator

I coach for the kids. I love being around them. I like everything about it—their energy, their competitive spirit, helping them reach their potential, watching them grow and improve. That's what makes me happy. Now, I am a competitive person, and I'll race you or try to outdo you on just about anything, but what really makes me tick is taking a group of players, making them better, and trying to beat another team with them. I like all the non-sport-related things that come with coaching, too, such as helping players with personal problems, grades, and all the daily things that come up.

You have to understand this about coaching: It is such a giving thing. When kids tell me they want to coach, I always ask them, "Can you care more about your players and how they feel than you do about yourself and how you feel?" You've got to be a total giver to be a coach. It wears you out because you give them everything you've got, and it's hard for them to understand that you need something back, too. Some kids will give back, but a lot of them won't.

You need to possess three skills to be an effective coach. You have to be a communicator, a teacher, and a motivator. I have known coaches who are great with Xs and Os and can teach the game with the best, but they struggle with communicating. Teaching the Xs and Os is only one part of the job. On ome level you have to develop relationships with players. You don't have to be their best friends, but you must have some kind of relationship with them in order to teach them. They need to know that you care about them becoming better. When I get new players, the first thing I do is talk to them, get to know them, and let them get to know me better.

Communication comes in the form of establishing a relationship with your players based on compassion and care that allows them to get to know you. You are not just "Nell, the coach." You are "Nell, the coach, who drives a Tahoe and has three dogs." You develop a relationship so that any player can come and talk to you as her coach and as someone who cares about her off the floor as well.

Players don't talk to a coach initially because there is a barrier. The line of communication has to be opened, and the coach has to be the one to open it. It doesn't have to be a wide-open, expansive area. The players simply need to have the comfort level to walk in that door, sit down, and say, "Coach, this is what's going on." You will not be successful if you don't have that relationship with your players. It doesn't happen in a day; it takes time. But it has to happen, and when it does, your players would run through a wall for you. This is trust, and it is a tremendously powerful thing between a coach and an athlete.

> You need to possess three skills to be an effective coach: You have to be a communicator, a teacher, and a motivator. Teaching the Xs and Os is only one part of the job. On some level you have to develop relationships with players. You don't have to be their best friends, but you must have some kind of relationship with them in order to teach them.

Once you have that open line of communication, your players will listen to the Xs and Os and you'll be able to motivate them more easily. They won't do anything for you until they know how much you care about them, and you have to be sincere. Sincerity and compassion must start on day one, and they feel that from you. If it is fake, you will never be successful, no matter how good you are with strategies. If you are genuine in your concern for and interest in them as people, then you can motivate them and they will want to play for you. One of the biggest compliments I ever received was when some of my Olympians told me I was compassionate.

Motivating Individuals

Once you have established open lines of communication with your players and proven that you care about them, you can't disregard those concepts when you're trying to motivate them. In this day and age, kids are sensitive;

they don't want to be embarrassed. They give you what they've got, and even though it might not be very good that day, it's what they've got at the time. If you embarrass them in front of others or upset them, you'll eventually lose them.

I learned an interesting lesson as a commentator for ESPN. After my first weekend of doing studio work, the producer and I sat down to watch the tape of the show. Five other people were in the room. He evaluated me, saying things like, "See, right here you could have gone a little harder," or "You were too soft right there." I remember feeling embarrassed and upset because I had done my best and other people heard his critique.

The first thing that came to my mind was, "This is how my players feel." When I'd watch film with the team and single out players, their shoulders would drop and I always wondered why. After all, we were only watching film and trying to get better. It wasn't personal. Now I understand what they were feeling, and I have never forgotten that lesson. Now when we watch film as a group I know exactly what I am going to say, and if I want to get a little harder on a player I do it in a one-on-one situation. When you watch video, to motivate them, watch all the highlights as a team. If you want to teach them, do it one on one. You will lose your connection with them if you embarrass the athletes in front of their teammates, and if you lose them, it's hard to get them back.

Even the Olympic team members were sensitive about how they practiced. Keep in mind these are the best players in the world—but if you stay on them, they start to question their ability and confidence. I talked to them individually when I wasn't pleased with a performance. In a quiet voice I might say, "I need a little more out of you," or "I don't like the way you are doing that. This is how you need to do it."

Coach–Player Interaction. I learned a lot about coach–player interaction by working with Leon Barmore. He didn't have any fancy techniques for motivating his players. He was simply consistent with his priorities—go to church, go to class, visit your family, and play basketball. That steadiness in maintaining a value system s not only motivating, but it also teaches players the importance of consistency. With Leon, discipline was ever present, and you always knew where he stood. He would go to the office every day and work hard; he would go to the gym prepared; he would go home to his family. Seeing that level of dedication is very motivating.

Leon's dedication was apparent in his actions. He studied the game and prepared meticulously for practice. He wrote out detailed practice plans that outlined down to the minute how much time he wanted to spend doing what. When he got on the floor, he expected practice to go exactly the way he saw it in his head. If it didn't, he was not afraid to get on the players. He got very animated in his dislike about how things were going.

Leon was always an effective motivator because of his consistent intensity in practice and games and his caring way with players. If a player had a tough day and was struggling in practice, he would call them later on the phone and say, "This is Coach Barmore. I want you to know I love you and I know you worked hard today, and you're going to have a much better day tomorrow. You are going to be a great player." That was all that kid needed. She would come to practice the next day ready to work hard because he had showed that he cared about her.

He cared about his staff, too. One time on a recruiting trip he and I got into an argument about how to handle a recruit's parents. I told him what I thought we should do and he disagreed strongly. I had to remind him that I was one of the good guys. The next day I walked into my office and there was a bouquet of flowers with a note saying, "To one of the good guys." I still have that note. That's how he came back and snagged you, and that's something I learned to do with my team. I am a note-writer to my players. If I criticize a player one day, she'll have a note in her locker the next day saying, "Looking forward to a good practice today. Keep your head up. I believe in you." Something as simple as that keeps them going.

Motivating Role Players. We all have athletes at the end of the bench who work hard and are team players. Understand that although there is no "I" in team, there is a "me"; the athletes interpret everything you say in terms of "What does this mean to me?" All players love to get individual tapes of themselves because they love to focus on themselves. Find ways to motivate and empower role players, too—maybe they get to start a drill or eat first at the restaurant—and give them positive feedback. You have to make sure they know that the team wouldn't be as successful without them. I huddle my teams together at the beginning and end of practice to talk about things, and I always find something good to say about a role player. I very rarely mention a starter's name at the end of practice because they always get their names called out during practices or games, but I make a point to positively call out one or two non-starters during one of those huddles.

Motivating a Team

Communication is one of the most important facets of motivation for players, both in practice and during games. I like to post thoughts for the day for players to see when they come into the locker room, such as, "Today I gave all I had, and what I kept I've lost forever," or "You never get this game back again. You might get October 29th again, but it won't be this year. Give it everything you've got today," or "Nothing great was ever achieved without enthusiasm. Always have that energy when you hit the floor." I'm always on the lookout for quotes like that. I find them in self-help, motivational, and quote books, but some of them are old standbys. Sometimes you don't think the players read them or care, but amazingly, often they write them down or mention them to me months or years later. Your staff will appreciate them, too.

Courtesy of Nell Fortner

Teaching the Xs and Os is only one part of the job—you also need to establish open lines of communication to allow both player and coach to build respect for one another.

One of my favorite quotes is this: "If you are going to be someplace, be all there!" One day in 1996, during national team practice, I was responsible for the perimeter players, and they were just going through the motions—Sheryl Swoops, Teresa Edwards, Katie Smith, these great players. I was getting upset and felt like I was wasting my time, so I called them together and said, "Look, our head coach, Tara, is not going to stop and say, 'OK, let's just forget practice and go to the mall because you all are tired.' Don't spin your wheels. If you are going to be someplace, be all there!" They looked at me and said, "Say that again." I repeated it. "If you are going to be someplace, *be all there!*

We have to be here right now—this is it, nobody is changing, and we're not leaving this gym for another hour and a half. This is where we are, so give it everything you've got." Those players have always remembered that quote, and they tell me they use it themselves.

Pregame Talks. Pregame talks can be very important, depending on the game and what is at stake. I remember the talk I gave in 1998 before the gold-medal game in the world championships, a tournament the United States had never won; we had to beat Russia to qualify for the Olympics. I started talking about a dream every one of those players had had as a kid. "Think about when you were growing up and you were playing in the backyard. You were out there bouncing the ball, you were 10 years old, and you heard the announcer call out your name as you went in to shoot the lay-up and heard the crowd roar. You dreamed about this moment and you're sitting here right now on the verge of competing for a world championship. Those dreams start when you are little and now you are here—it is *now!*"

I'm not a fan of using rival match-ups or special games to fuel motivation. You have to be careful with that tactic because your players should want to beat *every* team they play, regardless of whether it's the first game of the year, the last game, or the school's biggest rival.

Halftime Talks. My halftime talk is usually very concise, depending on how the team is playing. I gather with my staff outside the locker room, get their feedback, look at the stat sheet, process it all, and then go in and tell the players what they need to hear. I never have spent a lot of time talking at halftime—maybe four minutes—because they are trying to get a drink, use the restroom, and gather their thoughts. Figure out what the most important points are, give them a little boost, and be done. Two or three things are about all they can handle. If the team is getting killed on the boards or defending poorly, you can control that with more effort and hard work—and a much stronger, harder tone. Otherwise, try to relax them and give them some confidence. They still have to play, so you don't want to overload them. At times I have gotten angry, and that's done no good. You can't chew them out since the game is not over and you want them to feel good. You have to be smart about when to be hard on the team.

Postgame Talks. My postgame talks are also short and sweet. After a win, I briefly cover a few of the high points; they are ready to go and highly motivated. If you lose, the talk needs to be even shorter. Try to get them to leave on a positive note, and then go watch the film and prepare for the next practice. A long speech after a loss is horrible for everyone because no one wants to hear it. Both players and coaches are disappointed, tired, hungry, and not in the mood to learn anything. Do your teaching the next day.

Playing Time. I have never taken away playing time as a motivation method. Once the game starts, that's it. You're set. I don't punish the team to motivate a player since the team's goal is to win games. Game time is not the time to mess around. If I want to punish a starter, I do it in practice—I'll move them to the second team, and that gets their attention. They want to practice with the other starters to build chemistry, and if you take that away from them they worry about whether they will start. Sometimes they'll try to sub themselves back onto the starting team, but I'll make them stay on the second team until I'm sure they are back with me.

Have Fun. Some coaches badger their teams. Even if they have great players, all the coach does is yell. The players must think they are terrible! That coach motivates those players by scaring them into thinking about what will happen if they lose. It is about total fear. I would hate to play for that type of coach—where is the fun? You have to find the fun in playing; it is a *game.* Most days we'll finish out practice with a fun drill just to remind us that it is a game. Never lose sight of the fact that you started playing sports because you wanted to have fun; as long as you can keep that element in it you have a great chance of success as a coach.

> You have to find the fun in playing; it is a *game.* Never lose sight of the fact that you started playing sports because you wanted to have fun; as long as you can keep that element in it you have a great chance of success as a coach.

Rewards As Motivation. Every player likes to be rewarded, and it rarely matters what the reward is. For instance, veterans are rewarded by not having to help the trainer carry equipment. That job is for the rookies; as the players move up in seniority, they carry less and less equipment. Or they may get a steak dinner for taking a charge in the game. The pros loved to shoot half-court shots at the end of practice for the chance of some kind of reward. They would ask me to put some money down to give a player if anyone made it. They love that kind of motivation. Sometimes you do whatever it takes.

Most players love the chance to skip conditioning activities. If I wanted to reward a certain result in a drill, I would tell them what it counted for before-hand. If they achieved that result, they got a free pass (which the manager kept track of) to skip a conditioning activity whenever they wanted to. I always offered rewards for our free-throw drills, and I think it helped. Knowing they could earn a free pass if they made 25 out of 25 free-throw attempts made them focus. We led the WNBA in free throws for three years in a row.

Days off are much bigger rewards. I give my team a monthly calendar that includes practice times, games, other team obligations, and days off. I do not vary from that schedule if at all possible, which allows them to make plans and shows that I respect their personal lives. If I do have to change the schedule, I give them plenty of notice. I never add a practice on a day off; if I add anything, it will be a day off. Taking away a day off will turn your team against you quickly.

My professional team always wanted to wear open-toed shoes on flights. Since I normally didn't allow that, they would ask if they could wear them if they won. I have never understood that; I think they should play because they want to win, not so that they can wear different shoes on a plane. But I do know that a player is a player, and players need motivation. It doesn't matter if they are 10 years old, or 20 or 40. They think like players and they act like players, and they stay that way until the day they quit playing.

Coaches can be disciplinarians and still be compassionate and motivating. As long as you are clear, concise, and exact about your expectations and the players' roles, you will have discipline. That doesn't mean that every day will be easy, but open lines of communication give both player and coach the opportunity to build respect for one another. And that mutual respect is what gives coaches the power to motivate players effectively.

7

Decision Making

*Gather information, analyze options,
and choose the best course of action*

Jan Harville

Photo by Bruce Terami

Coaching is teaching, plain and simple—that's the way I figured it when I began in 1980, and it's as true now as it was then. When I first started coaching, at the University of Washington, I had never coached or taught before in any group setting, so I felt a little insecure in my teaching methods when 120 women showed up on the first day of freshman crew practice. I needed help! A colleague passed along something he had learned from a respected education professor, something I've kept on a slip of paper in my desk for more than 20 years.

The essential elements of being a great teacher are:

1. Being systematic
2. Working hard
3. Being honest

This advice reinforced the importance of developing a system and has kept me organized ever since. It quickly became clear to me that the most important element of a strong system is good decision making.

Coaching decisions define your program just as personal decisions define your life. They identify what kind of leader you are. Do you make conscious decisions in tough situations, or do you avoid taking action and thus make a decision by default? Great coaches, like great leaders, make those tough decisions at the right time. Every day we are greeted with numerous opportunities to draw on our experience and reinforce our goals and standards with our decision-making process. Learn and practice the process; you'll find yourself taking charge of your program and life, as well as earning the respect of your athletes.

My background before coaching included two areas: academic and athletic, both of which exposed me to many high-level decision-making situations. After graduating from the University of Washington with a degree in medical technology, I worked for six years as a clinical microbiologist. In this career the work is based on the process of identifying microbes in a systematic way. Evaluating, prioritizing, and performing identification tests are part of the logical process of microbiology, and those skills are equally important in coaching.

My athletic career began in college, where I was a pre-Title IX rower, after which I was a member of seven U.S. national teams and two Olympic teams (1980 and 1984). Rowing on the national team exposed me to a high level of coaching with respect to training, selection, and performance, which impressed on me the importance of process to the end goal. I learned that one of the most important characteristics of a great coach is to make fair, timely, and considered decisions. After years of coaching and working with some of the world's best coaches, I've learned a few things about decision making.

Decision-Making Process

How do you start the decision-making process? I use the steps that follow, which I've adapted from Joe Landsberger's Study Guides and Strategies Web site, www.studygs.net. Though you may be able to shortcut these in some situations, the process is usually the same. Some problems and decisions are very challenging and require a lot of thought, emotion, and research, and all of them require flexibility and creativity. Following these steps should help you in the systematic process.

Making Decisions

1. Define and evaluate the situation.
2. Gather information.
3. Develop and analyze options.
4. Choose the best course of action.
5. Implement and review the decision.

Define and evaluate the situation. Analyzing the circumstances includes acknowledging goals, desired outcomes, and the required timeline. This is a critical first step because it defines the parameters of your decision.

- What is your goal?
- What is the issue or problem?
- Is this the real issue or a symptom of a larger problem?
- Does the issue have ethical dimensions?
- What prevents you from reaching your goal?
- What conditions must the solution satisfy?
- Will the solution affect something that must remain unchanged?
- Who is or should be involved?
- Does it need an immediate solution, or can it wait?
- Is there a risk in ignoring it?
- Are there any other challenges?

Gather information. After you define the issue or problem, start looking for the supporting information, which may include facts, data, constraints, opinions, and assumptions.

Facts and data may include information from research, results from experimentation and studies, interviews with experts and trusted sources,

---

and observed events, past or present. The constraints or boundaries, which may include budgetary limits, required events, or minimal resources, may be hard to change. In fact, if a solution is surrounded by too many constraints, the constraints themselves may be the problem.

Opinions of involved, powerful, or respected individuals or groups are important to the success of your decision. You must be able to recognize truth or bias in their opinions as well as in your own. A bias is a preexisting attitude or judgment that diminishes your ability to objectively evaluate information. Assumptions can save time and work since it is often difficult to get "all the facts," but they also have a risk factor: They must be recognized for what they are and should be discarded when they are proven wrong.

Develop and analyze options. Develop all the possible options. Be open to finding new perspectives, and brainstorm with the information you have collected. List or think through the options. Analyze each and take notes. Describe those that need more information, that offer new solutions, that can be combined or eliminated, that will meet opposition, or that seem promising or exciting.

Evaluate each alternative on your list objectively, considering all criteria. Although a seemingly reasonable solution may solve the problem, it may need to be discarded if resources aren't available, if people won't accept it, or if it causes new problems. Consider the costs and benefits of each option. Assess the possible consequences of and reactions to the decision so that there are no surprises. Involving others will help you avoid overlooking something or perhaps confirm your analysis. Depending on the type of decision you are making, you may want to involve other coaches, your assistant, athlete representatives, or perhaps an involved individual. Call on those people who are candid and knowledgeable enough to provide objective feedback, not those who will merely tell you what you want to hear.

When weighing the options, single out the most important criteria, consider costs and benefits, identify advantages and constraints, and prioritize alternatives.

Choose the best course of action. Nine times out of ten, if you've done your homework, choosing the best option is relatively easy. That tenth time is the hard, sometimes prickly, one that presents many variables, negative outcomes in all options, conflicts between your determining criteria, or a challenging situation because you know that someone is not going to like you. The trick is to weigh the plusses and minuses of your options against the priorities, goals, philosophy of your program, team standards, and the desire to stay consistent. Eliminate alternatives systematically by comparing and discarding those that are least appropriate.

When deciding, don't regard any option as the "perfect solution." If it existed, there probably wouldn't be a problem in the first place. Consider your intuition, because you may have an instinctive feel for the appropriate decision. Then review your choice with a respected adviser. Is there something you missed? After a careful review of all the options, you may be able to combine solutions or find a compromise.

Making your decision in a timely manner is important. A rush to judgment without taking time to get the facts and analyze them ultimately takes control out of your hands. On the other hand, delaying or avoiding hard decisions doesn't make them go away; it only takes the control away from you and weakens your position as a leader. When you get frustrated about a tough decision, ask yourself what else you can do. Is there any more research or analysis that can be done? Are there any more options? Are there any more criteria available to help weigh the options? Is there any reason to wait? If not, then you know that you need to make the best decision possible, without delay.

Implement and review the decision. Consider taking these steps in creating an "action plan" and monitoring the progress of your decision:

- Follow a step-by-step process as required.
- Communicate your decision to those who will be affected by the change.
- Identify any needed resources.
- Create a time line for implementation.
- Assess the effects of your decision.

Do the results meet your expectations and goals? If not, is it possible to revisit other options? Review your experience to learn about yourself and what you consider important. If it turns out that you made a wrong decision, don't let it undermine your confidence. Simply acknowledge your mistake, learn from it, and move on. With each decision, you will learn important lessons that help you readjust the next time. The more decisions you make, the better you will become at making the right call.

Coaching Decisions

Let's take a few typical coaching situations and go through the decision-making process to see how it can work. I've encountered the following dilemmas in my coaching career.

Program priorities. Avoiding conflicts between academic and athletic priorities when coaching at an academic institution is difficult. You must be flexible in order to stay on course to achieve your goals. It pays to take time to go through the decision-making process with each situation or problem.

Consider the following example: An athlete told me that she needed to miss an important practice during racing season for a required school field trip that had just been scheduled.

Here are the facts: The team philosophy states that academics come first. Athletes are required to be at every practice, and they know the practice and race schedule before they register for classes. The athletic department's academic adviser helps with class registration to avoid conflicts, but in this case the athlete didn't know about the field trip requirement when the class was scheduled. The athlete was a good student, honest and reliable. She was in the top varsity eight, thus missing practice would affect several lineups for the upcoming race—the practice was an important one with specific race preparation. Finally, an immediate solution was required because the field trip was scheduled for the next weekend.

From the athlete I determined that her class grade would be affected significantly if she did not participate in the field trip. We discussed the time parameters of the trip and of practice. She hadn't discussed any other options with the professor; however, she did overhear another student have an excuse denied. I asked how flexible her professor was and suggested that she talk to her about the situation. Perhaps there were alternative trips she could take to fulfill the requirement. If not, there appeared to be three options.

First, the student could suggest a compromise to her professor that let her leave an hour late, drive her own car, and meet the group at the field trip site. This would require a compromise on my part in starting the practice a half-hour earlier and excusing her from the second part. This was my top choice because it allowed me to balance the academic needs of the student and the training needs of the team. However, this solution was dependent on the professor.

Second, I could allow her to miss the entire practice. This would affect the lineups for several of our crews, disturbing the matching, rhythm, and speed of the boats and affecting our ability to attain peak performance. I could switch workouts with the one scheduled for the day before, in order to put the racing emphasis on the practice when the athlete could be there, but the training would be somewhat compromised by reduced recovery time and less dependable water conditions. This option reinforced the priority on academics but had a greater adverse effect on the team's preparation.

The third solution was not to allow her to miss practice. Let her negotiate with the professor herself to solve her academic problem. This put the team interests over those of a single athlete. The major problem here was that it conflicted with the philosophy of the program. It would also probably cause the athlete to become stressed about the situation, which would not help her performance.

Fortunately, the professor was understanding when the athlete talked with her. They agreed that she could leave late and join the field trip after practice. This allowed me to let her meet her academic commitment and still participate in the most important part of practice. The professor and I compromised, but both of us were able to meet our goals.

You must be flexible in order to stay on course to achieve your goals. It pays to take time to go through the decision-making process with each situation or problem.

This example reinforces the importance of communication and information gathering in the process of making a decision. Compromise and creativity can solve many problems. I've been able to get more creative with alternative solutions with more experience. Just remember that each situation usually has subtle differences that require a new review of the facts, with potentially different options and priorities or a new final outcome.

Developing or revising a training program. Creating or revising a team training program requires meticulous data collection and review of numerous details, conditions, and options. Every coach has done this in some manner in her career. Several years ago our coaching staff reviewed the fall training program because it appeared to be an area in which we were weaker than some of our competitors. Our goal was to see if we could increase the level and efficiency of our team's fitness during this period, with a minimal time-demand increase.

The following were the facts of our situation:

- Fall is a training period in the sport of rowing.
- The priorities were endurance training and skill development.
- The goals were to improve the team's aerobic conditioning level and our efficiency of training, and to increase intensity to provide a better aerobic base preparation for winter and spring.
- Our program had been successful (our men and women were in the top three teams in the country) but our ergometer (indoor rowing machine) scores were not as good as other programs in the fall.
- Our secondary goal was to improve ergometer scores in the fall training period.
- Constraints included practice limits (NCAA and academic demands), class schedules, race and travel schedules, holidays, finals, and required athletic department meetings.
- The timeline was to finish the review so that a new plan would be ready by the beginning of fall training.

I worked with our men's coach, who had successful coaching experience with training programs at the collegiate and Olympic level. We each did a day-by-day summary of our fall training for the previous three years, then categorized the types of workouts and how they were done. On a calendar, we penciled in required events, and we listed our fall performance goals and

Photo by Joanie Komura

Good decision-making and organization are keys to creating a successful team.

priorities. We reviewed ways to measure our progress and discussed different ways to make the workouts motivating and interesting. We asked some of our top athletes for feedback about workouts they liked and didn't like, and why. We included ingredients from some of our competitors' plans as well as from the U.S. national team schedule, and we talked with several experts in the country who specialize in aerobic training and physiological testing.

From all these data, we developed some options for modifications, including changing the volume of training in each area, adding more specific individualized workouts, increasing the specificity of training (more rowing-based workouts), utilizing more automatic criteria for selection for fall races, increased emphasis on testing performance, and changing testing dates. We discussed variations of these options with respect to our athletes' academic commitments, likelihood of participation in optional workouts, motivation, interest, and injuries. Then we compared these options to what we were currently doing successfully; we didn't want to give up anything that was working well.

Developing our final plan was like putting a puzzle together. We had to keep all the required events in place on the calendar, then pencil in team and optional individual workouts. Our final plan included more individualized workouts, which required more work by the coaches in designing them and interpreting the testing. We added more workouts on the rowing ergometers but made minimal changes to the on-water training since we believed that we were already achieving close to maximum results. We changed our testing dates and criteria slightly to be more effective in giving training feedback to each athlete and allow easier adjustments to individual training. An important part of the process was discussing the changes and new program with the athletes when the season began; they needed to be excited and motivated in order for the plan to be successful. We reviewed the rationale for the changes, goals, testing dates, and qualification standards. The clearer the pathway to success is, the easier it is to follow.

The process of analyzing our fall program took a lot of time, and the resulting plan was not drastically different from the one we had been using. But we were happy that we had taken the time to make sure that our changes were based on fact and that the plan had a reasonable chance for success. As it turns out, test scores for both men and women were better than in previous years and the athletes liked the changes, especially the individualization. Both our men's and women's squads finished in the top three in the country that spring. Never be afraid of change if you're looking to improve.

Athlete Selection

Athlete selection is an entire decision-making topic unto itself and is probably the most important characteristic by which athletes judge coaches. Are we fair? Are we consistent? Do we stick with what we say? Do we treat everyone the same? Do we seem to have favorite athletes? Do we communicate our expectations clearly? Athletes will respect you if you stay consistent, whether they are the most decorated superstar or the last walk-on athlete. Winning doesn't hurt either.

First, I suggest having a system in place that allows the athletes to respect your decisions. By that I mean set up a system of testing and evaluation that covers all your priorities by making it clear, by the most objective means possible, which athletes are the best. My main goals were to make the varsity eight able to go as fast as possible and to have the best rowers be obvious to me and to the team. You know you've achieved success when athletes ask how they can improve rather than claiming that you made a selection mistake. Some of the selection criteria I use include the following:

- Performance under pressure
- Intra-squad "selection" racing
- Individual performance in small boats
- Ergometer times
- Consistency in workouts and dependability
- Improvement and potential for improvement

- Attitude
- Maturity
- Past successful experience

Other sports may require different criteria, but these are the general guidelines I follow. I have to weigh the amount of time needed by the crew to row together, which improves team matching and rhythm skills, against the time needed to make fair selections. With experience and trial and error, this usually becomes clear. But even using all these steps and priorities, athlete selection is still never easy and exceptions always seem to challenge the system.

I had one such exception a few years ago. We were in the midst of final selection for the varsity eight shortly before the first big race of the season when one of the top performers suffered a back injury and wasn't able to participate in the final two weeks of selection racing. She was cleared for full participation only two days before the team left for the competition. The question was whether to place the athlete in the boat based on her performance up until her injury or wait a week and work her back in after the race.

In evaluating the solution, my two main goals were to be fair in selection and to race the fastest crew possible. I wasn't sure how the athlete's back would hold up under intense exertion after time off. She had missed an important element of the selection and preparation process, but she was near the top in three measurable selection categories. I rated the confidence of the athlete and the crew's confidence in her, and noted that she really wanted to race. The injury wasn't her fault; it was out of her control.

A big concern was whether this athlete was fit and healthy enough to hold up during racing, which was such a huge risk with the type of injury she had had that even our trainer could not guarantee her health. I also took into consideration discussions with other staff coaches, a couple of team leaders, the trainer, and the athlete in question. The other major consideration was the fairness and credibility of the selection process.

The first option was to place her in the varsity boat; she could potentially make it faster. She deserved the spot to that point in the process but was unable to complete the final difficult testing and verifying process. One risk was that her back might not be completely healed and she could have a relapse by jumping right back into intense racing. If this happened, it would noticeably slow the boat or, if she couldn't race, cause a forfeit. The other big problem was risking the team's respect for the selection process by showing apparent favoritism to the injured athlete. There were no opportunities to continue the selection process until after the race.

The second option was to hold her out of the race and wait a week before having her row with the team, which would allow her to work back into intense training more gradually, hopefully with less risk of reinjury. After we returned from the race, we could start her rowing in the second eight for a few days before giving her a chance to race in the varsity eight. This would eliminate the risk of a poor race performance if her injury had not healed and would preserve the selection process. However, the varsity eight's speed might not be as fast with an alternate rower. Both options required clear communication with the athlete and team.

I chose the second, more conservative, option even though it was difficult for the athlete and likely limited our speed. She was upset about not racing because her back felt so much better, so we had to have a couple of discussions during which I explained all the criteria, goals, options, and possible consequences. She still didn't like it but understood and accepted it. She proved herself by winning her selection races a week later. She gained confidence by earning her seat, her crew had confidence that she belonged, and the athlete who had temporarily replaced her knew that she had been beaten. The varsity eight went on to win the NCAA championship that year and the second eight placed second, which verified the process.

This decision sounds straightforward when looking back, but weighing these options at the time required a lot of clear thinking. Emotions were running high. The team needed to understand that the plan was the best option for both the injured athlete and the team. This example illustrates the importance of communication in producing confidence in the solution. Because a plan needs to be trusted to be successful, it must be presented clearly. Once confidence is created, success has a chance to follow.

Expectations and Consequences

What happens when an athlete breaks a team rule? Do you treat every athlete the same way, or do you make exceptions for the better ones? I work extremely hard to set a universal standard for consequences. I may change them as the season goes on, and different team goals may be factored in, but expectations and consequences do not vary for individual athletes. Team standards can be reinforced only if they apply to everyone, and coaches who are consistent earn respect from their athletes.

What about athletes who break a team rule in the middle of the competitive season, when in team sports almost any consequence will affect every player? It is very hard to weigh the punishment of individuals against the "innocent" punishment of the team. I had one such case a few years ago: Four athletes from our top two eights were found to have been drinking alcohol on a road trip. Drinking is prohibited for all athletes at our institution while on official team travel, and each team's coaches must determine the consequences. I confirmed the report and the facts by talking with witnesses and the athletes involved. The issue was deciding what the consequences should be and who should be involved in determining them.

After expressing to the team my disappointment and reinforcing the rules and the seriousness of the situation, I asked our elected team leaders to give me a recommendation. I gave them guidelines about what to consider in their decision. This was very stressful and difficult for the leaders because it required them to weigh what was appropriate punishment for the individuals (who were their good friends) with the almost certain effect it would have on their own crew's race performance. This serious transgression of team rules hadn't happened before to my knowledge and I wanted to be sure that it did not happen again.

I almost always involve the team leaders in decisions about consequences so that the team has a stake in the process and the outcome. The consequences that they came up with covered several areas; the one that had the greatest impact on the team was to hold all four athletes out of racing in the next competition. This decision changed all the lineups for the upcoming weekend's races, which could affect each race's outcome by slowing boat speed. The other recommended disciplines involved community service and apologies.

I was satisfied with the severity of the punishment. It required that the entire team step up in the next race to meet the challenge of changed lineups, which generally result in slower speeds. I wanted the crews to get something positive out of this experience. I told them not to look for excuses or allow themselves to become victims of this situation. I said that if everyone contributed a little more, the sum of those contributions might be enough to overcome the changes. In the end, the team was successful, with excellent performances in each event. What had been an extremely serious problem became a chance to develop a sense of responsibility in not only the team leaders and the transgressors but in the entire team. This reinforced my coaching philosophy of teaching athletes to take responsibility for themselves, their team's actions, and their performances.

Again, communication was critical in this situation. The process needed to be clear, the lesson to be learned needed to be articulated, and the fact that something positive would come out of it needed to be emphasized. The offending athletes were contrite, the leaders took responsibility by making a tough decision, and the team met the challenge presented.

> You must make conscious decisions about what you say and do, not merely act by default. Your personal decisions affect the credibility of your coaching decisions. Be reliable. Be consistent. Be accountable.

As a coach, the decisions you make about your actions are important to your position as a leader. You are a role model and, given a choice, it's better to be a good one. Your athletes notice how you act in public, what you talk about, your use of alcohol, and the respect you show for others. You must make conscious decisions about what you say and do, not merely act by default. Your personal decisions affect the credibility of your coaching decisions. Be reliable. Be consistent. Be accountable.

You will make better decisions if you follow a systematic process. It doesn't matter whether the process is this model or one that you develop yourself. My goal is to provide you with one model that works with examples that relate to coaching. But be sure that you have a model. Be flexible, but be organized. Take responsibility for yourself, your decisions, and your program.

> *"I cannot, for want of sufficient premises, advise you what to determine, but if you please I will tell you how. . . . My way is to divide half a sheet of paper by a line into two columns; writing over the one "Pro," and over the other "Con." Then, doing three or four days' consideration, I put down under the different heads short hints of the different motives, that at different times occur to me for or against the measure. When I have thus got them all together in one view, I endeavor to estimate the respective weights . . . [to] find at length where the balance lies . . . And, though the weight of reasons cannot be taken with the precision of algebraic quantities, yet, when each is thus considered, separately and comparatively, and the whole matter lies before me, I think I can judge better, and am less liable to make a rash step; and in fact I have found great advantage for this kind of caution, in what may be called moral or prudential algebra."*
>
> *—Benjamin Franklin, letter to Joseph Priestly, September 19, 1772*

The better the decisions you make, the more successful you will be. You will be respected for your considered opinions and decisions, and that respect will encourage your athletes to listen to and follow you. A great coach is a great leader who guides her team to success.

8

Self-Discipline

Maintain consistent direction, effort, and composure without external controls

Mary Jo Peppler

Courtesy of the American Volleyball Coaches Association

What is self-discipline and how do you get it? Some people have lots of it, but most people want more of it. How much of it do we really want? If you had it, what would you accomplish?

Self-discipline can assist us in getting something that we want. That something that we want will be difficult to achieve, will take hard work, and will demand amazing amounts of focus and diligence.

We can think of discipline as a template that develops in direct proportion to how well we support it. I look at discipline as a component of training, just like learning skills or developing fitness. Its muscles must be flexed, and if it is properly challenged, it will fail and succeed at regular intervals.

The focus of all training is on attaining a goal. Until we understand the goal and have a clear idea about how to achieve it, any efforts we direct toward getting it will be random. Once we clearly enjoy the idea of what we want, we are almost home. I know of two ways to attain things that we don't have—breathe it or plan it. Here is a story about the first way.

Some time ago, a fast-food chain had a promotion. For a 25-word essay, some lucky winner would own a go-cart. In a rural Texas town, over 60 miles away, a small boy, a friend's nephew, set his sights on that go-cart. Nobody can say how Tommy started to live his dream, but in one moment, he set his template and breathed life into it. He jumped into it 24/7. He wrote the essay and started to prepare for getting his go-cart. His parents worried about what to do when he did not win. It never occurred to Tommy that he would not win.

Thoughts, dreams, behaviors, and choices are most intimately connected to reality. Tommy did not have to make himself live and breathe his go-cart. His mother did not sit him down and say, "OK, Tommy. Stop everything now and think about winning the go-cart for 10 minutes!" He did not have to be disciplined to give it energy or to keep a positive outlook. In one grand moment, he was fully committed. Body and soul. One hundred percent. He looked only forward and never doubted the outcome.

So the first, and I think easiest, way to attain a dream is to breathe it. Embody it. Act as if it were so. As children, most of what we create in our world is done in this manner. It is not so farfetched. It is not even unnatural. In fact, I think it is our natural state of manifestation. It is the way our right brain, our creative genius, makes up our world. This way mimics and embodies. This way lives it, buys it, breathes it. It is magical. It can be easy but it requires a leap of faith.

In this first way of creating reality, you must be a dreamer. You don't have to understand how to accomplish a new dream. You just have to breathe it. Tommy did. We can say he had faith. For Tommy, it was easy. He told everyone that he was going to win. In one moment he was fully committed, and he was not separate from the result. He owned it. Then he won.

Can dreams come true? For as long as I can remember, I knew I was going to go to the Olympics. As a small child I must have become enamored with the event. I don't remember when or how. I never visualized what sport I would play. I never visualized competing or winning. I did visualize marching into the stadium. Many years later, the memory of marching into that Tokyo stadium in 1964 still quickens my heartbeat.

The second way I know how to accomplish something is more linear. It demands discipline. It is the way our left brain, our scientific genius, makes up our world. This way dissects, practices, experiences trial and error, and moves through a process. This way plans and progresses on a schedule. It grinds away day by day. It fails and succeeds at regular intervals. It builds block upon block and links these blocks to the goal. This is the way we accomplish things as adults. It is difficult and requires discipline.

But discipline isn't really what gives results in this method. Discipline is only a step along the process. An important step, indeed, the keystone step on the trail. But what really matters here is commitment. Discipline helps us get to commitment. It is through commitment that we can fully direct our willpower to make the quantum leap that will yield success.

Here's how it works. We set a goal. We lay out a plan or a process that should yield results. Then we go about following that plan. Along the way, we forget that the plan is unyielding in its demands on us. In this method, if we waver from the plan, it will erode our belief that the goal can be attained. The belief is all that holds us to the realization of the goal.

> Discipline is a component of training, just like learning skills or developing fitness. Its muscles must be flexed, and if it is properly challenged, it will fail and succeed at regular intervals.

Whatever the goal that we are pursuing, something must bind us to it, weave us into its *energy signature,* the full body of its manifestation. When we choose the process style of accomplishment, we take those pieces of the dream in small bites. We bite off some of the skills that we will need (our weight training, for example). We tear away part of a strategy. Somewhere along the way we have eaten enough. We arrive at the goal when we release ourselves from the process. The release is the tricky part. It requires that leap of faith. Until then, all we have is our process, our hard work, and our diligence. Our discipline is what binds us to that future.

There are four phases of the process: external discipline, transition, self-discipline, and commitment.

Applying External Discipline

The first type of discipline that we need when we embark on a journey to accomplish something is external discipline. In sport, you require external discipline until you agree to join the dream of success. The dream will be fairly specific and will demand certain behaviors. If it is a team sport, success will require awareness of and respect for teammates.

An athlete will need external discipline as long as she isn't committed. At times, others will need to force the athlete to follow the plan of training. The amount of external discipline necessary at this stage is in direct proportion to the degree to which the athlete buys into the individual or team goal. If an athlete's level of commitment is too low, she may not submit to the program. In this case, she may quit, get injured, complain, perform minimally, or even denigrate the experience from within. Regardless, through external discipline, those who will not join will be revealed and eliminated.

Your goal as a coach at this stage is to get the athlete to join the dream. A good example of how discipline develops a person's level of commitment is the military. Not everyone chooses the military as a career. Those who do make that decision have submitted to the discipline and have bought into the dream. The system and the coach can transform the person. Both will reveal the benefits of participation along the way.

Those who enter the process without clear goals or drive can still be won over. The results of discipline can engage the dreamer's highest self. The athlete can feel a sense of power from the structure, and the hard work starts to transform her physical reality. Soon, the hard work starts to feel good, and the victim in her gives up because the athlete starts to receive better benefits than the victim can offer. It is in this moment that the athlete's future opens to her.

External Discipline

1. Externally enforce the training.
2. Enforce adherence to the structure and follow through on consequences.
3. Give extensive feedback on progress.
4. Watch for signs of more commitment.
5. Sell the program and training to the players.
6. Show the players and team how they can be successful if they keep working.
7. Be aware that you will encounter limitations in belief.
8. Let the training sell itself by the participants' improvement

The athlete at this level is a beginner. Her skills of training and focus are undeveloped. As a beginner, she will need high structure and discipline and unerring supervision. She will falter. She will need to understand the consequences for failing to adhere to the program. She will need to be tested so that she can see her progress at regular intervals. As the coach, you can see the athlete's progress at this level when she works hard without having to be pushed, when she trains successfully without supervision, and when she starts to do additional work on her own. The player who is becoming more committed will start to explore her options to become even more successful.

At this stage of training, it's helpful if you have sales skills. Training will be somewhat in a holding pattern until the athletes buy in. Your goal is to move the athletes toward self-responsibility and then self-discipline.

Imagine being a used-car dealer. You have a car to sell with a rebuilt engine. The body is good, and it has a clean interior and low mileage. It is a great car for the money and will probably run for many years to come. Compare this to the coach's task of giving a sales pitch to players to join the team and give their best competitive effort. We have good personnel, we will work hard and be in better shape than our opponents, and we are better competitors because we have great game plans.

As the used-car dealer, you should be aware that the customer probably has some negative ideas about buying a used car. The customer may think that buying a used car is a risk because it probably has something wrong with it. To change the template that drives the customer's belief, you might offer to have the mechanic check it out, or you might be able to produce its past service records. Maybe you could offer some guarantees.

As you sell the template to the team, you will also have to engage the athletes' past template. You will need to diffuse any resistance. Players may think that their school never has a winning season, or they may have a specific opponent that they have never beaten. They may think they are inferior players. To change the template that drives the players' belief, you may need to show them stats indicating too many serving or hitting errors, which have kept them from success in the past. They may need to replace one skill with a better skill or be shown a different manner of performing it. For instance, they might learn better techniques, or learn a stress-reducing routine so that they could play successfully under pressure, or learn how to make better choices so that they could take the best swing in difficult situations and not make so many hitting errors.

A player will resist changing her beliefs, just as the customer will be skeptical until she accepts enough of the new template to buy the product. In both cases, the sale is not ensured. What sport and the military have to offer that the salesperson lacks is the authority to administer discipline. Through external discipline, the coach and the athlete, or soldier, are given adequate time to generate the required energy to accomplish exceptional tasks. It gives everyone time to buy in. It allows players to feel their bodies get stronger from the training, or perform skills more reliably, and in general be successful where they previously failed. This is a powerful motivator. It is a period of building momentum. Then, when you see the athlete's commitment start to rise, you can expect that the athlete is ready for the next level.

Transitioning From External to Internal Discipline

As an athlete matures, her need for external discipline will diminish. While she is developing, however, she will demonstrate changing levels of commitment to the dream. This progress usually happens in increments. Therefore, levels of discipline, external or internal, will have to be varied. When an athlete is immature in this area, she will need a high level of external discipline and structure, which means clear instructions, consequences, and an active feedback loop.

Self-discipline starts to flex its considerable muscles when an athlete buys into a program. Then, she will not resist the specifics of working toward its goals. In that transition, external discipline gives the athlete and the coach a period of grace. One day the athlete will be self-motivated, and the next day, not so much. This is a period in which both the athlete and coach struggle with control of the direction of the training and the amount and type of work that are required. Often, this period is not so graceful at all, because power struggles ensue while the athlete struggles with her ability to attend to the moment-to-moment challenges of her workload as they relate to her goals. Both coach and athlete also need this time to agree on the specifics of the goal or what the final product will look like. Until the athlete merges with the coach or the program, she will need extensive external discipline.

Once you start to observe behaviors mentioned earlier in the chapter, such as internal discipline and greater commitment, then more of the training can be delegated to the athlete herself. This is possible because her commitment level has increased to the point of self-responsibility. At this level, the athlete starts to understand that she is only hurting herself when she does not follow her program. If she does not believe in the training, then she will not adhere to it. If she does not recognize her progress as a result of that training, she will become discouraged and need more external help. But when she is bought in, she will automatically start to discipline herself.

Transition

1. Watch for signs that an athlete is growing toward commitment.
2. Support her in her independent discipline by recognizing her progress.
3. Assist her through disappointment by refocusing.
4. Move back and forth between external and internal control.
5. Focus more on the goal than on the structure of the discipline.
6. Recognize discipline for what it can do for the athlete's progress.

When the athlete gradually replaces external discipline with self-discipline, her workload will feed her. The successes and even the failures on the journey will feed her. She will have more energy and more of an ability to stay optimistic. She can truly start the journey toward her success.

Ultimately, any type of discipline is flawed because it keeps the person who is being disciplined inept. As long as the experience is happening to you, while it is imposed on you, it is not your dream. When discipline is administered externally, the participant is dependent on the administrator of the discipline. When discipline is administered internally, the athlete becomes a victim to the structure of the discipline. Either way, only the discipline, not the dream, is being pursued.

When discipline is present, the athlete is not operating from her full power base. She has not achieved full integrity with her goal yet. She is compromised. She does not have enough energy to actually become the model. She still relies on discipline to glue her to the goal. The energy it takes to engage discipline is the very energy required for propelling forward into the champion that is being pursued. The athlete relying on discipline is chasing instead of being.

Acquiring Self-Discipline

The athlete who comes to the level of self-discipline wants to accomplish the goal. She buys into the training plan. She has learned how to work hard and can sustain herself through periods of drought. She uses failure as a motivator instead of letting it frustrate her or give her a reason to quit. Certainly, the self-disciplined athlete will have lapses of frustration and disappointment, but she will rebound. She will feel her emotions deeply and then will take the power of those emotions and recommit to the goal. She just needs to refocus.

Self-Discipline

1. Let the athlete manage parts of her training and participate more in choices.
2. Keep the training on task while keeping the big picture in mind.
3. Keep trying to break through an athlete's limited thinking.
4. Let self-discipline glue the athlete to the dream.

This athlete is still not committed. Commitment is the ultimate goal of training. Once she's committed, all things become possible. Discipline keeps us on track, keeps us woven into the grid of the champion, until we heal our lack of commitment. It is medicine for our passion. We have to keep taking the medicine until we are healed or until we succumb to the disease. Self-discipline is the pivotal step in becoming committed. When an athlete attains a working relationship with self-discipline, she has learned how to use its primary tool: self-talk. It is through self-talk that she works when she would rather rest, sleeps when she would rather party, and eats well when she wants empty calories and rich desserts. Self-discipline is about winning those internal arguments between your athlete and your couch potato. When we positively direct our inner dialogue during repetitions and work, during rest and recovery, and during all our waking moments, our self-discipline becomes an agent for our healing.

Creating a new reality, in the form of a dream or goal, can be difficult. Athletes who lack the commitment will become discouraged, blame others, or want to quit, especially when that reality is not readily attained. As the coach, you must then hold onto the dream for both yourself and for your athletes. You must let evidence contrary to the dream give you the opportunity to display your courage, your passion, your faith, and your work ethic. When necessary, you and the team must pretend that things are better. At these times, self-discipline must lock out the evidence of failure.

> Athletes who lack the commitment will become discouraged, blame others, or want to quit. As the coach, you must then hold onto the dream for both yourself and for your athletes. You must let evidence contrary to the dream give you the opportunity to display your courage, your passion, your faith, and your work ethic.

Excellence is not ordinary reality. To attain it, you must shift to a place where what you want to happen is actually possible. Throughout time and culture, different things are ordinary, and different things are possible. We are limited by what is possible in our time and place. Today we live easily with many things that were impossible in another time. Conversely, many things in other times are not possible today. To get to a reality that is beyond our current capabilities, like winning a championship or beating a specific opponent, you must be healed of the affliction of your limited beliefs. The evidence of your disease, the voices externally and internally that tell us you are sick or that you cannot do it, must be silenced. At this moment, the self struggles to be lifted above the influence of the sickness, the limitation.

In the beginning, self-discipline is the athlete's medicine. In the end, when she is fully committed, she doesn't need medicine because she is not separate from the thing that she had been chasing. But while she is chasing, her chances for healing are intimately woven into the self-discipline of her internal dialogue. It is the strongest tool for transformation. The struggle to overcome the collective inertia of the old model is the greatest challenge of the self-disciplined athlete. This inertia is considerable because everyone reinforces what can't or hasn't been accomplished. It is absolutely necessary to release the lock on whatever old idea is limiting the athlete and enter the new one idea. Sometimes this begins as simply as only pretending. Until an athlete has enough energy invested in the new model, she will continue to be sick and need to keep taking the medicine of self-discipline.

Healing

1. Help athletes release the old and limiting model of performance.
2. Be willing to shift toward the new and desired model.
3. Focus on self-talk.
4. Move toward full commitment by celebrating and focusing on what is in tune with the model.

To create a new reality, an athlete has to be linked to its new template with self-discipline. Almost everything of value that we accomplish hasn't been done before, at least not by us. The new template doesn't have to be logical. In fact, it usually is not logical. Each time we create something in sport, it is new. It has never been done before; each situation has always been altered from the last time, from any other time. For most future winners, there is no evidence to support their intended success. Especially in the United States, success stories in sport are in direct contradiction to reality as we consent to it. Many winners come from unlikely places.

Everyone in training must be willing to shift what they think is possible. Self-discipline is the glue that attaches the seeker to the future model. You can help players find the catalyst that allows them to believe in the attainability of the new model. First, sell the program. Second, take an active role in helping to shape each athlete's interior climate. Athletes struggle with positive inner dialogue. When the athlete gets to the level of self-discipline, your feedback loop should focus on a player's inner conversations. This step is the most neglected one in sport training. For this reason, most athletes are not healed. They do not understand that how they represent their experience to themselves, in each moment, is really what self-discipline is all about. Remember that the function of self-discipline is to move the athlete into commitment.

Negative self-talk stops the athlete from becoming enchanted. Without commitment, passion cannot flow freely. Commitment makes an athlete's actions clear, energetic, passionate, willing, fearless, and on task. She becomes whole and healed.

Achieving Commitment

When an athlete becomes committed, she will be willing to do whatever it takes to accomplish her goal. She understands that the program works. The committed athlete looks much the same as the athletes at other levels. The biggest difference between a committed athlete and an uncommitted one is a willingness to fail. The committed athlete does something different with her experiences and her internal dialogue. She stops trying to improve and instead practices how to respond. Her training is linked to performance rather than development. When she fails, it is not personal; it is a problem to be solved.

Before an athlete is committed, the reality of her unrealized goals will limit her. She will have lots of evidence to negate, and little evidence to support, the dream. Through the process of discipline, an athlete can incrementally try on her goal. She can practice feeling and thinking like a champion. She locks into that grid with the extraordinary energy of self-discipline. She holds it tightly. The committed athlete is released from this effort. She doesn't need to be glued to the goal, because she has embodied it already. This frees up an extraordinary amount of energy.

Commitment

1. Reinforce any evidence that supports the new model, and join the energy of those who have the most passion.
2. Deemphasize any evidence that does not support the new model.
3. Do not judge any phase of the process. Move away from linear evaluations and move toward becoming a champion.
4. Be sure the individual and the team are committed to the ultimate model.
5. Use willpower to accomplish goals.

Ironically, the person who is truly committed will be damaged by discipline. Her commitment affords her a level of self-esteem that she will have to relinquish when she submits to discipline. The same discipline that may build personal momentum in the uncommitted athlete will suck the life out of the already committed one. As the coach, you must stop the eager player from working too hard. This is in sharp contrast to a player who needs discipline and tries to get out of doing her part. The committed player will need to be sold on the benefits that discipline offers in a program so that she will want to follow it. Before that happens, a committed player will be damaged by discipline.

Once fully committed, the seeker embodies the dream and never judges her ability to attain it. Once committed, the player's willpower eagerly takes orders from the dreamer and works hard without inner dialogue or argument. This is accomplished with minimal energy. There is no question of lost possibility or deficiency. However, this is so difficult today that it is the stuff of fairy tales and child's play. It is rare in our culture to step outside ordinary reality and embrace our future self now. This is the reality that wins a go-cart. Most adults will question and talk themselves out of doing the work. When we question, we will need discipline. Through discipline, we can accomplish more than anyone thought possible. Discipline can build an incredible momentum that is empowering beyond previous beliefs. Discipline brings us the growth of commitment; with commitment comes the gift of willpower. This is the growth and the gift that can pull up a new reality.

Commitment differs from discipline because it is directed completely from within. Commitment doesn't whine or talk itself out of training. It doesn't question. It is simple, beautiful, exquisite intention. Once an athlete is committed, intention and goals are merged. Willpower becomes an agent for the accomplishment of the work. It is woven into the fabric of success. It merely needs to be given directions and it follows through without argument.

Children easily access commitment. They seem to understand instinctively that they have a direct relationship with the creation of events that will then happen to them. They believe, they have faith, and they act accordingly. Children don't question Santa's existence until they have lost their innocence. From that point on they will need more discipline, and from that point on they will have more trouble gathering enough energy to manifest their dreams.

On the level of full commitment, we can bypass our skepticism, our limitations, and our lack of confidence through a steady diet of unobstructed training and competing. Everything becomes congruent. When we are successful, we come full circle and enliven what we lost as children, we can want to serve an ace and then actually serve an ace. We can feel and play with thinking and doing with complete innocence. We remember that the relationship of intention and goals does indeed easily merge. We know what we must do, and without challenging it (willpower), we do it.

Every successful team that I have ever been involved with has had key players who burned with their passion. These fully committed players had the ability to transform the entire team into champions. Teams that succeed accept that passion and help it grow. It becomes contagious. Remember that each player will give more or less of their approval to participate in the team's goals. The players who give more have to dominate the energy signature of a team for it to progress and become exceptional.

Working With Teams

As difficult as it is to get a single player to embrace the full commitment of excellence, a team sport magnifies the problem. Team members need a private reason to join a group template. Each participant must give her personal approval to join the dream. Each individual must compromise her own personal ambitions for the greater accomplishments of the team. The willingness of each team member will set the limits of the team's accomplishment.

In the beginning, the team experience happens to the players, with varying amounts of personal approval. This erodes personal power. Nothing magical happens with damaged personal power. With the tool of discipline, you can gain the consent of the individuals who must partake in the group template. Again, the model of the military shows how forced discipline can create momentum. The soldier who emerges through external discipline to self-discipline to commitment emerges as a warrior.

In some ways, team sports are easier than individual sports because the momentum of the team can generate an amazing tidal wave and everyone will go for the ride. But team sports are also more difficult than individual sports because, almost always, each player will have to compromise her self-interests. Regardless, most players will fall away before they reach the promised land because their victim will be unwilling to give up and join the dream. The hard part about team sports is getting full participation from all members. Each player must fulfill her role, and that role is often not everything that she wants from the experience. Normally, excellence is not attained without work. When players are in need of discipline, they need hard work. When players are committed, they love to work. Either way, they work.

When a team repeatedly loses, it suffers from a damaged vision. When fixing the team's broken dream, start with the individual. The individual's approval is the hardest to keep and the easiest to lose. When times are hard, there is only one question to ask: "How do you get your passion to pour into you?" Less committed players need discipline in order to get through frustration. More committed players instruct their willpower to get them back on track.

Spiritual hope is a defining human trait. It feeds us when there is no food; it breathes for us when there is no air. When hope engages the dream, it gives the power of miracles. Athletes who are fully committed are always capable of hope. When members of a team link their hope together to gather enough energy to create a shift in consciousness, the team embodies the future.

When there is struggle, remind yourself of the dream. When the critical mass of any group starts to eat the dream, the mass will shift and extreme performance begins to embrace them. No one knows what the last piece of energy looks like that is needed for gathering a critical mass for a shift. So we must stay ready, poised with our attention and effort in each moment. Each season it is different. Each champion stalks and feeds her model in a new way. Each process connects the dots in a unique pattern to solve the puzzle, to answer the challenge.

Each champion moves relentlessly toward solving the puzzle. Each stalks the dream. The values, work, external discipline, self-discipline, commitment, team culture, and myriad distractions of a season share a common thread. Everything that is embraced and valued by a championship team will be performance directed. In this way they are disciplined. When a championship team steers off course, it self-corrects or yields to external leadership. Most teams are socially directed as a group and individually self-centered, and they push each other toward the mean. A full level of engagement is required for this kind of passion. Not everyone can be a champion. It is special.

Team Commitment

1. Get each player's permission to help her fulfill her role.
2. Find your team's specific way to stalk the dream.
3. Keep the team on task.
4. Entice the critical mass of the group to move toward a greater performance.

Nothing is accomplished until enough energy is breathed into the model of what you want to accomplish. When energy is reorganized in a way that it becomes locked with the desired outcome, enough energy is present. Until then, the energy for that lock is not available. All efforts toward the outcome will build and gather. But the critical mass that is required for a projected shift is also constantly eroded through off-task behavior and thinking. Most adults cannot generate enough energy to create extraordinary things. Many adults who do accomplish amazing things do so through process. At the very heart of this process is discipline.

9

Focus

*Develop a vision and stay cued in on it
despite setbacks and distractions*

Lorene Ramsey

Courtesy of Lorene Ramsey

Coaching was not an option when I began my teaching career after graduating from Illinois State University in 1959. Then, after eight years of teaching physical education classes and developing intramural programs for girls in high school, I became interested in teaching at the college level. In 1968 Illinois Central College hired me, along with two other teachers, to begin the physical education and intramural programs. Because opportunities for females had been limited, only eight women signed up for our basketball team. When practice started it became obvious that we had a limited number of true athletes among our few players. Since I had never coached competitively, I was as green as our players. In our first three games before the Christmas break we lost by 33 points to Bradley University, by 25 points to Spoon River College, and by the score of 44 to 12 to Illinois State's *fifth* team.

Focus was very easy in this situation. I focused on becoming a better coach by attending the practices of the successful high school and college boy's and men's coaches in the area. At our practice I focused on talking about the good accomplishments that we were attaining and almost never focused on the negative. The players focused on our two goals: first, "Play a little bit better every night," and second, "Basketball will be fun for us."

Focus Defined

We can define focus as directed attention, a point of concentration, or a center of activity. In other words, it's the focal point—the task, person, or event you place above all others for a specific time. For instance, being focused means looking past minor distractions so that you can see clearly the major issues at hand. It means putting on hold the little problems that come up in order to concentrate on solving bigger problems.

Having focus is ignoring your ringing telephone so that you can devote your attention to the upset player in your office. It's delegating paperwork to assistants to free up time to develop a practice or game plan. It's not spending all your time worrying that your rival's budget is larger than yours, but instead working to make the most of what you do have. It's forgetting about the shot clock that goes out in the middle of the game and instead figuring out how to stop the opponent's inside game.

Focus could also be referred to as "the essence of concentration in which you are using your senses to make small adjustments in timing and rhythm to match the work and eliminate extraneous movement and mental activity" (Morehouse and Gross: *Maximum Performance*, 1977). For players, the following equation is a simple way to think of focus:

$$Concentration + Intensity = Focus$$

Learning What to Focus On

Many coaches complain about the time demands of coaching. I have never heard coaches say that they have enough time for their jobs. When we began our programs at Illinois Central College, I was the only coach for softball and basketball. I also taught four physical education classes in each eight-week period. Furthermore, community college coaches have to recruit new players and help place current players in four-year schools. Life was certainly different then compared to my last year of active coaching, when I only coached basketball.

How do you focus on anything when you have so many duties? My solution to the problem certainly wasn't ideal, but it was the only one I could come up with at the time. I call it the "hole in the dam" theory. You give your attention to the one or two biggest holes in the dam until you get those situations resolved. Then you focus on the next most urgent situation.

Your focus will change as you mature as a coach, particularly if you spend many years in the profession. In the meantime, strive to sort out the occurrences that you have no control over and put them aside in order to work on the things that you can manage and change. Also, set a limited number of goals that you can concentrate on and achieve. I tried to assign areas to assistants that matched their strengths and would relieve me of some time constraints. I concentrated on practice planning, scouting reports, academic counseling, game strategy, and some public relations. I focused on player relationships during every practice, road trip, game, and any time I saw the team members on campus.

Even if you have excellent focus skills, they will be wasted if you do not have a good grasp of what to focus on. The successful coaches I've observed focused primarily on their players—*all* of the players. Dean Smith, former University of North Carolina men's basketball coach, once said that he tried to talk to each of his players about something other than basketball when they entered the gym. He wanted them to know that he cared about them as people. I thought that was a great idea and have tried to talk with each player each night about something other than basketball or softball. They will understand that you are interested in them as people. It's critical to talk with the players who don't start or who see the least amount of playing time as much or more than you talk with the starters, letting them know that they are as important to you as those who contribute in more obvious ways.

Coaches' and players' relationships with parents are definitely influenced by the parents' focus. Playing time and team success, or lack of it, do influence parents and their relationships with the coach and even the team. I usually tell my players early in the season that I would like to talk with all their parents but that I'm not the *least bit* interested in their coaching theories. I also tell them that parents have to love only one of them while we coaches have to love them all. I stress that this point makes our outlooks a little different. I am sure many of our players relay this message to their parents, which isn't a bad idea, because it makes parents aware of the differences in our point of reference. It also becomes obvious to the parents that the player understands the difference between the coaches' and the parents' outlooks. Parents can be an asset to the development of the proper attitude of their daughter and the team if they have the right focus.

An important point of focus for any coach should be improvement. Coaches are exactly like players. They're either working at improving and are getting better or they're slipping back and getting worse. My focus on improving came from attending and speaking at clinics, attending other coaches' practices, reading about the sports I coached, and engaging in many conversations with other coaches. In college coaching you must also work at selling your program to the fans, the media, and the administration that controls many areas related to it.

Teaching Focus

To be successful in coaching today you must have an unbelievable drive, high energy level, and an obsession for the game and each player. Your focus on the game will be apparent to your staff and your team, and to some degree it will rub off on them. However, simply demonstrating focus is not enough. Although the players and staff will recognize that quality in you, they may not have learned the skills necessary for focus. Part of a coach's responsibility is to teach each person in her program skills that will help not only in athletics but also in life. Focus certainly fits that description.

Staff. One way I teach my assistants focus is by assigning them specific responsibilities; that way they know what to focus on. The more ownership you give coaches of a particular aspect of the team or program, the more focused and therefore more proficient they will become in that area. In 1998, I used that strategy to help our softball team win the NJCAA Division I championship. Even though I was the head coach, I worked solely with our four pitchers, allowing equal time for each one. Sue Sinclair, our head volleyball coach and assistant softball coach, was in charge of preparing our team to play defense, and Tom Gilles and Shelly Lindsey worked only on hitting. Our team's total improvement was quite striking. I believe we all did a better job because we were better able to focus our thoughts and energy on the aspect we had been charged with directing.

I did the same with basketball my final season of coaching, dividing out the duties of press situations, man-to-man defense, academics and player issues, and guard skills. Obviously, we all worked on other areas as well, but each person focused on developing strength in one area.

When you assign responsibilities to assistant coaches, you should attempt to motivate them by giving them written material, tapes, or any pertinent information. Then give them the opportunity to coach the area they have been assigned, including some or all practice situations, without you breathing down their necks. Micromanaging your assistants is not productive, does not teach focus, and does not give them a sense of responsibility. Give them tasks they can accomplish, and as they earn your trust you can increase their responsibilities.

Players. One of the first ways any coach teaches a player about focus is when she says, "Watch the ball." It's a simple but important lesson in learning what to focus on. Worrying about an upcoming exam during practice doesn't help a player learn the material or improve her basketball skills. Wanting her parents to support her athletics endeavors is OK, but wondering if they are watching as the game hinges on her free throws with no time remaining on the clock isn't where a player's focus should be at that time.

> Players especially need help learning to focus, which doesn't mean ignoring aspects of life. It means learning when to think about them. Focus is a skill just like shooting a basketball is a skill.

When I first started coaching, I would explain a skill or strategy that I wanted to implement and then ask the players if they understood what I was talking about. The entire group would almost always say yes. It didn't take long for me to learn that in many cases several players didn't have a clue about what was expected. In order to get them to focus on and retain everything that was said, I frequently picked a player at random and asked her to explain what I had just discussed. They are punished by the embarrassment of not being able to give the correct explanation, but coaches can add other punishment that fits the situation to further encourage complete focus on everything that is said by all coaches. Many coaches like to reward players for their focus. One way is to give a short written test, true-and-false or multiple choice, on what was covered at that day's, week's, or even month's practice, and then reward the top three players in some fashion.

Practice is the most important time that coaches have with players, and all of us want our players to be as enthusiastic about their performance during the last month of practice as they were during the first few days. Several unique methods can be used to obtain a focus on practice that eliminates clock watching.

I listened to a presentation by a nationally successful swimming coach several years ago in which he described how he got his swimmers to focus on practice results. He had not been happy with the intensity or focus of his team members, so one night at practice he gave each of them a jar to keep in their lockers and told them that they were going to have a contest. After each race in practice, the winner would get a jelly bean to put in the jar. Of course, the members of this men's college swimming team laughed at the silliness of this idea. However, not too long afterward the swimmers began counting how many jelly beans they had in comparison to other members of the team. One night a fight broke out because one swimmer had accused another of stealing his jelly beans and putting them in his own jar. What had seemed silly at the beginning became motivation to focus on practice results in order to reach the goal of being the best practice swimmer.

We coaches always try to get our players to focus on being good teammates, yet we do little to teach or reinforce the behavior. During one softball season we had two very good starting pitchers. Our third pitcher, Tonya Perry, pitched her regular batting practice turn and was always available for extra practice of anything that would help a teammate. Her attitude was very upbeat even though her playing time was limited. We didn't give a "most valuable player" award on our basketball or softball teams, but I gave Tonya a plaque honoring her as most valuable teammate. I think that award promotes everything that players and coaches want from a teammate, and it places the focus on individuals who put other team members and the team's welfare first.

Team. One of the most important parts of coaching is establishing goals, because they help focus and unite the team. However, having too many goals can be as destructive as having none. Sometimes in athletics we do focus on too many goals. A sign in our locker room that brings that point home reads:

FOCUS
If you chase two rabbits, both will escape.

Goals must be realistic. Coaches should meet with players individually to identify each one's goals. They may be focusing on goals that are unrealistic or entirely different from the coach's goals for them. They may be focusing on goals that are not even conducive to team success. I have always felt that players should have a few goals that they can accomplish rather than so many that focus becomes skewed and little progress is accomplished.

As far as team goals are concerned, usually teams discuss which goals they would like to reach. Our basketball team frequently passes the same goals down every year:

1. Win 20 games.
2. Win the regional tournament.
3. Win the first game of the national tournament.
4. Win the semifinal game.
5. Win the national championship.

In 2003 the goal for the basketball team changed. In the semifinal game of the 2002 NJCAA Division II national tournament, the team got into foul trouble, played poorly, and went down to defeat by 1 point as they lost a 20-point lead. The seven players returning from the 2002 team had only one

Courtesy of Lorene Ramsey

The time-out is adjustment time. Begin and end the time-out with your main focus points to help drive them home.

goal: to win the national championship. They believed they should have accomplished that in 2002. This became the single-minded goal of the entire team as the new members of the team embraced the feelings exuded by the returning players. The players never took their focus off the goal. They weren't distracted by the three losses early in the season, the injuries that occurred during the season, or their 28-game winning streak.

When you reach your one and only goal, it's a great feeling. Unfortunately, if you don't reach your one and only goal, it's a disaster. For the 2003 basketball team, having one goal worked—we won the national championship. Personally, I prefer to have three or four goals that are more reachable in addition to the national championship goal. Then if you reach some of the goals but don't win the national championship, you still have a feeling of accomplishment.

Coaches are responsible not only for a team's outlook or focus but for controlling the people and environment that surround the team and help direct and establish the proper focus. We use our walls for inspirational slogans, articles, and pictures. When you walk into the locker room, no matter how barren it may be, and see a sign that says, "Those Who Bring Sunshine to the Lives of Others Cannot Keep It From Themselves," you should be affected in a positive way, at least on one occasion. Another sign we have is one of Isiah Thomas' sayings for his team: "Toughness, Togetherness, Intensity."

Our gym has banners that list all national tournament appearances for our volleyball team, golf team, and our men's and women's basketball teams. All seven national championship softball and basketball teams have large, full-color pictures in the lobby. We talk to our players about their opportunity to add their picture to the group.

Encouraging the faculty, staff, and administration to become part of the group surrounding the team can also add to the team's focus on the proper goals. Our Illinois Central College presidents, Dr. Tom Thomas in 1998 and Dr. John Erwin in 2003, both attended the national tournament, and both were invited to speak to the team before some of the tournament games. They had attended many of our games during the season, which makes the players feel that what they do is worthwhile. Their talks were an inspiration to the team and added to their focus on the game. Many other faculty and staff members have been positive influences throughout the years. We have also included talks with nutrition teachers, the academic adviser, coaches who have special skills, counselors, and anyone else who can help players or teams become all that they are capable of becoming.

Changing Focus

Probably the toughest job in coaching is getting a team that is beset with bad luck, poor morale, and a losing streak to refocus on the positive. After beating a team that had beaten us by 33 points, I told the team after the game that our ugly ducklings were about to become Cinderella. We used the ugly-duckling-to-Cinderella comparison several times, and as we left the hotel to play the national championship game, one of the parents presented us with an ugly stuffed duck dressed in an ICC jacket and said, "This is the last of the ugly-duckling era. Tonight it's Cinderella time." Even the parents were focused on the positive.

If you coach long enough, you will probably experience a season when it seems like everything goes wrong. Mine was the 1992 basketball season. We started with 17 players; however, that didn't even last until the first day of practice. Our number one recruit, who had demonstrated no physical problems, came to the first day of practice and announced that she had rheumatoid arthritis. It had worsened, and her physician said that she would never be able to play basketball again. A few days after practice started an excellent post player was not performing as an excellent post player. In fact she was getting winded without much continuous running. We sent her to the doctor and found out that she had a serious thyroid condition; not only couldn't she play basketball, she eventually found it necessary to drop out of school. The last major catastrophe occurred in December, when our starting point guard tore her Achilles tendon and was out for the year.

We were down to nine players, so I called one of my softball pitchers to come out and play point guard. The previous year she had inquired about playing basketball, wanting to know if I thought she would play much. Since we had an experienced All-American point guard, I had told her that she probably wouldn't see much playing time. This time I convinced her to come out, telling her that her chance of playing was excellent.

The team was following our 1991-92 team, which had been 31 and 2 but had lost in overtime in the regional championship game and didn't get to the national tournament. People who followed our team constantly reminded the players about not measuring up to that team, but the coaches remained positive. I have always said that coaching is disaster control, and it certainly was for us that year.

We experienced our seventh loss at the end of January, on the road at Kirkwood Community College, by 33 points. The three-and-a-half-hour bus trip home was dismal. The effort in the game had been very unfocused, and our season was on the verge of disaster with this latest setback. What to do? My assistants felt that we had been very positive and had tried everything. We never discussed missing the players who were out for the season, and we rarely mentioned past success—but that was about to change. At practice the next afternoon, I reminded the players that past teams had more than 500 wins and an 80 percent winning rate while learning many of the skills that we were teaching them. It was time for them to take responsibility for games like the previous night, when it was too much work to put forward even a decent effort.

In a brief meeting with the captains before practice, I asked them to conduct a meeting to try to get more team communication and effort and a return to the "we" focus instead of the "I" focus. When they finished with their meeting, they were to come into the office and inform the coaches that practice could begin. One of my assistants asked how long I expected this meeting to last. I told him that in the past, players-only meetings had lasted 20 to 30 minutes but that with the way this team communicated we'd probably be on the practice floor in 10 minutes. Two hours later the captains came into the office and practice started. Evidently all the players had participated, freely discussing what they liked and didn't like about each other. In the end, they blamed only themselves and vowed to change the atmosphere. What a difference! Talk about focus and effort—it was there. How long did it last? When Kirkwood came to play us the second time that season, we won by 13 points, which was a 46-point turnaround. How important is getting everyone on a team to focus on the right goal? In this case it was worth 46 points.

In March 1992, we won our first national basketball championship. The point guard who wasn't talented enough to be told that she would play the previous year scored 18 points in that national championship game. How focused was she? She had come into the gym every morning at 7:00 a.m. and worked on her shot for an hour. Our president, who came in to run in the mornings, saw her and told me about her dedication. She had never said a word to anyone about her extra efforts.

In cases where team meetings don't work, coaches must go to plan B. I have used many approaches. Among the more successful were having the entire team read the book *See You at the Top* by Zig Ziglar and bringing in former players who have succeeded in various ways to talk to the team without the coaches present so that the players can feel free to ask questions. Showing a movie that might motivate them, such as *Hoosiers,* is also a good approach. As a coach, you need to know your team and what might motivate them.

Game Focus for a Coach

The amount of focus a coach has during a contest is obvious to a spectator. I can tell when opposing coaches are unfocused because they merely sit on the bench and wish for a different outcome. A coach should be concentrating on the game, thinking of tactics and strategies that will help her team be successful.

During a game, there is a huge amount of information to process—from your own observations to players, assistants, opponents, officials' calls, players' reactions to officials' calls, statistics, the scoreboard, and the fans. To be successful, you have to learn to concentrate on certain parts of the game, such as substitutions, changing tactics, or calling a time-out. That way you will have a positive impact on the game and you will teach your players and staff by example. I also pay attention to the players' mental and emotional states during a game to make sure they are focused on the right things. Are they positive or negative? Are they communicating well with each other or do they look like five individuals running around? Are they executing the game plan or do they look confused?

> The amount of focus a coach has during a contest is obvious to a spectator. A coach should be concentrating on the game, thinking of tactics and strategies that will help her team be successful.

An experienced coach prepares her team in practice for any unexpected circumstances that may come up during a contest. Players will most likely observe the coach's reaction closely and respond according to her demeanor. It's wise to practice for possible unusual situations, such as a late arrival to the playing site, poor officiating, player injuries, lighting problems in a facility, and in some sports, weather delays. A prepared team is more likely to maintain focus on the game when distractions come up.

Show your team a videotape of a game performance when they were focused and successful, and then show them a game when they were not focused and therefore unsuccessful. That visual will go a long way in helping the team understand the need for focus. They will see the difference clearly—you won't need to say much—and they will strive to repeat the focused behavior.

One of the best messages about the total focus it takes to be all that you can be is the "Pyramid of Success," which was devised by John Wooden during his days of great success at the University of California at Los Angeles. He defined success as "peace of mind that is a direct result of self-satisfaction in knowing you did your best to become the best you are capable of becoming."

The base of the pyramid is made up of the cornerstones of *industriousness* and *enthusiasm*. Filling in the base are *friendship, loyalty,* and *cooperation*. Building on the solid foundation are the principles of *self-control, alertness, initiative,* and *intentness*. The next three blocks are *condition, skill,* and *team spirit*. Near the peak are *poise* and *confidence*. *Competitive greatness* is the top block, and the mortar that holds it all together is made of *patience* and *faith*. We hand out copies of the pyramid to our basketball campers and our athletes and recommend that they put them in their lockers as a reminder of what can help them be better people and players. I also have a copy, because coaches need a little inspiration, too.

Focus won't make you 6'6" tall, and it won't make a slower player lightning fast or a great leaper out of an average player. But focus will help you and your players become all that you can be, which is all any coach or player can aspire to!

10

Stress Management

*Find positive coping strategies and
keep perspective when under pressure*

Jill Sterkel

Courtesy of Jill Sterkel

Managing people is a stressful job. Even if the manager has a lifetime of experience in her sport; even if every person under the manager's direction is hardworking, conscientious, mature, and gifted; coordinating the operation while keeping everyone working together is a challenge. But when the operation is the pressure-cooker of college athletics where the "workers" are females between the ages of 17 and 22 who are just beginning to learn who they are and what is important in life, personal stress management quickly becomes an important facet of coaching.

I started swimming at age 5, so the sport has been a huge part of my life. I was interested in marine biology when I arrived at the University of Texas in 1979 and thought I wanted to be a scientist, but I discovered that I wasn't passionate about it. Halfway through my junior year, when I learned that I would have to complete my final year and a half of the marine biology program in Galveston and would be unable to continue my swimming career, I changed my major to kinesiology and physical education and caught the coaching bug. While growing up, I had never considered being a coach—even though I had great coaches and I enjoyed going to workouts and being with my friends—primarily because most swimming coaches are male. In fact, I never swam for a female coach. I didn't think coaching was something I couldn't do; I just never thought it was something I *would* do. My college coach, Paul Bergen, taught me to be a student of the sport and gave me the confidence to believe that I could coach. Once I started taking classes related to coaching, I knew that's what I wanted to do.

Challenges in Coaching

After graduating in 1984 with a degree in physical education and a minor in biology, I was a student-coach for a year before serving as an assistant coach at my alma mater from 1986 to 1991. Although my life was busy, working in my first full-time job, being an active swimmer, and pursuing my master's degree in sport administration and management, I didn't consider it too stressful. Assistant coaches are an important part of a team with crucial responsibilities, but rarely does something major land in their laps. The head coaches I worked for would talk about how they didn't sleep well and I wondered what their problem was, because I always thought everything would be all right. Obviously assistant coaches don't shoulder the same kind of stress as head coaches do. It's hard to understand that when you haven't experienced it.

In my first head coaching job at Indiana University in 1991 people embraced me because I was new. I encountered some stress, but it was a safe place to learn to be a head coach. The program had not done as well as the administration had hoped, but we were well supported because they wanted to build a successful program. However, I stayed there only one year because the head coaching position at the University of Texas opened up. I had to make the tough decision of whether to stay at Indiana and learn more about coaching or go to the University of Texas, a high-profile program. When athletic director Jody Conradt hired me, my understanding of stress as a head coach began.

Before I left, one of the coaches I worked with at Indiana asked, "Do you really want to be a head coach at Texas?" At first I was offended, but looking back I now understand that he meant, "Is this what you really want to do? Because you are going to have to do it at such a different level. It is going to consume your life."

In my first years at Texas, part of me believed that I had to work twice as hard as the coaches who had been in the profession for a while. I thought people would feel that I didn't have the experience to be a head coach. In addition to the workload, worrying about what people thought of me increased my stress level.

Recognizing Stress Responses

My view of stress as a head coach can be summed up like this: Input comes in from a multitude of sources within the program, and you try to think of ways to weed through it all and have it come out OK. With so much thought going into each aspect of the program, it's easy to internalize every decision that comes across your plate. You can mull things over too much and let them percolate inside, which can be very destructive.

Many people who are stressed make rash decisions or dig their heels in and refuse to change their minds. You have to be consistent and strong in your convictions when dealing with young people, but at the same time you must adapt to each person as an individual. You can sometimes get to a point where you think, "I am going to do it this way and forget about everyone else." The more stressed some people feel, the more rigid they become and the less inclined they are to ask for advice.

I was so stressed out at the University of Texas that I literally made myself sick. I developed the Epstein-Barr virus, which can occur in conjunction with chronic fatigue syndrome. Although not all stress manifests itself this dramatically, coaches must learn to recognize the symptoms of stress in their lives—for example, feeling short-tempered or tense, taking their feelings out on the people around them, or not performing properly. Then they can develop the coping skills that allow them to manage stress.

> Although not all stress manifests itself dramatically, coaches must learn to recognize the symptoms of stress in their lives. Then they can develop the necessary coping skills that allow them to manage it.

Once the head athletic trainer and the athletic director noticed that I was having a problem, they met with me to discuss it. I told them I'd cut back and slow down, but they said, "No, you won't. You are going to go home and get some rest." I didn't want to leave, but it was the best thing for me even though I didn't know it at the time. And I had been a head coach for only five years. I took four months off, spending it at my parents' house in southern California and literally pulling the plug.

Causes of Stress in Coaching

One main cause of stress in coaching, as in any management position, is being unable to control other people's lives. Your success as a coach is in part determined by athletes who make their own decisions. You have to learn to manage it all and keep it together. Every day something different happens when you have, for example, 26 young women in your program. They are individuals with varying needs, desires, and dreams, which come and go on a daily basis, and the stresses in their lives emerge in various forms and fashions. Coaches are constantly managing the daily events in a large group of people's lives.

Recruiting is also intense and can sometimes feel never-ending. You call prospective student-athletes weekly, travel to see them compete, make home visits, and entertain them on campus. After scouring for talent and spending months developing a relationship, it comes down to a teenager's decision—which could be based on important things like academic programs or the team's camaraderie, but may be based on something as trivial as the color of the uniform or the climate.

Tasks such as daily paperwork and administrative duties—managing equipment, arranging travel, developing training plans, filling out compliance forms, and keeping track of the athletes' academic standing—can create challenges because they are so time consuming.

A coach's responsibilities are never done. It is a 24-hour-a-day, 7-day-a-week job. Because so many young people are involved in what you do, events and decisions in their lives—such as parents going through a divorce or uncertainty about whether they want to compete anymore—can affect what you do or how you do it. Don't assume that all the great athletes in your program are perfect individuals with no problems. And at many levels, coaches also have the additional workload of teaching—my hat is off to them.

Handling Coaching Stress

The stresses early in my head coaching career were caused by a lack of balance in my life and by my failure to understand that other people can help: those on my staff, in the department, and contacts made through networking. I felt like I had to do everything myself, and I was not good at prioritizing. By managing stress in the following ways, I've learned to become more adaptable, both personally and with the athletes.

Develop a Network. When I was starting out there were very few female coaches, and consequently, no established network for support. At times it was very lonely, and I felt like nobody wanted me to succeed. I thought asking for help would make people think that I didn't have it all together. Being in a high-level position was a double-edged sword: I felt like other head coaches knew what they were doing with their programs and that I should, too. Often coaches want to make everything perfect, although that is impossible.

One strategy I've developed for dealing with stress is to use other people as a sounding board. You must develop a good network of people you trust to talk to about issues in your program, whether it's someone nearby or a long-distance phone call away. That person might be one of your assistants, but often they do not encounter the same stressors that you do as a head coach. People will help if you ask, but asking can be the hardest part.

Difficult as it is, when you first get into coaching, try to be aggressive about seeking advice, networking, and using the resources available to you. I was lucky enough that our department had another female head coach, Bev Kearney, who served as my rock. She had been in coaching long enough that she understood everything I was feeling and could talk me through things as they came up. I never would have stayed in coaching without her support.

The UT men's coach, Eddie Reese, also is a valuable resource who helps the women's program succeed. A legend in swimming, he has been an Olympic coach three or four times. (I even swam with him during one of the Olympics.) A successful men's team helps the women's program become more successful—we learn from the things they do. Enjoying the support of your counterparts is an important part of coping with stress.

Participate in as many networking opportunities as you can. For example, a women's swimming coaches group, with a core of 12 primarily NCAA Division I coaches, meets once a year for four days. We call it "The Summit." We have an agenda, so those who have specific topics they want covered can send them in to be included in the meeting. We talk about decision making, recruiting, discipline problems, and other issues. The first time I went to the meeting I thought, "Wow! Other people have the same kinds of problems I do. I thought I was the only one struggling with my program." It was an incredibly valuable experience for me. This yearly summit is exciting and powerful, and its members have been getting together for the past seven years to share experiences as some of the few female swimming coaches.

The USOC also put on a coaching summit a few years ago for female swimming, track-and-field, softball, and soccer coaches. They brought in a top person in each sport, an up-and-coming coach, and an assistant. At first I wasn't sure that I could learn from people in other sports, but the similarities in what these coaches deal with are unbelievable. It opened my eyes to the fact that coaches are not alone. The more you network and use other people, the better off you'll be.

Prioritize. I also have learned to prioritize things in my life. Think about what's most important to you; at the top of my list are family, health, and relationships. Two mornings a week I either work out with my team at an outdoor pool or participate in some of the medicine-ball exercises with the team in the weight room, and several mornings a week I take my golden retriever, Jake, for long walks. During those walks with the dog, I let my head go and enjoy the solitude. Sometimes I don't think about anything, or I can mull over thoughts and make plans. That is my personal time to unplug and relax and also enjoy my dog and the outdoors. Discover your top priorities, and make time for them in your daily schedule.

Further down on the priority list are the everyday occurrences. When an athlete gets injured, it can be a huge stress. You wonder, "What are we going to do? We were counting on this person to do this and now this can't happen!" Awful as they are, you can do nothing about injuries and illnesses. You have to figure out a way to make the team be even better, learn from the situation, and hope it doesn't happen again. But then you need to accept it and decide what needs to happen so that everything falls into place. You can spend time worrying about things you can't do anything about, but you will never win that war. The sooner you learn not to fight those battles, the sooner you will reduce the stress in your life.

Delegate. Part of a head coach's job is learning how to delegate and then actually doing it. When I was ill, my assistant coach was amazing, handling many responsibilities that I hadn't let her do before because I hadn't delegated as much as I should have. If you don't delegate, those in a position to help you can't do as much as they could. Learning how to prioritize helps you realize that not everything is an emergency. True, some things have to be taken care of immediately, but things in the middle of the list may not have to be done that day.

You might need to adjust your delegation strategies depending on the size of your staff. For example, swimming staffs are typically small—most women's-only programs have only a head coach and an assistant coach. I've handled this differently by having a co-head coach, who has been with me for five years. Our program also has an administrative assistant, a manager, and a volunteer assistant.

A strength coach can also have a great deal of input into your training program. We brainstorm with ours, and she puts the pieces together and develops the program.

Be Yourself. My father passed away at the end of my recuperative period in California. Obviously it was a very emotional time, and for a two-week period I decided I wasn't coming back to Texas. I decided I didn't need this stress in my life. But my mom said, "It's not good to make that kind of decision right now. Why don't you sit on this and think about it? Make sure what you are doing is what you really want."

Courtesy of Jill Sterkel

Use other people as a sounding board, and develop a good network of people you trust to talk about issues in your program.

I stayed home for another 10 days, and then one morning when I woke up, I had changed. I had let go of the stress about coaching and what people expected of me. Jody Conradt noticed the change when I came back. I had decided, "I'm going to coach the way I want to, and that's OK. If I'm not successful enough to stay at Texas, then that is OK too." I let go of all the baggage that holds you back or makes you do things you don't want to do. I was free to be me. Then I could wake up every day and look in the mirror and say, "This is who I am, and this is what I'm going to do." I went through a metamorphosis to become myself.

As a coach, you hear and read what people say and think about you. I was trying so hard to be all the things that everybody else wanted me to be, but I didn't take time to talk to other people about these issues. There is a perception that coaches have to behave or do things a certain way. However, if you are not true to yourself you will never be consistent and things won't work out right. By letting go of those perceptions and coaching the way I feel it needs to be done, I am being true to myself.

Managing Athletes' Stress

The stress I feel as a coach is different from the stress I felt as an athlete. As a swimmer, stress helped me swim faster. It was information I could take in, and I had control over it because it was about my performance and me. I felt in control of my environment.

Athletes at all levels have the stress of balancing the various aspects of their lives—school, their social life, sports—and trying to keep them all in an orderly fashion. Too much stress in one area would carry over into the others. I used to get stressed out about being up late studying for exams because I still wanted to perform well in the pool the next day. That might not happen because I was tired, though, and then the ball would start rolling, making it more difficult to keep stress under control. But as a competitor I still felt like those things were within my power to control.

Managing their everyday lives is stressful for the athletes. They get worked up about academic tests, boyfriends, relationships with each other, how well they are performing, and things at home, such as a sick parent. At the college level, a coach plays yet another role in addition to being an educator, a motivator, and trying to get athletes work to their potential—she is their mom or dad away from home. Because of proximity, college coaches are probably more interactive with student-athletes than their parents are.

Create a Supportive Enviroment. Athletes have to understand that they can come talk to you. They seem always to be afraid to talk with the head coach, but it's up to her to make them feel comfortable and supported. Individual meetings offer great opportunities to get to know each other. The more the athletes can feel your support through talking, the better you'll be able to help them through everything.

Team meetings can be used to talk about the sport, team dynamics, and other issues. Younger student-athletes often don't have the skills to deal with things like conflict resolution and they may need help gaining perspective on what's happening to them. I believe it is part of the coach's job to help them learn how to do those things and spend time with them so they feel OK about it. Talking to someone can make you feel like 10 pounds has been lifted off your shoulders. Talking an athlete through a problem can help her learn how she feels about it and what she thinks she can handle.

> A coach needs to be an anchor in the storm, a steady, dependable presence regardless of what's going on. That strength not only calms the athletes, it teaches them how to handle their stress.

Our life-skills program at Texas includes a class for female freshmen on how to cope with different things. Talking and expressing themselves is one way of coping for the athletes, so we try to create such opportunities for the team. We also try to give them some ownership in the program by offering elected positions such as team captain and recruiting, equipment, birthday, social, and community-service coordinators. Through these jobs they support and help each other. Plus, they gain experience and leadership skills.

A coach also needs to be an anchor in the storm, a steady, dependable presence regardless of what's going on. That strength not only calms the athletes, it teaches them how to handle their stress. When I get stressed I become quiet, not because I'm mad but because I'm thinking and trying to figure out something. I very rarely blow up. Remember, as a coach you are a role model for coping behavior.

Avoid Causing Stress. I always feel like I'm in control of how my stress comes out. I will speak firmly if the team is not performing the way I think it should, but choosing your timing and tone of voice is important. If I make the team start something over at practice, I'll explain why; they'll know I'm irritated, but I don't behave in an out-of-control fashion. Athletes need to know what to expect from their coaches. With some coaches, their behavior on a given day is anyone's guess. Are they going to yell? Are they in a good mood or a bad mood? It's hard to enjoy working with people like that.

My philosophy of coaching is that it shouldn't be fear based but more of a partnership: "You're telling me you want to be this good and I want to help you get there." That doesn't mean there won't be some days when you're on the athletes, but that's different from saying, "You're a piece of junk!" Participating in a sport should be an enjoyable experience. Causing unnecessary stress for your athletes won't make them perform better and or help you as a coach in the long run. Most days you should be excited about what you're going to do.

Stress can help raise a coach's level of performance, in a competition situation or in life outside of sports, as long as she is in control of it. That means keeping expectations in perspective. If people around her think that she can achieve a certain level of performance, that expectation can manifest itself as stress—but in a good way, inspiring and motivating her.

I loved stress when I was swimming. It gave me adrenaline, and I was always in control of it. But learning how to control stress as a coach is a daily job. When it gets out of control, you lose perspective, and that's when it becomes dangerous: People snap, get sick, burn out. Defining your philosophy of coaching and what you want to accomplish prevents unnecessary worry. Everybody wants to win, but how are you going to get there? You can't do or be what somebody else dictates. By doing what you believe in, you'll win the battle with stress.

PART

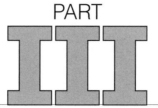

Program Implementation and Management

11

Organizational Skills

*Establish systems and procedures
to maximize the use of all program resources*

Diane Davey

Courtesy of Diane Davey

I am proud to have spent my entire 29 years of coaching at Plano Senior High School. Our players were crowned four times as the University Interscholastic League Texas Soccer State Champions. These titles represent players, families, and friends in the Plano community, but they also represent a great deal of organization by our staff. As a result of our team's success, I was named the National Soccer Coach of the Year in 1991 and 1997 by the National Soccer Coaches Association of America, and the National High School Athletic Coaches Association selected me as National Soccer Coach of the Year representative in 1998. These honors have created expectations of me that I can only maintain by managing time efficiently and meeting personal standards of performance.

I was honored in 2002-2003 as the Plano Independent School District Secondary Teacher of the Year and was honored by the Texas Exes, a University of Texas organization, as one of 12 recipients of the Texas Excellence Award for Outstanding Teachers in 2003, receiving a Lillian B. Rhodes Teaching Award. Both of these awards brought many opportunities to share my experiences with students and student athletes. Preparation for these events was paramount and a direct outcome of getting and staying organized as a coach and teacher.

Early in my coaching career, I realized that exceeding expectations, producing ultimate results, and sustaining optimum performance are accepted standards of excellence for all coaches. However, no scientific formulas for a coach's organizational skills exist. Each coach must develop a comfortable style of systems and procedures that allows her to meet standards set by players, parents, administrators, and community members. If I wanted to maintain a stellar coaching career, it became increasingly apparent that developing consistent, professional organizational and communication skills would ease the road to success. Managing organized chaos, multitasking, and meeting deadlines are requirements for dealing with players' ambitions, colleagues' expectations, administrative demands, and the general public's desires. Organizational skills give coaches a positive perspective each day. Although repetitive duties are the norm, predictability, along with a level of expectation, enhances classroom and athletic environments.

> Develop a comfortable style of systems and procedures that allows you to meet standards set by players, parents, administrators, and community members. If you want to maintain a stellar coaching career, develop consistent, professional organizational and communication skills to ease the road to success.

Administrators want coaches to reflect the mission statement of their school. The community wants coaches to serve their needs and represent their city's values. In order to meet these expectations, coaches must follow a consistent pattern of organizational rules. They need structure and a system they can depend on, like arranging materials in a logical fashion and establishing a purpose. To administrate a team, activity, or event and implement efficient strategies for success, coaches need to stay committed to those preplanned procedures. Predictability and trust are virtues for team-centered coaches, for whom being organized is critical to their success.

The world of technology assists with professional management skills. Software packages provide organizational solutions; I use a simple one to monitor and manage my yearly schedule. Each morning I glance at my weekly calendar and observe my daily schedule. Coaching software can assist with controlling long- and short-range schedules, reduce paperwork, and provide an avenue for communication with strategic personnel.

Poor organizational skills can lead to poor coaching performance. The public expects coaches to be organized, punctual, to have immediate answers, and to be correct 100 percent of the time. Having a daily plan of action and sticking to it is paramount.

Developing a Strategic Plan

Enthusiasm starts at the top, with the head coach. During my coaching career, I have committed to building a balanced soccer program that represents our school's values, remains competitive, and reflects the attitude of our community. I wanted our soccer program to be able to sustain itself through the toughest as well as the best of times. I wanted academic excellence, school spirit, and sportsmanship to remain at the forefront. And I wanted continuous player development that would lead to achievement in all areas, from the playing field to the classroom to the community, and throughout life.

I have spent many hours during my coaching career seeking information about top-ranked teams and using that valuable input to enhance our women's soccer program. Capturing coaching ideas from every possible source is essential to building a successful career. I have a library of books on motivation and organizational skills, which I often share with other coaches, both seasoned and new. Another valuable source of information came from evaluating the organizational skills of successful high school and college coaches throughout Texas. Through this research, I have enhanced my organizational skills.

In the early 1980s, Anson Dorrance, the head women's soccer coach at the University of North Carolina, began a soccer dynasty that would lead to his team winning 17 of 22 national championships. I had been fortunate to coach a NSCAA high school All-American, Tina Luft Patterson, who later played for Coach Dorrance. When Tina returned to visit her high school alma mater, I solicited information about UNC and areas of emphasis in their program. Sharing organizational skills with other coaches and former players is a wonderful way to build a dynamic coaching career. After a series of these conversations, I began a lifetime of capturing information to assist in my quest to maintain a consistent women's soccer program.

Almost three decades ago, I started my coaching career at Plano Senior High School as an assistant coach in basketball and track. Fortunately the head coaches paid attention to detail and were great mentors. Our head basketball coach, Rita Barnes, was known as an accomplished coach throughout the state. Our track coach, Rochelle Davis, was a former all-American member of the U.S. Track and Field Federation team and a member of the U.S. National team. Both women proved to be competitive and influential in the community, and they offered me valuable learning experiences in organizing players, parents, and the media. Their dedication encouraged me to draw on their expertise to develop my own organizational strategies. Their positive professional influence led me to believe that every young coach should serve as an assistant coach.

I had aspirations of building a successful soccer program and a desire to serve as a role model as a teacher and a coach. I learned quickly that I had to define administrative duties in order to build and oversee a program. I needed parameters for my teaching and coaching duties, and I needed to develop the kind of confidence that would create public trust.

Getting Ultimate Support

The longer I coach, the more I delegate responsibilities to other people. Delegating allows you to stay organized and get more accomplished without overburdening yourself. My staff members (including coaches and trainers), along with alumni and parent volunteers, are willing to assist with projects that have clearly defined objectives and will benefit our program. I believe in energizing, empowering, respecting, and supporting individuals and groups who assist in promoting high school athletics. Simple praise and recognition of their assistance encourages them to continue to contribute time and energy to the program. Delegating and organizing others can create many opportunities.

I recently sat in on a meeting with our media-guide committee. I scanned the meeting and realized that the room was filled with parents I have known for at least four years. They trust that our soccer program's staff will make a difference in their daughters' lives. The seasoned parents were passing down the "work spirit" traditions involved in producing our media guide to a group of new parents. Each person contributes expertise in the form of financial advice or sales tactics for the fund-raising portion of the guide. They energize each other by sharing new ideas and putting new twists on old ones.

When you are leading a parent group or seeking community support, be clear and organized. Use precise language, hand out written guidelines, and establish time frames for project completion. Give the participants ownership in the project and allow them to work in a self-directed manner. Recognize their needs and differences, and capitalize on their strengths. Listen to others' points of view, and try not to reinvent the wheel unless it is warranted. Look forward to exchanging ideas and finding solutions. If conflicts arise, find a way to turn setbacks into triumphs. Empower your athletes' parents and offer genuine respect and encouragement for their leadership.

When I delegate responsibility, I also foster enthusiasm by offering verbal or written praise and extending kindness. I am always willing to assist in any appropriate manner, whether it is to provide physical strength or emotional uplifting. Those who invest their time to assist me with organizational tasks deserve recognition. Honesty, communication, and the commitment to see a project through to completion bring honor to all participants.

I also seek assistance with our soccer program from community members, many of whom are looking for opportunities to promote school activities. They are motivated to make the community a better place by contributing to the promotion of high school sports. Forming lasting partnerships with supporters can be beneficial; their participation can make a difference, and in return they enjoy the satisfaction that comes from contributing to our program and the community.

Delegating Tasks

I must constantly remind myself that other people have talents that they can put to use to promote our sport. Since delegating tasks allows me more time to work with our players, I welcome interested and qualified people to assist with projects. I rely on parents to do many tasks that would otherwise be left incomplete. And although I trust and respect them, I am responsible for follow-up procedures. Delegating responsibilities and checking on progress can be an art. Recognize the strengths and weaknesses of your helpers (along with your own), and seek out those who will successfully complete projects because of a genuine interest in your sport.

When delegating tasks to parents or my staff, I ask myself, "When do you want it? How soon do you want it? How important is it to the overall success of your program?" Ultimately, I assume responsibility for organizing and completing the task. I must entertain, inform, and educate my potential helpers and inspire them to complete the job within the allotted time frame.

You must think strategically when tackling important tasks. Developing dependable resources can simplify the most difficult task. Critical thinking and problem solving can improve most situations and produce resolutions that can keep you heading in the direction of an important goal. Think critically. Look to improve the situation by relying on people who want to outperform. There are no secrets to success, but working with people who can market, promote, and assist with your program will help. For most coaches, being organized means relying on the help of others.

Creating a Daily Schedule

Our annual schedule revolves around three seasons: preseason, in-season, and postseason. Coaching duties vary with the season, so know your schedule for the day and stick to your agenda unless your priorities change. Honor your time allotments for projects and meetings, and make your plan for the day efficient and productive. Your daily schedule can be directed toward long- or short-term goals, but it needs to follow a plan.

Preseason. Our preseason begins with player selections in August, during which time we are limited to a one-hour training session per day for a two-week period. In an average year 80 to 100 girls want to participate on our varsity and junior varsity teams. We explain in detail the tryout procedure; we want each player to understand the process and to recognize that she will have a fair opportunity to compete for a spot on a team.

Having a written, detailed, daily record of tryout results is important to our staff and for future players. After each skill-training session, our staff reviews each athlete's results and targets specific assessment skills for the next session. Mile-time measurement is an indicator of a player's game fitness. We post a list of mile finishers along with their time of completion, which gives players an idea of how they are competing. Fitness testing is followed by technical and tactical assessment. All assessments are charted, and the accumulated results can be shared with interested parents. Competition placements are recorded and posted for players to review prior to the next tryout session.

During our two-week tryout period we notify players who are not selected to be on a team that they will need to complete a schedule change. Because we want to have their continued support, we acknowledge their courage in making an effort to be a part of our teams. Once we have narrowed our teams to a manageable number, we begin our official preseason program.

Since we are limited by our state governing body, the University Interscholastic League, to a one-hour training session per day during the preseason, our players do strength training two days per week for three months, then step up to three days of strength training for the two months of postseason. We work on agility, ball control, fitness, and small games during the first three months. We develop concepts for position play, learn the rules of the game, build character and school spirit, and have team-bonding sessions. Our players are trained to honestly assess their own and their teammates' skill levels. Leadership is taught by dividing our players into groups, each led by seniors, who share with their new teammates their attitudes about tradition and excellence— two important ingredients for success.

Throughout the preseason our staff records individual and team statistics that will assist us in the selection of starting players. In November, two months prior to our first game, we begin the next phase of training. We gradually increase the number of players involved in small-sided games from 3v3 to 11v11. We use the increase in numbers to look at player combinations that will work well together on the field of competition.

During this period, fitness training becomes more game oriented and our emphasis on technical skill begins to give way to tactical skills. Our goal is to have the players prepared for 11v11 competition when our season begins. Because numerous scoring opportunities result from set pieces, training for them becomes part of daily sessions. Combination play is emphasized, and players begin to train in small groups. We keep accurate records, daily notes, and practice films to assist with the selection of starting players.

In-season. During the season, our staff meets several days prior to game days to determine team objectives and strategies for the upcoming game. We do a match analysis of game film on our opponent and review our scouting reports. Using the match analysis, we match up personnel and draw conclusions about our game plan. Then we prepare a written game plan for our players and hold team meetings, to which our staff and team captains contribute, to discuss our opponent's strengths and weaknesses. The players are given an opportunity to review statistics and highlights from previous games. As a result of these efforts, our players will be ready to compete.

On game days we review the opponent's strengths and weaknesses and focus on our game plan. We have a team meeting before each game to answer any player questions about the opponent. At game time we implement our week's worth of preparation and make adjustments. At the conclusion of the game we begin our preparation for the next opponent.

In addition to game-preparation duties, daily coaching tasks include a system of weekly checks:

❏ Prepare and confirm any community speaking engagements.
❏ Check the weekly weather forecast to predict when we can schedule outside training sessions. Confirm potential use of the indoor facility in case the weather is inclement.
❏ Confirm match sites and times with opponent.
❏ Confirm officials' assignments and means of transportation.
❏ Confirm announcers, video technicians, and photographers.
❏ Confirm community halftime events.
❏ Check video equipment in preparation for games.
❏ Announce game times and sites through local newspaper, television, radio, or Web site coverage.
❏ Update scorebook after each match.
❏ Update Web site based on previous game performance.
❏ Double-check the list.

Off-season. During the off-season my assistant coach and I host senior-player exit conferences in which we ask them to evaluate our program; these serve as learning tools for our staff for the next year. Next we do upcoming-player evaluations, assessing their play and making recommendations for the following year. In practice, we reemphasize our strength-training program, play small-sided games, and begin to develop team bonding for the next season. During this time, I visit training sessions at local schools and clubs and host clinics for parents and players. I educate others and myself about our program and reorganize our booster club for the following season.

Managing Your Time

About 20 years ago I met with Donna Lopiano, who at that time was the director of women's athletics at the University of Texas. (She is now executive director of the Women's Sports Foundation.) Her ears were connected to a headpiece and her phone was lighting up as I tried to talk to her about starting a women's Division I soccer program at the university. I am sure her mailbox would have been full had e-mail available in the early '80s. Our brief conversation was to the point; she was a master of time-management skills and the epitome of a multitasker. I learned a great deal about organization and time management in less than five minutes.

Often, coaching at Plano Senior High School is like taking a quantum leap. Teaching multiple classes, attending meetings, and reading and responding to e-mails can be difficult tasks to juggle. I set aside time in the early morning to prepare for the day. During this time, I address meeting times and content, answer communication requests in a timely manner, and return all telephone calls. I use mass e-mail, conference calling, and voice mail to minimize the number of contacts.

A computer and a little knowledge can simplify a coach's life. Gone are the days of calling each parent and worker when a game is cancelled or rescheduled. Changes can be communicated with a simple mass e-mail message or by issuing an update on a coaching software package such as Assistant Coach. Parents can check the site prior to game time, and we can immediately post game results for interested parties and for newspaper publication. Text messaging is another way to communicate game results. Today, coaches are expected to dispense up-to-the-minute information.

Time management has always been essential for productivity in my coaching career, and I have discovered that there are ways to conquer it. You have a choice: Work long hours or work smarter. After developing sound time-management skills, I am less overwhelmed and more confident. I can spend less time on administrative tasks and more time on team preparation.

Time management begins with establishing a calendar to address yearly work priorities, which can be broken into manageable increments, such as seasonal and daily priorities. I use software to organize my coaching duties, preparing a personal "plan of attack" each year. Coaching our soccer team and teaching my classes are paramount. I start with the big picture: How does the soccer-season schedule relate to the school calendar? I develop a simple calendar and begin to integrate priority time lines with daily and yearly events and commitments. I identify what is most important and highlight the urgent items.

My plan of attack works well for me; planning puts me in a comfort zone. Developing a comprehensive plan and completing it moves me toward a higher level of accomplishment. I select my priorities, sorting the urgent from what is most important, and consolidate a to-do list. As deadlines approach, the urgent tasks rise to the top of the list. This procedure gives me control and focus, preventing those feelings of being out of control and overwhelmed that can reduce productivity.

> Time management is essential for productivity in any coaching career. You have a choice: Work long hours or work smarter. After developing sound time-management skills, you will be less overwhelmed and more confident, and you'll spend less time on administrative tasks and more time on team preparation.

Multiple tools can assist coaches with time management. Technology makes it easy to schedule our professional and personal lives to the second. Simple or complex calendars can be found in cell phones, planners, and on handheld and desktop computers. Select the most efficient mode of technology to ease time management, and keep your software updated. I function best with hourly time increments. Watches and phones can alert me to time and destination details. Calling systems are available for the ultimate time manager. Check your television—perhaps you can program an alert for a meeting or appointment. Of course, you must be able to program your chosen "technological assistant," and learning how can be fun as well as valuable.

Keep your schedule visible and handy and review it often, confirming times and places for meetings and tackling the important jobs first. Deal with daily interruptions while staying on course. My office door is generally open because I believe it is my job to be accessible to athletes and students. But when I am on a mission or deadline, I close my door and post a note stating the times I will be available. I have also been known to find a quiet hiding place in the library where I can stay focused on my project.

Set realistic long- and short-term goals by identifying each step in the process. Sort the relevant from the irrelevant for goal completion. I try to remain focused but flexible when the unexpected arises. I establish a time line and deal with frustrations and setbacks, perhaps reestablishing priorities. Try developing goals with anticipated outcomes, then writing them down and sharing them with others; this process helps you remember to stay on task and makes you become accountable for your actions. When you complete your goals or accomplishments, check them off your list and reward yourself.

Manage pressure by being organized so that you do not create chaos for yourself. Set parameters and time limits on your tasks, and then figure out the places or activities where you lose time and eliminate the loss. Also take the time to identify and focus on the activities that give you the greatest return for your time commitment. Recognize your competency and ability, then learn to delegate the tasks that you do not have time to complete. Do not stress about unimportant tasks; instead, reduce the stress by effective planning. Once you've done the planning, don't procrastinate. Finally, evaluate your accomplishments at the end of the day.

Time Management for Athletes

Our staff recommends that athletes take control of their own destiny. We educate them about "getting it together" and provide them with an understanding of the tools to build time-management skills. We teach our athletes skills that lay the foundation for a lifetime of success. As adults, we recognize that being a student-athlete in high school is similar to being caught in a whirlwind. Athletes who are academically responsible must

Courtesy of Diane Davey

Teach your athletes today the skills that lay the foundation for a lifetime of success.

maintain a rigorous schedule in order to meet all of the demands of school and sport. They juggle academics, tutorial sessions, training sessions, work, family, and church commitments. They also need to balance their lives with friends and personal time. Our players appreciate learning skills that will lead to a balanced and organized life. We prepare a blank calendar for them in which they can organize all their activities. Having a weekly schedule with planned daily activities helps them meet daily challenges. We address strict adherence to the calendar and a include check-off list for completion.

Students must place activities and goals on their calendar. As Sean Covey says in his book *The 7 Habits of Highly Effective Teens,* "Put first things first" by prioritizing through goal setting and "drawing a map to avoid the road blocks which knock you off course." Student-athletes can avoid high stress levels and feelings of anxiety by completing priorities. When they use the powerful habit of prioritizing, life becomes more balanced, and balance leads to higher degrees of success.

Ultimately, each of us in coaching must develop our own system to stay organized. Our efforts should reflect the needs of our athletes and gain the respect of the community. While maintaining structure, we must use creative avenues to avoid roadblocks to success. We must not be afraid to try a new path, but at the same time we need to display a feeling of consistency and commitment. Being organized from top to bottom is a huge achievement for both players and coaches.

12

Staff Management and Mentoring

Delegate responsibility and
offer opportunities for development

Pat Summitt

I got into coaching because I needed a job. During the fourth basketball game of my senior year at the University of Tennessee at Martin I tore my ACL, and the first orthopedic surgeon I saw after the injury suggested I give up playing the game. Thirty years ago a knee injury could be career ending. I wanted to compete in the 1976 Olympics, but I knew that even if I were able to play again, eventually I would be entering the working world. The injury turned out to be a positive experience because it forced me to think about my future. When I was a teenager, females were almost locked into being teachers or nurses. Although those are great professions, they didn't hold my attention like basketball did, so I chose to pursue a career in coaching.

I decided to get a master's degree for two reasons: to be able to coach at the college level and to gain coaching experience as a graduate assistant. The University of Tennessee offered me a graduate assistantship, but as timing would have it, the head coach took a sabbatical and never returned, which thrust me into the position of head coach at the age of 22.

Being in a position of authority at such a young age made for an interesting situation. My only training had come as a college player when I helped our coach, Nadine Gearin, with the offense, and through conversations with my brother, Tommy Head, who was a high school coach. I had never conducted a practice, had no budget for a staff, and certainly had no experience with staff management. I recruited graduate assistants to help me and have been learning how to hire, organize, evaluate, and work with staff ever since.

Hiring and Organizing Your Staff

Regardless of the size of your staff, an organizational chart is vital to efficient management. It shows the chain of command and the flow of communication, and the visual representation of the program minimizes confusion by showing supervisory responsibilities. My staff would argue that our organizational chart is a circle with me in the middle and that everyone else's responsibility is to keep me happy. Hopefully, the chart in figure 12.1 is closer to reality.

When organizing your staff, remember to consider support personnel and others you work with on a consistent basis. Trainers, strength coaches, academic advisers, compliance officers, and members of the media relations, marketing, and operations departments are all part of our program, even though they are not members of the basketball staff. A clear plan that details the proper flow of information and channels for contact reduces the risk of miscommunication and ineffectiveness.

Hiring your staff may be the most consequential aspect of management. Hire good people and your headaches will be greatly reduced. My philosophy has always been to hire bright, talented, loyal people who have a passion for coaching and working with young people. Surrounding yourself with great people is important because they have a significant impact on your success. When I was a child, my parents would ask me, "Who are you hanging out

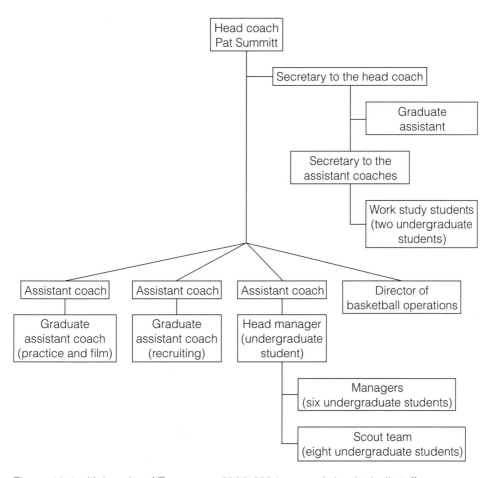

Figure 12.1   University of Tennessee 2003-2004 women's basketball staff.

with?" and "What do their parents do for a living?" They impressed on me at an early age the importance of associating with good people.

Having that philosophy is one thing, but successfully implementing it is another. Learning to gather appropriate information about the applicants and make sound evaluations is a lifelong process. When beginning the hiring process, first determine which qualities and skills are most important for the new staff member's success. Filling positions on a staff is like recruiting for your team: You recruit those who will embrace and thrive within your philosophy and who meet the needs of your team.

Next, assess your staff's strengths and weaknesses and look for someone who can balance the ledger. You may need a recruiter who has great people skills, a knack for assessing talent, and is personable and dynamic. You may need a floor coach—someone who can break down the game and communicate it to the players on the floor. I would never want to have three assistants cut from the same mold. On our current staff, Holly Warlick, my longtime assistant, provides talent assessment and teaching on the court. Nikki Caldwell, an assistant coach since 2002, brings recruiting and people skills, while Dean Lockwood, assistant coach since 2004, imparts organizational and teaching skills. I am the jack-of-all-trades and master of none.

When I hire assistants, I look first for loyalty. I also want someone who is on the cutting edge in the field. I want to know their background and their knowledge of the game. I look for someone who can relate well to everyone—especially to the student-athletes—and inspire them. More and more, I find that student-athletes need people who can connect with them and be on their level at times. The right person can also bring them to a different level when it comes to developing their skills.

> Hiring your staff may be the most consequential aspect of management. My philosophy has always been to hire bright, talented, loyal people who have a passion for coaching and working with young people. Surrounding yourself with great people is important because they have a significant impact on your success.

Camps are an integral part of my evaluation process. Most of the people we hire, from managers up to assistant coaches, have worked at our camps. It gives me an opportunity to evaluate their work ethic, enthusiasm for the game, energy level, and ability to teach and relate to players. I have also hired several former players as assistants after they had gained coaching experience in other programs. Because they have been through the program, they understand the expectations and our system and can speak from experience, all of which helps us in recruiting as well as with the current team.

Staff diversity is important. Some of our players might be more comfortable talking to a male, some a female, some an African American, others a former player. Nikki is not that far removed from being a player, so when she speaks about the game it is from a more recent perspective. Although Holly is a former player at UT, she can connect the past with the present. She relates well with the current players and that is one key to our ability to be successful.

As for the rest of our staff, a secretary is one of the more important hires you can make. They need to be warm and friendly because they create the first impression of your program for most people. They need to be attentive to detail, have good people and phone skills, and be fully committed and loyal to the program and philosophy. Our graduate assistants and managers must demonstrate a tireless work ethic and a passion for the game and the program. I interview them and run a personality profile as I do for any staff position. We do background checks by calling their high schools and any coaches they have worked for, and we require letters of recommendation. A high level of responsibility and dependability are crucial traits for our graduate assistants and managers.

Assigning Staff Duties

During the season the day-to-day duties of assistant coaches are almost too numerous to count. Duties are assigned based on the strengths of each assistant, but we also share some responsibilities to make sure we have all the areas covered. They correspond with recruits and high school and AAU coaches, work on game-plan strategies and recruiting tactics, and continually communicate with other parts of the athletic department and the university. They also spend quite a bit of time in practice sessions with the team, breaking down videotapes, traveling to games, and evaluating recruits.

As a head coach, breaking down videotapes of our opponents has become an important factor in determining how much time I will spend with a remote control in my hand. Some head coaches take on the primary responsibility of scouting. Some staffs have one person designated for this task, or one person assigned to scout a particular opponent. That person would then prepare reports for the rest of the staff and team. Although we assign assistants to scout each opponent, they are still required to watch at least one tape of the opponent in order to become familiar with them and identify their tendencies. What is most important is that the scouting report represents and supports your philosophy.

During the off-season, every member of our full-time coaching staff must be involved in community events, such as speaking to alumni or corporations, participating in athletic department fund-raisers, participating in a local charity, and teaching at coaching clinics. High school, junior high, or club coaches might enlist parents to aid in similar fund-raising and community tasks. I like to speak to civic groups and generally choose five charities to work with each year. Community involvement is a great way not only to give back to the community but to build your fan base.

Graduate students serve as administrative assistants for our program. They take statistics at practices and games and help with filming, recruiting details, and other administrative tasks, but according to NCAA rules they cannot coach. One of the responsibilities of our graduate assistant is to write down anything of significance that I say. Of course, some days the page isn't very full.

Managers are important to day-to-day program operations and can simplify a coach's life. I won't hire anyone who hasn't first worked in our summer camp, where they were involved in tasks similar to what they would perform in our program. That exposure gives our staff a chance to watch them work and gives the potential managers a better idea of what the job entails. I explain that their position is essential to the smooth operation of the program but that no job is too big or too small. Among their tasks are laundry, packing gear for road trips, videotape exchange, and helping with recruiting and camp mail-outs. That most of their tasks are thankless and behind the scenes does not diminish their importance on our staff; they are our peers and should be treated with respect.

Also important to our program are the "practice guys" who provide strong opposition for us in practice. Our players meet them playing pickup games on campus, and then we have them work our camps; we are very selective about who we choose. We explain that they cannot bring their egos to the court and they must follow certain rules: On drives to the basket they have to pull up, some days they can't block shots, and they have to be coachable. Most important, they have to be committed to our team's improvement. They get nothing for their efforts but practice gear—although they were mentioned in *Sports Illustrated* recently—but they know how valuable they are to the team's success.

Not every team at every level has the resources our team receives. Any coach who has a limited budget for salaries should seek out undergraduate help. There are some great students who want to be involved. Maybe they played in high school and are not interested or talented enough to play at the college level, but they want to go into the coaching profession. Those students can be a great resource to your program and provide an excellent opportunity for you to pass on your expertise and experience in the profession.

Often the first personal contact the public has with our program is with the office staff, and we want that impression to meet the highest standards. We want our basketball offices to run like a corporate office. We expect the staff's attire to be appropriate for welcoming the university president should he walk in, and we expect their phone skills and manners to be impeccable. Our office staff has to understand that every call is important, even if it comes at 7:59 a.m. or 5:01 p.m. We receive a high volume of calls, and at times it is difficult for the staff to manage the phone lines without calls rolling over into voice mail and still provide good service to visitors who stop by the office, but those are the expectations.

Katie Wynn, my secretary since 1981, oversees the office staff in addition to handling my correspondence, schedule, and the entire coaching staff's speaking engagements. Her organizational skills, attention to detail, and people skills are second to none, and I continually receive feedback about how great she is to work with. Student workers from the work-study program are another source of help in the office. We try to get at least two every year, and they handle much of the recruiting and camp mail-outs. Work-study money is available for students at most colleges, and I highly recommend recruiting extra office staff from that pool.

Setting Expectations

Outlining the expectations of each position on your staff in terms of job duties, professionalism, and personal conduct, so that everyone is aware of each other's responsibilities, can head off potential problems. In addition, I suggest forming guidelines for dress code, punctuality, relationships with players, language or profanity, and office hours. One key philosophy in our program is that the student-athletes are our top priority and deserve our full and immediate attention when they come in the office.

Once they understand their specific roles and responsibilities, trust your staff to get their jobs done professionally. You must give your staff the freedom to do their jobs, just as you must give players the freedom to perform. The similarities in facilitating the smooth operation of a staff and molding a cohesive, successful team are undeniable. You want to key in on players' strengths and allow them to do what they do best. In the same way, your staff members need to feel that they are trusted, respected, and expected to utilize their talents for the betterment of the team.

Instilling trust and confidence in your staff gives them a sense of ownership, which then feeds their investment in the program, feelings of belonging and contributing, and a sense of urgency when needed. Instead of feeling like a puppet, capable only of following orders, they will rise to their potential and understand that their actions enhance the performance of the team and the program.

Courtesy of the University of Tennessee Women's Media Relations

Surround yourself with great people—they have a significant impact on your success.

Involving Staff

Once you have hired your staff and set clear expectations for them, you've got to take care of them. Your staff is a small team, and just like on the court or the field, the focus must be on the team. Forming bonds of loyalty and respect is imperative not only to your success but also to creating an enjoyable workplace.

Few things foster loyalty in a staff member better than a head coach who exhibits allegiance and respect through her actions, including entrusting them with responsibility and going to battle for them. Some of the biggest battles I've fought have been about raises for assistant coaches. Taking such action shows that you value their contributions to the program. Administrators—unless they have been coaches—might not always appreciate the importance of an assistant coach. One way I take care of my staff is by using summer camps to supplement their income. Regardless of title and salary, all staff members put more time and commitment into the job than their compensation merits.

Another way to take care of your staff and keep them motivated is to keep things interesting. Just as players get bored with routines, staff members also can become complacent when their jobs lack variety. Change their routine the same way you change practice. Many people need a change of pace to keep them sharp, so offer them new challenges.

Changing who runs drills on the court is an excellent way to infuse variety into day-to-day routines. It keeps your staff on their toes and involved in practices and gives the players another voice to listen to. Often the same staff members run the same drills, and depending on their responsibilities, they might work closest with a particular group of players—but switching duties around gives even the same routine a different feel.

I have learned not to have coaches be limited to working with the guards or the post players every day. They can become very territorial. Although they may have a specialty, they should be involved in the coaching of every student-athlete. Individual workouts during the off-season offer opportunities to work with different players. Giving staff the leeway to choose which drills they present also keeps practices diverse. By allowing them to be creative, you teach your staff to teach the players. I might go to them and suggest, "Why don't you organize the drills that you think would be most beneficial in practicing the motion offense and shooting."

Coaches are always seeking new drills because they want variety. You have to be creative and involve your staff in finding new ways to present the same information. That's very healthy for the players and the staff. When coaches continually run the same drills, everyone gets bored. Look for new ideas, new drills, or a new way to accomplish the same goals. The players may not even realize they're practicing the same skills. You should even put some variety in your stationery, both for your staff's sake and to keep the recipient's attention. Recruits, for instance, receive frequent mailings, and utilizing different materials keeps the correspondence from becoming stale.

Make sure you and your staff take time off and get away from the job. Just as athletes need some time in the off-season to recuperate mentally and physically from the rigors of the season, the staff also needs to take a break to keep from becoming stale and unenthusiastic about the job.

In any job, you need to have fun and enjoy the process. The people who work with you need to remain passionate about their jobs; the student-athletes need to enjoy practicing and playing the game. Our philosophy is that when we step onto the court, we're intense and work hard, but we also have to learn to laugh at ourselves and enjoy every day. It's a game, and it's easy to have fun when you're winning; however, you don't always win in life, so you have to learn to handle the disappointments as well.

Picking an Avenue of Communication

Communication, with your staff and the outside world, is vital to managing a program. Whether this is accomplished through face-to-face meetings, memorandums, emails, or phone calls, the channels of communication must be clear and effective. Communication eliminates mistakes.

Every fall we have a department-wide meeting in which everyone presents their timetables, deadlines, responsibilities, and issues that need to be resolved; at the same time, they gather any information they need. This meeting sets the stage for the new academic year and helps get everyone in sync. I meet with each member of the basketball staff individually to review job responsibilities and expectations. At the Division I level we are fortunate to have a director of basketball operations. I spend a great deal of time meeting with her throughout the year to discuss team travel plans, practice schedules, and every aspect of the program she oversees.

I also try to have a fall retreat with my three full-time assistants to go over Xs and Os for the coming season and discuss individual workouts. Before that we would have spent time early in the summer thinking about offenses, defenses, and strategies for the coming year. We might meet at my house or work at the office in the morning and play golf in the afternoon. We mix it up each year.

Our regular staff meetings, however, don't have predetermined times. I don't believe in meeting merely for the sake of everyone being at the same place at the same time. Because we work together so closely, we discuss much of what we need to as situations arise. Everyone has to be flexible because of time demands, and we may have an impromptu meeting if needed. At the same time, you also need to recognize when the group would benefit from a more formal meeting.

Each day after practice I either sit down to talk with my assistants or I'll ask them to have their suggestions for the next day's practice on my desk by morning, which helps me in my practice preparation.

Communication with student-athletes, other members of the athletic department and university, and the community is also important. Everyone must have no doubt that a message from one member of the staff is representative of the entire staff. Cohesiveness eliminates confusion and division among the athletes and provides a consistent message to others. The staff may have spent four hours behind closed doors hashing, rehashing, or disagreeing about a situation, but the moment those doors open, everyone must be together philosophically.

> Everyone must have no doubt that a message from one member of the staff is representative of the entire staff. Cohesiveness eliminates confusion and division among the athletes and provides a consistent message to others.

I am a strong believer in the Predictive Index, a personality-profile tool that has been valuable to us for the past eight years. It gives an accurate portrayal of a person's strengths and assesses their patience, energy level, and ability to pay attention to detail. I have personality profiles for each member of the staff, as well as team members and recruits. We study the personalities and identify the communication techniques that will be most effective with each person. Understanding and motivating someone is much easier when you know what lights that person's fire. The tool also helps identify the best leaders and the most competitive people on the team.

Dealing With Conflict

You won't always make a perfect hire, and all staff members won't always be in agreement. Conflict among staff members will inevitably arise, even on the most cohesive staffs. Resolving those issues as soon as possible is critical.

Staff conflict can be one of the most detrimental things that can happen to a program. Friction or a lack of communication makes day-to-day life difficult and unproductive. Staff members don't have to spend all their free time together or be best friends, but they must be cohesive, work together well, and enjoy the process. At times that means periodically putting their own feelings aside. This sets a positive example for the team members, who often have to do the same thing.

Causes for conflict can stem from differing personalities, moodiness, motives, roles, boredom, or many other reasons. Staff members might become territorial about duties or players or feel locked into what they are doing and need a change. The entire staff needs to be in tune with each other so that they can identify an edgy member and work to ward off tension or disputes before they become full-blown. This could mean taking the time to talk with that staff member or help with a particular task. Early intervention does wonders to ease tension, make the staff more cohesive and fulfilled, and improve a program's efficiency. The first step is dealing with the issue one on one or having the individuals involved meet to discuss their problems. Sometimes conflict stems from a simple misunderstanding, in which case the resolution is relatively painless.

If such actions do not resolve the issue, talk with everyone involved to gather as much information as possible about the situation, but do not involve more people than necessary. You have to be loyal to your staff; for example, you should not talk to one assistant about a conflict with another. Mediate a discussion with those involved to help facilitate a peaceful and productive solution. Sometimes those in conflict have to make a concerted effort to resolve their differences and put the team's needs ahead of their personal agendas or opinions.

If conflicts or philosophical differences cannot be resolved, the only solution might be a change of personnel. I've never fired an assistant, but I have helped them find other jobs. I don't want to hurt anyone's chances of staying in the profession, so I try to get them other positions in which they can be successful.

Evaluating Staff

Our annual staff evaluations are done as required by the university, but I may also call one-on-one meetings to give staff members feedback throughout the year. Occasionally, if I sense unrest in the "basketball camp," I'll organize evaluations of the entire staff. More than anything I want the players' feedback, and the following procedure has helped pinpoint turmoil with great accuracy.

I have the athletes complete a blind evaluation of each staff member, including the head coach, assistant coaches, director of basketball operations, academic adviser, strength coach, athletic trainer, and media relations person. The purpose of this evaluation method is to measure the student-athletes' perceptions of each staff member, because all of us should be doing what we can to make the team successful. The questions used for each evaluation follow on pages 148-151. On the actual evaluation form, an athlete would circle the selected answer to each question (superior, above average, average, below average, poor, N/A), and space for comments follows each answer.

Staff-Evaluation Questions

Academic Counselor

1. How much confidence do you have in your academic counselor's knowledge of the curriculum at UT?
2. Do you find your academic counselor to be accessible?
3. How comfortable do you feel about speaking to your academic counselor?
4. Do you find your academic counselor helpful during registration periods?
5. How much confidence do you have in your academic counselor's knowledge of the academic policies of UT, the NCAA, and the SEC?
6. Do you receive academic information in a timely fashion from your academic counselor?
7. Do you feel that your academic counselor does a good job of communicating about academic issues with you and your coach?
8. Does the academic counselor inform you of and encourage you to use academic support services (e.g., tutors, language and math labs, special needs)?
9. Does your academic counselor inform you of and administer specific forms that you are required to fill out (e.g., designation of degree forms, petitions, senior standing sheets, graduation applications)?
10. Does your academic counselor pay close attention to details?
11. Do you have confidence in your academic counselor's ability to inform and instruct you?
12. How would you assess the professional image of your academic counselor?
13. How would you rate the overall effectiveness of your academic counselor?

Athletic Trainer

1. How much confidence do you have in your athletic trainer's knowledge of conditioning and rehabilitation?
2. Do you find your athletic trainer to be accessible?
3. How comfortable do you feel about speaking to your athletic trainer?
4. Do you find your athletic trainer helpful as a teacher and educator in her field?

5. How much confidence do you have in your athletic trainer's ability to be an effective motivator?

6. Do you receive feedback in a timely fashion from your athletic trainer?

7. Do you feel that your athletic trainer does a good job of communicating with you and your coach?

8. Does your athletic trainer pay close attention to details?

9. Do you have confidence in your athletic trainer's ability to inform and instruct you?

10. How would you assess the professional image of your athletic trainer?

11. How would you rate the overall effectiveness of your athletic trainer?

Media Relations Director

1. How much confidence do you have in your media relations director's knowledge of her field?

2. Do you find your media relations director to be accessible?

3. How comfortable do you feel about speaking to your media relations director?

4. Do you find your media relations director helpful and available for the team?

5. Do you have confidence in your media relations director's ability to inform and instruct you?

6. Do you feel that your media relations director does a good job of communicating with you?

7. Does your media relations director pay close attention to details?

8. How would you assess the professional image of your media relations director?

9. How would you rate the overall effectiveness of your media relations director?

Assistant Coach (A separate questionnaire is filled out for each assistant coach.)

1. How much confidence do you have in your assistant coach's knowledge of basketball?

2. Do you find your assistant coach to be accessible?

3. How comfortable do you feel about speaking with your assistant coach?

(continued)

4. Do you find your assistant coach to be loyal to the UT basketball staff and program?

5. How much confidence do you have in your assistant coach's knowledge of the policies of UT, the NCAA, and the SEC?

6. Do you receive important information in a timely fashion from your assistant coach?

7. Do you feel that your assistant coach does a good job of communicating with you and your teammates?

8. Do you feel that your assistant coach genuinely cares about you and is concerned when you have a question or need?

9. Does your assistant coach inform you of and encourage you to use academic support services (e.g., tutors, language and math labs, special needs)?

10. Does your assistant coach pay close attention to detail and properly prepare you for competition?

11. Do you have confidence in your assistant coach's ability to inform and instruct you?

12. How would you assess the professional image of your assistant coach?

13. How would you rate the overall effectiveness of your assistant coach?

Head Coach

1. How much confidence do you have in your head coach's knowledge of basketball?

2. Do you find your head coach to be accessible?

3. How comfortable do you feel about speaking with your head coach?

4. Do you find your head coach to be loyal to the UT basketball staff and program?

5. How much confidence do you have in your head coach's knowledge of the policies of UT, the NCAA and the SEC?

6. Do you receive important information in a timely fashion from your head coach?

7. Do you feel that your head coach does a good job of communicating with you and your teammates?

8. Do you feel that your head coach genuinely cares about you and is concerned when you have a question or need?

9. Does your head coach inform you of and encourage you to use academic support services (e.g., tutors, language and math labs, special needs)?

10. Does your head coach pay close attention to detail and properly prepare you for competition?
11. Do you have confidence in your head coach's ability to inform and instruct you?
12. How would you assess the professional image of your head coach?
13. How would you rate the overall effectiveness of your head coach?

Avoiding Mistakes in Staff Management

No one can hire and manage a staff without making any mistakes, but there are a few ways to improve your chances considerably.

The most important and obvious safeguard is to hire the right person for the job. A thorough interview process is key to making the best decision. Gathering information from a variety of sources is crucial. Although recommendations play a big role in evaluating a candidate, by no means are they the only factor. Communication with the candidate and a careful review of the application materials also are important. I have made the mistake of relying too much on recommendations rather than spending time gathering information from the individual. However, be careful not to bulldoze ahead based on your intuition without considering warning signs if you receive similar assessments from several trusted sources.

Another important aspect of staff management is listening. Communication involves a flow of information not only *to* your staff but also *from* your staff. Gathering feedback makes the staff feel like valuable members of the team and is an important resource for generating new ideas or gaining the inside track on a specific situation. As I have grown in my job, I am now better at asking, "What do you think?"

Understanding when and how to confront staff members is one of the more difficult lessons to learn as a manager. A key to good management is recognizing flaws in the system or behavior that isn't conducive to the program's success, and then talking about and correcting the situation. Just because you are going down the wrong road doesn't mean you can't turn around and go back.

One of the more common topics I discuss with my peers is the difficulty of confronting others. Through sharing ideas on how to do so more effectively, I've learned that confrontation doesn't have to be as hard as it seems. It is not about attacking people; it is about teaching and coaching them. If your guidelines and philosophy are in place and the staff's actions don't measure up, your responsibility is to let them know that and facilitate a change in their behavior.

If I have to address a concern with someone, I prefer to do so directly. Any student-athlete or coach would rather that you talk with them one on one. Sometimes in the course of a game or practice, however, you may feel that the feedback you have for one player is pertinent to the entire team; you may want to make that point to everyone by discussing it with the player in a group situation. Similarly, at times it is necessary to talk to the entire staff together. Be sensitive to when and how you address your concerns; you never want to embarrass anyone or break their spirit.

Having an open-door policy is also key to effective staff management. Whether that is literal or figurative, being open in your communication style offsets some potential problems. Head coaches have to work hard to develop a good rapport with each person in their program. It takes time to build relationships. They don't just happen.

Mentoring

Much has been written about the importance of being mentored as well as being a mentor. Gathering information from successful people whom you respect is important, as is sharing information with other coaches at all levels. When I started out in coaching I didn't know much, so I didn't have much to give back to the game. Now I try to take time to share my knowledge.

I've had the good fortune to learn from many people, each with different strengths. In grammar school and junior high I played for men who were great teachers, from whom I learned both strategy and discipline. I played for two women in high school and college, and I wouldn't have this job if it hadn't been for their support.

Without question, though, Billie Moore, a former coach at UCLA, has taught me more about the profession and about being a professional than anyone else. Billie convinced me that things should be done a certain way. She taught me the importance of setting high standards and developing a philosophy to follow during tough decision-making times to keep from lowering those standards. I learned to stand by my principles, to always strive to do the right thing, and to avoid operating in the gray. I see things as black or white; maybe that can be a fault at times, but that's how I think.

Talking to Billie early in my career, listening to her knowledge and experience about how to manage situations that seemed like crises at the time, was very beneficial. Her feedback was simple. She would say, "Think about this. Are you lowering your standards? Is this what you're all about? What is your philosophy?" She forced me to think about my own philosophy and become consistent in my thinking and in what I would do day to day. Billie also ran great practices, which I used as a reference point for my practices.

By providing mentoring opportunities, coaches help their staffs continue to learn and grow. Our staff periodically gathers with coaching staffs from other universities to get fresh ideas, hear new ways to solve problems, and learn how other successful programs operate. We also spend a lot of time brainstorming with our men's basketball coach, Buzz Peterson, and his coaching staff.

I am also proud to serve as a mentor to former assistants and players who are in the coaching profession. I try to help them find a place where they can be successful based on their goals, philosophy, and talents, and I make myself available when they seek information or advice or just need someone to listen to an idea.

I consider it a compliment to our program that so many players, managers, and graduate assistants leave here with aspirations of coaching, teaching, and recruiting. I believe it's because they have really learned the game, but also because they understand more of the total package of coaching. I remember Holly, back in her playing days, asking me, "What do you do in the office all day while we are going to school?" She hasn't asked me that question since she began working here.

Although we run a competitive, highly visible program that brings with it a certain amount of pressure and stress, the staff members need to enjoy their work and the atmosphere in which they work. You want them to look forward to coming to practice or to the office. Every day should be new, different, exciting, and rewarding. My staff has taught me that you can work incredibly hard and still have fun. You can be competitive, but you don't have to be serious all the time. Ideally, your players and staff will look back on their careers with fond memories. Good management goes a long way toward fulfilling that goal.

13

The Assistant Coach's Role

An important yet underappreciated asset to the program.

Lele Forood

Before arriving at Stanford in 1974, I was the high school state tennis champion in Florida. At that time, not only were there no athletic scholarships but there was also no recruiting. Because of the necessity to earn money to pay for college, I turned pro after my sophomore year, but I went back to Stanford and graduated in 1979 with a degree in sociology while continuing to play pro tournaments. I played full time on the tour through 1984 and was ranked 30th in the WTA singles and in doubles reached the semifinals at U.S. Open. My coach through both my junior and professional careers was Frank Brennan Jr., who later became my boss at Stanford.

When I left Stanford in 1979, the head women's tennis coaching job was available, and Frank Brennan ultimately accepted that position. After retiring from the tour I had been living and working in Paris as a tennis promoter, getting the first women's pro event off the ground in Strasbourg, France. After two years of tournament promotion, I no longer wanted to live abroad, so I returned to San Francisco and coaching just kind of happened! Frank hired me as an assistant in September 1988; but not knowing if I would like the profession, I took the job strictly on an interim basis for three months. After 16 years, I am still on the job.

I wasn't sure I wanted to be a coach then because, after turning 32, I didn't know if I was ready to be around college-aged kids. But when I got back on the Stanford campus, everything was familiar, it was easy to get back into the tennis routine, and I found out I liked the college-aged people. They had so much energy. So I served as an assistant for 13 years until the fall of 2000 when Frank retired and I took the head coaching position. When I came back to Stanford in 1988, the tennis team had already won five national championships through the 1980s, including the previous three consecutive championships. By the time I started as the head coach in 2000, the team had won five more, so I was coming into a successful yet challenging situation.

Qualities of a Good Assistant Coach

My vision of my role as an assistant coach was based on what I wanted a coach to be when I was competing. As a student-athlete at Stanford, I expected mainly tennis knowledge from a coach. I didn't want someone to tell me what to do all the time; I wanted some freedom to make decisions. I wanted to have a say in some of the things that affected me as a player, such as travel plans, where we ate, what time we got up, and how we spent our free time off the court. It was the turbulent '70s, after all!

As an assistant coach I consulted not only with the head coach but also with the older players on the team about where we would stay and when we would leave and return on trips. The assistant coach always walks that fine line between the team and the head coach; therefore, it is imperative that the assistant coach relate strongly to both sides. The assistant coach is most likely the first person of authority that a team member will go to with questions and problems because the assistant is usually more accessible. A team member will often feel that she can bounce ideas off the assistant or discuss problems and thereby get answers without involving the head coach. The assistant can make or break a great rapport within the group structure, and it is her job to relate to the team members as well as support the head coach. This is not always easy, but it is part of the responsibilities of an assistant coach.

> The assistant coach always walks that fine line between the team and the head coach. Therefore, it is imperative that the assistant coach relate strongly to both sides. The assistant can make or break a great rapport within the group structure, and it is her job to relate to the team members as well as support the head coach.

Any coaching job is largely a teaching job, so the assistant has to be a good teacher—this is the most important skill for an assistant coach. When training athletes younger than the pro level, and oftentimes at the pro level, coaches must teach physical as well as psychological skills. The assistant must teach each athlete how to improve her game, and the assistant must be able to follow through on that teaching. This is where a coach's acceptance by the athlete originates, and the assistant coach will get her respect according to her ability to positively affect and improve that athlete.

Second, you have to be able to relate to the age group you are working with. In a collegiate situation, you have to understand that the athletes are in an important developmental period. They're under pressure to play big-time sports, but you also want them to get a good education to help them in their future. The college years are also their most important social years. The pressure is on the student-athletes to do a little bit of everything, and the assistant coach (who is typically close in age to the athletes) probably remembers those days best and can relate. Therefore the assistant can keep an empathetic perspective about what the schedule and demands on the student-athletes should be, which will enrich the relationship between the assistant coach and her charges.

Although it's important for you as an assistant coach to be able to relate to the athletes from their perspectives, you must also get beyond their collegiate playing career and have some experiences that will enhance your coaching ability. In that way I don't think it best serves a program to have the top assistant be too close in age to the student-athletes. I would never hire anyone who was out of college for fewer than five years. I don't believe in having anybody that close in age and experience to the players they would be working with. Unfortunately, because of their financial situations, many programs do need to hire people just out of college. A team relates differently to a person they just played with, and it's difficult for that person to establish authority. I prefer someone that has been removed from being a player and

Photo by David Gonzales

Good communication skills are undeniably a great asset to both head and assistant coaches.

now has other experiences and is mature enough to handle the responsibilities of the assistant coaching position.

Loyalty is also a critical requirement for an assistant coach. No one should take a coaching job unless she can fully subscribe to the school she will represent and the style and policies of the head coach that she will be supporting. The head coach instills loyalty in staff by giving the assistant responsibility to operate according to her particular styles and expertise. In return, the head coach expects that the assistant work to keep team relations smooth and that she report potential problems to the head coach so that a joint decision can be made to resolve the conflicts. If this is not the way the assistant handles her responsibilities, some very clear divisions will arise within the group, and the team members will be put under undue stress by having to take sides. Fortunately, in my experience I had such a good relationship with the person I was working for that the issue of loyalty never came up.

I try to take care of my assistants so that they will stay with the program. I don't like the notion of having turnover every year or every couple of years. Continuity is good for the program, especially in the recruiting area. If you constantly have to bring someone else in to fill the assistant's role, it requires time and effort to find the right situation and develop camaraderie with the other coach. That time can always be better spent in improving your team and program. Stanford strives for continuity by providing physical education teaching opportunities for the assistants so that it's financially palatable to stay in the assistant coach's position. Now you can have a career as an assistant coach until you are either ready to move on or ready to move up to the right job, not just any job.

Communication and conflict-resolution skills are great assets for an assistant coach. So much of the job involves communicating with the student-athletes and giving and receiving ideas, techniques, and experiences. You have to be prepared to explain things and keep the lines of communication open while the head coach concentrates on directing the program. As mentioned earlier, often student-athletes will go to the assistant coach when they think they are not getting the right thing from the head coach. In that sense they can try out ideas or bring up issues in a safe environment with someone in a position of authority, especially if student-athletes feel that such an action might compromise their position with the head coach. The assistant coach needs to have the skills to work through any trouble spots and explain the position of the coaching staff in most of these situations.

Assistant Coach's Responsibilities

Assistant coaches have varying responsibilities according to their other commitments and the number of assistants available for their programs. Assistants bring stronger and weaker skills to the job, and a good head coach will make sure that a new assistant starts out in a comfort zone by giving her responsibilities that suit her strengths. The assistant coaches' responsibilities at Stanford have a lot to do with the fact that there is a major physical education teaching requirement involved, so some coaching duties have to be minimized because many of the assistants' noncoaching hours are spent teaching. For example, an assistant's recruiting responsibilities take place only when the recruits are on campus. Recruiting for collegiate tennis is not as complex as it is for most sports because we don't recruit many players to begin with, and it's pretty easy to recruit student-athletes to Stanford if they have the grades to qualify!

I had very limited recruiting duties early on. My first year involved adjusting to the players' personalities and needs, hitting with them on the court, and getting comfortable in the role. Frank, my boss, used me largely as a trainer with the team. Since I was so familiar with Frank, he knew where I should start out to become comfortable with the job. It was a good move because he knew my strengths. He added more responsibilities for me later.

Because only two of us work full time, my current assistant coach's responsibilities are not too different from the responsibilities I had as an assistant coach. The only role he does not have that I undertook when I was an assistant is "travel coordinator," which is a role I keep for no particular reason, even though it is time consuming. Otherwise he is responsible for all the equipment, plays the sets with players at practice, and has a variety of other tasks. (My days of playing sets with our players ended somewhere around my turning 40!)

Other duties of assistant coaches might include helping with camps, organizing and participating in fund-raising activities, completing paperwork (although rarely budget work), preparing practices, and doing other "miscellaneous duties" as assigned by the head coach, which is a popular phrase for doing whatever I may need the assistant to do. I started out with limited responsibilities in these areas, but over time I gained valuable experience in all of them. It is crucial for assistants who aspire to head coaching positions to become familiar with all of these areas; that way, the first year as head coach will be much less stressful. My current assistant, who has a background in group teaching at clubs, is skilled and creative in practice ideas; therefore he has a large responsibility in this area. Again, it's important for assistants to speak up and share their expertise and for head coaches to utilize the talents of their assistants.

Sometimes as an assistant you are an intermediary and can solve the issues yourself, and sometimes you should bring them up with the head coach. What gets reported to the head coach is at the discretion of the assistant coach. If it's a significant issue, it becomes the assistant's responsibility to inform the head coach and then to be part of the solution. As an assistant, I didn't bring everything up with the head coach if I thought it was trivial, or if I thought I could make somebody understand with a brief conversation why we had to do something a certain way. With bigger situations, head coaches can take the decision back to the team and let everybody know why they are handling the concern a certain way.

My assistant, Frankie Brennan (son of the head coach I worked with), has come into my office and said, "The team feels that you're spending too much time working with a particular player and there seems to be a little resentment by the other players." After he informs me of that type of situation, we'll try to figure out how to address it with the team and whether it should be discussed individually with the people who feel that way or whether I need to talk about it in a team meeting. I may be spending more time with one player and didn't realize it. It always seems to help the team when he brings a problem forward and we come to a resolution that's good for all of us. I expect him to bring me information like that because discontent is something that won't usually be brought directly to the head coach. It is fundamentally important that the assistant present a united coaching front to the student-athlete while trying to solve any minor issues that they might present.

I think empowering assistant coaches is a vital management responsibility for a head coach. A happy assistant will have a positive effect on a program; I would say that you cannot be successful with a program without great assistants. That's why it's so important to choose wisely and make the assistant comfortable in her role right from the start. Not just allowing, but even requiring, input from assistants will make everyone feel a stronger allegiance to the program and help the team move toward the common goal. An assistant as well as the head coach can transfer that same demand for input to the student-athletes as well.

Unity Among Coaches

Lots of situations arise that test coaches' sense of unity. As an assistant, I joined the head coach in meetings with our players for several reasons. Obviously it's a safety precaution in case a player later makes an outlandish accusation about a coach. But more important, the presence of all coaches at a meeting makes whatever is said look like a unanimous decision of the coaching staff, especially when it involves announcing something such as a player's position on a team. If a player protests, we can respond with, "No, for the following reasons we have decided you are going to play this position." Of course the players have a hard time hearing news like this and will probably want to talk more about it later. With the assistant coach present at the meeting, she is able to confirm the decision to the athlete in any further discussion. I think it's important that the coaches act as one in these pivotal meetings with the student-athletes and that each coach present have something to say in that meeting, even if it is just a remark or two. As a head coach, I make sure my assistant coach is in all meetings as well.

When I was an assistant, the coach and I had at least one weekly coaching meeting so that we could go over that week's schedule, practice ideas, and travel details. We also used the time to take inventory on each student-athlete and the mood of the team in general. That has continued into my head coaching days, and I realize more than ever the importance of giving the assistant coach a forum for his opinion. If we do not start out with the same viewpoint, then we hash it out and discuss it until we come up with some conclusion that we are both comfortable with. Topics of discussion might involve practice plans, training ideas, or positions the players are competing in. I realize I need to be open to their suggestions if I expect them to continue to communicate openly with me. This is the appropriate time for an assistant coach to raise concerns with the head coach. The assistant coach is usually more of the sounding board for team members because, rightly or wrongly, they are seen as not the final authority figure; therefore assistants tend to learn more from the players than head coaches do.

Staff Guidelines

This is an interesting area of coaching, and times have changed in this area. I used to have a lot of interaction with our players when I first started as an assistant. I even socialized with them when that was not frowned on. Many rules changed at the end of the 1980s, and coaches had to be careful about contact with players. We stopped having meetings with players in hotel rooms while traveling, and just to be safe from any accusations, we tended not to have meetings one on one anymore. Then some years ago the athletic department instituted rules, probably for the better, concerning coach–student fraternizing. These department rules make it simple for us to regulate the dos and don'ts of socializing with our players.

You should develop guidelines for the staff to follow and go over them as early as possible during the interview process. Your assistants need to know your expectations of them. Make sure to include things that are important to you, such as having the assistants dress professionally, keep regular office hours, and maintain open and honest communication with the head coach about all aspects of the program so that the head coach is never surprised. Also, make sure they know they can challenge you in private about team policies, but they must provide full support to the head coach in public. Loyalty is a key quality for an assistant coach if she wants to move up in the coaching profession.

Moving Into a Head Coaching Position

Every head coach should realize that at some point her assistant coach may take over a program and become a head coach. Therefore the head coach should gradually give more responsibility to the assistant, who in turn must become comfortable with the various tasks. In my first year of head coaching I sent my assistant to an important national tournament with three of our top players so that he could show to the three players, the rest of our team, and the collegiate tennis community in general that not only could he do the job, but that I also had confidence in him to do a *great* job at the conference. They came back with all the titles at that event, and no one questioned whether the assistant knew what he was doing.

> The head coach needs to make sure her assistants are competent, challenged, and reasonably compensated. The assistant coach also needs some autonomy in order to develop a coaching style. As a head coach, you are not only training athletes, you are also training future coaches.

My experience of transitioning was not quite so easy. When Frank Brennan Jr. told me he was retiring, there wasn't a formal search for head coach because I was already the associate head coach, a job that I had held for two years. I was apprehensive about the management aspect of the team, not about whether I could coach this team to be national champions. My apprehension stemmed from my own lack of training during my days as an assistant, and as a result I, like everyone, am constantly working to improve myself and my performance.

I recommend giving assistants a variety of responsibilities to prepare them for becoming head coaches later. Ask them to develop the recruiting strategy, prepare team travel, develop the player notebook, run a team meeting, speak to booster groups, meet with administrators, and even speak with the media so that they will be as prepared as possible to move into a more public role as a head coach.

The head coach must make sure assistants are competent, challenged, and adequately compensated. Assistants also need some autonomy in order to develop a coaching style. A happy assistant is a valuable asset not only to the head coach but also to the success of the program.

Assistant coaches can make or break a program. There is nothing more exciting than working closely with another person or group of people to help young women reach their potential in a sport. As a head coach, you are not only training athletes, but you are also training future coaches. If a head coach is smart, she'll give hard-working assistants the credit they deserve. If the assistant coach is wise, she'll take advantage of every moment to learn as much as she can about the exciting profession of coaching.

14

Team Management

Develop a system, set functional parameters, and stimulate growth

Dorothy Gaters

Courtesy of Dorothy Gaters

Since 1975 I have been the varsity basketball coach at my alma mater, John Marshall Metro High School, in Chicago, Illinois. During that time, the program has won more games and state titles, male or female, than any other school in the history of Illinois basketball.

Despite our team's success and the various honors I've received, I am most proud of watching my players grow and excel. Some have earned honors from local, state, and national organizations; some have excelled at the college and professional levels; and almost all who want to attend college do so and graduate. I believe the methods I use to manage my program have as much to do with the success of my players as with what we do at practice or in games.

Proper team management is as important and necessary as good on-court coaching, but it is generally considered to be a less enjoyable aspect of the job. Managing all the facets surrounding an athletic program of any level could easily be a full-time job in itself—without ever setting foot on the court. At times it seems that the many day-to-day and season-to-season tasks get in the way of your "real" role as a coach. However, how you manage your program will affect what you do and how your team responds on the court.

Virtually everything about team management boils down to organization and communication. By developing systematic ways of organizing your tasks, your paperwork, and your communication with those involved in the program, your job will be much easier and more rewarding. Although team management also involves sport-related activities such as technical and tactical instruction, this chapter will focus on off-court duties.

Aspects of Team Management

One of the most important things I can do as a coach for my team is to be organized. Not only will players have a better experience in a well-run program, but they also see from example how to be organized and the benefits of doing so.

The areas of responsibility involved in team management are diverse, but almost all fit into one of the following categories: people, events and scheduling, documentation, resources, communication, academics, players' off-court development, and policies.

Having an overall view of what to manage is a big start. Understanding what is involved within each area will help you get a handle on the administrative aspects of the job. Developing a yearly calendar that details the tasks you want to accomplish will help you know what to focus on throughout the year. Organizing the foundation of your team management system for the first time may take several days of focused effort, but the benefits in the long run are well worth the time. Then, as you gain experience in coaching, you'll learn where to make adjustments so that your processes are fine-tuned.

People. Managing and working with a wide variety of people may be the most difficult aspect of the job. Certain characteristics--such as respect, honesty, and consistency--should be displayed when dealing with anyone. But your role differs with different groups.

With your players, you are the leader. With your staff, you are both the leader and a co-worker. With parents, you are another adult interested in the welfare of their children, yet you also are in charge of what goes on with the team. With your administration, you are the employee and must learn how to accept and respect their decisions. With opponents, you are an equal.

But of those groups, it is your team and staff that require the bulk of your management efforts. Getting your staff in place and running efficiently will help immensely with the rest of your responsibilities. Your first decisions concern staff make-up. Some of the parameters already may be in place at your school or organization, such as restrictions based on rules or budget for how many assistants, managers, and support personnel you can have.

Regardless of how large or small your staff, you should have a clear view of the qualifications, characteristics, and roles of each position. Make a list of every single thing that needs to be done throughout the year, then decide which position or person is best suited for that task. Failing to properly delegate will create undue stress for you and the team. Perhaps a parent or booster can handle travel arrangements, an assistant can monitor the players' academics, and a manager will have the necessary equipment ready for each practice. Knowing and communicating each person's responsibilities will keep projects from falling through the cracks, reduce overlap of efforts, and emphasize that everyone is important to the success of the team.

Choosing and managing players is another important aspect of team management. Roster size and makeup may also be predetermined. Your school may have a policy that guarantees a spot on the squad to anyone who expresses an interest. Or, you may conduct tryouts to choose players, in which case you must determine the structure of the tryouts: when and for how long will they take place, how to publicize them and to whom, the objective and subjective criteria for making the team, and how you will announce the results.

You may actively recruit players you want to join your team. This much freedom requires more effort on the coaching staff: determining the characteristics of players you want, deciding who and where the staff will watch and evaluate prospects, organizing communication, and following any rules that govern recruitment at your level.

In any event, putting together a well-planned squad requires that you consider the optimal number of players on the squad; the number of players needed at each position; and the goals and expectations placed on your program by yourself, your school or organization, and your players.

Events and Scheduling. The planning of a season's competition schedule and other events is as important as it is time-consuming. Tryouts, practices, games, meetings, fund-raising efforts, and group outings are important aspects of program, and working hard to be organized will lessen the stress that often surrounds the events, making them more enjoyable for everyone involved. Have a brainstorming session with the groups that will be involved in the planning of these events. Make a list of the different aspects of each event, and then begin assigning duties so that the burden of the event does not fall upon one person.

Developing a competition schedule takes forethought and an honest evaluation of your team. You want your schedule to be competitive and challenging, but you also want your team to have success. If you know your team will be more thin than usual on talent or experience, adjust the level of your competition accordingly. Knowing your team's potential and putting together an appropriate schedule is a critical part of helping your team continue to grow and improve.

Management of your home competitions will probably be what most people associate with your program rather than what you do *during* a competition. A game or tournament that is run professionally, efficiently, and hospitably will go a long way in improving the perception of your program. Your administration and staff will likely provide support in that realm, but consider all the details: facility and equipment needs; school or league regulations; communication with and locker rooms for officials and opponents; fair treatment and friendly greeting of opponents; staff for ticket sales, ushers, concessions, medical needs, officials, clock operators, official statistics, promotions, and facility management; and the timing and structure of the event.

Arranging travel plans for away competitions should be done well in advance to ensure your transportation and accommodations needs are met for the least amount of money. Hotels and charter bus companies likely will give you a better deal if you make reservations ahead of time rather than at the last minute. Circulating detailed, complete, and accurate itineraries to players, coaches, support staff, parents, faculty, and administration will decrease both your stress and the number of questions asked surrounding the trip.

The planning of the team's year and practices is also extremely important. My strategy is to plan from the largest segment of time to the smallest. First, develop an overall calendar that outlines the different phases of the year and its important dates: the beginning and end of classes, holidays, available windows of practice and competition, and important competitions. Then determine the timeframes of your team's preseason, season, postseason, and off-season. Break each of those segments down by what you want to accomplish, how often and long practices will be, and your competition schedule.

Finally, prepare a detailed daily practice schedule. I work hard to make sure practices are organized so that we can use the time effectively and efficiently. Your players will recognize when you have a cohesive plan to help them improve, and they will also recognize when you're making up the schedule as you go along. They will work harder and respond more positively when they see you putting the same amount of effort into the season that you expect from them.

Parents and boosters will help with determining what fund-raising efforts will be most effective considering the goal, the community, and the time commitment. Ask players their opinion, too, if they will be participating. Determining their interest in or excitement about one project over another will have a lot to do with the success of the campaign.

Other events—like meetings, team outings, or banquets—also require careful planning and attention to detail. Securing facilities, inviting guests, making meal arrangements, planning travel, and developing an agenda are manageable tasks when delegated and completed ahead of time.

Documentation. Forms and documents are as much a part of coaching as game-day tactics. Paperwork permeates our lives, but it also serves a number of functions, such as keeping us legal, facilitating help from another department, documenting our season, obtaining reimbursements, and remaining compliant with a governing body. Making sure you use and retain on file the documentation necessary to run your program is the mark of a professional, and it will improve your relationship with your administration.

Perhaps the most important documents are those involving the student-athletes: their medical histories and release forms, signed parental release forms, eligibility confirmations, emergency contact information, and miscellaneous information, such as injury or rules violation reports. Not having the proper documentation on file could result in huge, negative consequences to your program, including lawsuits based on medical situations, forfeiture of games due to ineligible players, or penalties from a governing body.

Other paperwork that should be used, filed, or submitted at appropriate times includes budgets, receipts, reimbursement forms, facility schedules, equipment inventories, practice and training plans, competition schedules and results, performance records for your team and facility, press releases, news articles about the team or a player, travel plans, policies, award nominations, organization membership and dues, job descriptions and evaluations, risk management plans, accident reports, and meeting agendas and notes.

Resources. Managing your team's budget and financial resources is tied closely with documentation, but here we're talking about the actual expenditure and allocation of resources rather than the procedures of making purchases.

The budget process can be intimidating and frustrating, or it can be rewarding. It all depends on your outlook, preparation, and expectation. There are varying strategies for preparing a budget proposal, from being as realistic as possible, to automatically increasing the previous budget by 10 percent, to following the "I won't get what I don't ask for" philosophy. Regardless of your tactics, you should be thoughtful and ready to provide a logical explanation of your requests, taking care to allocate appropriate funds for your program that fit in with your priorities and goals for the team. Among the possible categories in your budget are staff salaries, team travel, equipment, game-day expenditures (such as paying the officials and the table crew), marketing and promotions, recruiting, team building activities, and office equipment and supplies.

The choices facing coaches in regard to budget are endless, and the way a coach spends her budget reflects her philosophy: Purchase new uniforms or travel to an out-of-state tournament? Conduct a fund-raising activity to pay for a team retreat in the preseason or have better pre-game meals? New computer and color printer or new basketballs? Bring in more recruits for modest stays or limit the number of official on-campus visits and spend more on their accommodations and meals? Have monthly team parties or provide officials with post-game pizza?

Equipment is also a resource, and it is one that will save money if well-managed. Washing game-uniforms properly will save on wear and tear. Collecting and counting all balls after practice will keep them from "walking away." Taking care of practice gear, equipment, and team computers will prevent you from spending more than necessary on those items. Keeping your equipment room and records organized will lessen the chance of replacing something you mistakenly thought was missing or stolen.

Communication. This area can be the most difficult to manage well if you don't have a cohesive plan or accountability from everyone in the program, but good communication is vitally important. Thoughtful and efficient communication can help a good team overachieve, and poor communication can make a talented team average. Among the items that need communicating in detail are the practice schedule, game-day schedule, travel itinerary, dress code, equipment needs, and other activities. Here I'll cover what needs to be communicated. Later I'll talk about the different methods of communicating.

> Thoughtful and efficient communication can help a good team over-achieve, and poor communication can make a talented team average.

Players should be given a practice schedule, including start time, duration, and location, at least weekly so they can plan the rest of their time and responsibilities. Explain the game-day routine, such as when and what they should eat, when they should arrive at the locker room, and when they should be prepared for the team warm-up. For away contests, let them know what is appropriate and inappropriate travel attire, what individual and team equipment each member is responsible for, and departure and arrival times.

But communicating is more than just relaying facts and strategies. It is embodying the mission, goals, and philosophy of the program so that everyone is motivated to work together. It is checking in with your administrators to keep them apprised of any situation that might be brewing. It is a coaching staff that pitches in when one person is buried with a project. It is listening to all sides of an argument and settling on the best course of action. It is players supporting each other personally.

It also is staying connected to each of your players. Most coaches have frequent meetings with staff, but fewer meet with their players on a consistent basis. Holding regularly scheduled, one-on-one meetings with players once or twice a month is ideal. Most players associate a meeting with the head coach with being disciplined, but making them a regular part of the routine allows you both to bring up problems, highlights, or personal matters more comfortably. A player might not feel comfortable making an appointment with you on her own, even if she has something important on her mind, but a regular meeting will provide her the opportunity to talk about it without making it a big deal. Whether you watch videotape, discuss the next opponent, or just touch base with one another, meeting with players should be a high priority.

Academics. The emphasis you place on academics will be evident in how your players perform in the classroom. A lackadaisical attitude will likely yield lower grades, a higher number of ineligible players, and a poorer relationship with faculty and staff than a hands-on approach. Saying that academics is important and demonstrating it through your actions are two different things.

First, your grade policy should be communicated early and often, so players, faculty, and administration know what you expect of your athletes in the classroom. A minimum grade point average may be set by the school or league, but you may decide to place higher standards on your team. Perhaps the official grade point average is a 2.5, but you require athletes to carry a 3.0 to stay out of team study hall. Or, you may impose study hall on players with a C- in any one class.

Second, you must help student-athletes plan around activities such as practices, games, and team functions. Your practice time should be fairly standard within a quarter or semester so that players know when to schedule their classes. During times when your team travels every other Friday, scheduling Tuesday/Thursday classes is key. Also, knowing when major exams or projects will require more attention than normal will help you adjust team commitments to allow for the additional study time.

Third, you should conduct regular grade checks. Taking early steps to identify any student who is failing or having problems with a particular class often will nip larger programs in the bud. Talk with the athlete first to let her know you want her to succeed. If that doesn't help, set up a conference with the teacher to get a sense for the problem and help develop a plan. That could serve as motivation for the athlete to work harder and prove to the teacher that you place a high priority on academics. Call the parents in for a meeting if necessary. Hold the athlete out of practice and games if that would be motivating, or impose study hall. If none of these tactics works, suspend the player from the team until she demonstrates a commitment to her grades.

We also spend quite a bit of time talking about recruiting and college preparation: ACT and SAT testing; freshmen eligibility rules for NCAA, NAIA, and NJCAA schools; clearinghouse information; and filing applications for financial aid grants. I want all athletes to be informed about their options and responsibilities, both athletically and academically, in qualifying for college entrance and scholarships.

Players' off-court development. I believe strongly that it is a coach's responsibility not only to help players succeed athletically, but also to improve and succeed off the court. Athletics is filled with such emotion and passion, and it provides such unique relationships and bonds, that to dismiss your influence over your players is short-sighted. To ignore it not only lessens your impact on their lives but also could cause you and your team problems in the long run if players are unable to compete at all or to their potential because of off-court issues. Providing them with the support they may need is extremely important.

Each of your players, not just your stars, should know and feel that you care for them as people first and athletes second. You should show genuine interest in their families and outside interests. You should reveal some of your personality to them to show that the relationship is important to you. This is not to say you should be buddy-buddy with your players; that is not your role. Your role is to help teach them teamwork, responsibility, trust, hard work, ethics, and good citizenship, and you will do that best by consistently displaying the same characteristics.

One thing we do that helps show the scope of what our program is about is by having a team mission. Although part of our mission pertains directly to basketball, such as playing pressure defense and diving for all loose balls, it is about much more than just winning basketball games, because coaching is about much more than just winning games. I want our players to learn to give 100 percent effort during every possession of the ball in every practice and game, but I also want them to display good sportsmanship, to be good students, and to be good citizens at all times.

Many players today feel that it isn't cool to put forth maximum effort. They try to be too laid back. It is almost as if they are embarrassed to play hard. They don't want to get on the floor to tie up a ball or save the ball. I have heard my players tell other players: "Don't run so fast," or "You're trying to impress Ms. Gaters," or other things to discourage the player from showing them up. One thing I do to combat that during practice is to put different players in charge of the team during various drills. If the person can command the respect and demand proper effort of her teammates, it teaches leadership, accountability, and teamwork, and it makes my job of coaching a lot easier.

One of the best educational experiences provided to my players was a trip to the Netherlands in 1988. Giving your team the opportunity to travel outside of their normal boundaries, whether it is out of state or out of the country, teaches them so much about other places, other people, and other cultures that it truly broadens their horizons and helps to open their minds to other ways of living. As a coach, you may be giving your students many opportunities that they would never have had otherwise. The highlight of the year might be a trip they'll never forget, but providing them with a mission of good citizenship and good sportsmanship can also last them the rest of their lives.

Team Policies

Team rules are another aspect of team management, but it is of such importance I wanted to address them individually. The creation, adoption, and enforcement of team rules are extremely important in your efforts to help your players and program succeed.

I don't overburden our players with too many rules. However, I do recognize the significance of having rules in place to run a successful program. Many people think that being in an inner-city environment makes it difficult to instill respect for rules. I want to dispel that rumor. Actually, most kids want order and direction in their lives. As teenagers, they are searching for an identity and direction, and the coach can be a guiding force in developing character in these young people.

Team rules are necessary so that everyone knows the importance of working together as a team. We also set rules so that players understand they should not do anything to embarrass themselves, the team, the coaches, or the school. The correlation between what you expect from your players and what they do in other situations is very close. When players do not learn to be responsible and respectful, your program is in jeopardy from the start.

The first thing I want our players to understand is that I am the captain of the ship. I want to make sure each player knows who is in charge of the program, what is expected, and what happens if a rule or policy is broken. I like to joke that we have two rules:

Rule 1: The coach is always right.

Rule 2: Refer back to Rule 1.

More seriously, our team rules encompass behavior and performance in class, behavior toward teachers and others, dress code, attendance at games and practice, and punctuality. I set the standard of expected behavior early in the season. Players should arrive at any class, practice, and appointment on time and prepared. A committed and serious athlete understands the need to be punctual, and it is disrespectful to expect a group to wait on any one person. Players must be attentive and willing to participate. Players are not allowed to miss practice without notifying either my assistant or me. We have a dress code for what players wear to away games because we want our kids to take pride in representing our school and community, and we want to project a certain image of our program. We understand our responsibility as athletes and coaches to be leaders in the community and to behave as such.

There are two keys to enforcing rules. First, make sure the punishment fits the action. Second, be fair and consistent yet compassionate. That sounds contradictory, but it isn't. Showing compassion is different from being lenient and unpredictable. When you apply your rules fairly across the board, regardless of whether you are disciplining the best player to the least talented to everyone in between, your players will respect you and your rules even more. The key word is respect. I have had many teams with many personalities, but the best are those in which the majority of the athletes followed the rules because of their respect for me. They understood what I was trying to accomplish, not only for them but also for the entire team.

> Showing compassion is different from being lenient and unpredictable. When you apply your rules fairly across the board, regardless of whether you are disciplining the best player to the least talented to everyone in between, your players will respect you and your rules even more.

There are always exceptions to the rules. One of our team rules is that, at the beginning of the season, every guard has to run a mile in 6:30, forwards in 7:00, and post players in 7:30. Our athletes are usually in excellent shape because the majority of them participate in cross country, track, or volleyball, but I had a 6-foot, 2-inch, 200-pound player one year who had a bad combination of being extremely lazy and slow afoot. After trying to make her time every day for about two weeks, and not putting forth a full effort, she could see that I was unrelenting. For the next four days she worked extremely hard, but she could not make the time despite her teammates' steady stream of encouragement. Finally, I could tell that she was giving everything she had but was not going to make her time. With the first game only a week away, I decided to use a hand-held stopwatch instead of the stadium clock. She finally made her cutoff, with some creative timing from me. This young lady was a nonstarter on our team for her entire career, but her teammates pulled for her so much that I thought it was the right thing to do for team spirit.

I know of another instance where a 6-foot, 4-inch high school All-American in California never made her running time as a freshman in college and thus was not allowed to play in games her first year. The young lady lost more than 30 pounds in her wholehearted efforts, but in her discouragement she later quit the team. This program has still not reached any level of consistency, in part because I believe they alienate their players by not showing compassion or mercy.

Methods of Communication

Choosing the most effective and efficient method of communication for any given situation is an important piece of the puzzle. Written, verbal, or nonverbal communication may be the best option depending on the type of information or emotion being relayed, the recipient, the timeframe, and the setting.

It is easy to think you've told a team an important announcement when in fact you just told a few players you saw in the hallway. You may think everyone read the message board in the locker room to know what to wear to the fund-raising event, but an overwhelmed freshman may have forgotten to look for it and shows up in team sweats instead of dress clothes. Making sure everyone is on the same page when things go as planned is tough enough, but informing 20 student-athletes, five staff members, and the bus driver that the team needs to leave 30 minutes early for the next day's out-of-town contest requires a commitment to communication.

Meetings. Meetings are the best way to ensure everyone has heard the same information in the same way. People can claim to have not received an e-mail, or that their answering machine does not work, or that a letter has been lost in the mail. But if everyone is sitting in the same room at the same time, excuses are lost. It may take perseverance to plan a meeting around everyone's schedule, especially on short notice, but the clarity and efficiency are hard to beat.

Our most formal meeting is at the beginning of the school year. We get to know each player, discuss policies and expectations, and outline the schedule for the year. This first meeting sets the tone for the rest of the season and should be well-planned so that players see that the coaching staff is organized and ready for the year to begin.

Among the items to cover are your coaching philosophy, an overview of the program's history and future; team mission and goals; rules and policies; academics; schedule for the year; what to expect with regard to conditioning, practice, and games; expectations and responsibilities of players and staff; how team members, starting line-ups, and captains are selected, and the roles of each; fund-raising activities; and how to take care of ourselves physically, mentally, and emotionally.

We have brief team meetings before or after each practice to recap what we want to accomplish; relay any deviations from information we had previously given the players, such as a change in itinerary; or remind players of important details. We do not post this information on a bulletin board in the locker room. Players are more attentive when you have eye contact with them.

I also hold final meetings with seniors, players not returning the following year, as well as returnees. These meetings serve as excellent forums for an honest exchange of ideas and thoughts about what transpired and how to improve operations. We use them evaluate the year, discuss our off-season program for players who will be returning, and focus on getting our unsigned graduating players into a college or university.

Communication with players' parents is essential too. I like to meet every parent or guardian. These meetings can go a long way in helping establish support for your athletes. I have only a few examples of uncooperative parents; an overwhelming number of my parents support me and the rules of the program. I cherish the many long-term relationships I have with the parents of my athletes.

Handouts. One of my methods of communication is with handouts I put together for both players and staff to serve as guides for our team throughout the season. I would never include something in a handout that I had not already covered at length and in person, but they serve to document subjects already covered.

At the first meeting of the year, each player is provided with written information that we will discuss at the meeting. No one can remember the many details of such a meeting, so we give them a way to reference the information for themselves at any time. The rules and policies are printed in black and white, along with possible consequences for violating them, so that there can be no question about what is expected.

Throughout the year, I hand out emergency contact information; our practice and playing schedules; travel policies; player awards or recognition possible throughout the season; technical and tactical information on basketball; nutritional information; study skills and tips; important academic dates; and articles on conditioning, time management, stress management, and mental training. Some coaches may choose to include all of this material in a single notebook and give it out at one time.

Phones and e-mail. I have a wonderful assistant coach, Gwen Howard, who is one of my former players. Gwen is responsible for keeping tabs on and communicating with our players during the school day. She may call each player herself, send out a group e-mail, or initiate a phone chain. I often tell my players that they are responsible for more than themselves. Every player has the phone numbers of all teammates and coaches, and we sometimes use a phone tree to share information. It encourages responsibility and friendship among team members.

Self. Remember that communication also occurs with yourself. Your internal thoughts, ideas, and mental gymnastics are sometimes fleeting, and coming up with a way to capture them when they arrive in your mind will keep you from trying to remember too many things and worry about what you may have forgotten.

I always carry a clipboard or a spiral notebook with me. I keep our practice schedule on it so that I stay on task and on time. It allows me to take notes on what I want to cover the next day in practice or on what I want to address with the team or individual players at the end of practice. I can jot down a task I need to remember to do at work or at home, a play I think will work against an upcoming opponent, or a solution to a problem I've been thinking about. I even sleep with a writing pad and pen on my nightstand.

As you can see, team management encompasses all aspects of your program, is critically important, and is an opportunity to teach your players about more than sports. Your ability to manage your team and all that surrounds it will be a huge factor in how you are perceived professionally and how much stress and tension surround your program. Put together a system; consult with other coaches, professionals, books, or articles about how to organize and communicate effectively; and evaluate your system often so that you can tweak the procedures when you see a better way of management.

15

Athlete Recruitment

Finding the right fit of talent, temperament, and team needs

Terry Crawford

Courtesy of Terry Crawford

Recruiting is synonymous with challenges. In fact, this chapter's title could be "Challenges in Recruiting." It's the nature of the beast—as a college coach, you are asking 17- and 18-year-olds to make one of the most important decisions in their lives by sifting through mail, surfing the Web, listening to coaches, and getting solicited and unsolicited advice from everyone they know. You are relying on those teenagers and their overeager parents to tell you the truth about the athletes' goals, character, priorities, and accomplishments. With the explosion in the number of athletes and competitions, you have a seemingly endless array of opportunities to find that next diamond in the rough—consequently you're plagued by an ever-present feeling that you could be doing more. Plus, you are in a high-stakes game, with much resting on your ability to build the best team possible. Sometimes it feels like you might as well be in Las Vegas playing craps.

In the course of my career, I've had to change my recruiting strategies along with my jobs. Fortunately, the exemplary coaches I've worked with in both the collegiate and professional arenas were instructive and inspiring. At the University of Tennessee, where I did my undergraduate work, I had some wonderful mentors. During the years I competed in track and field, they piqued my curiosity about the profession enough so that by the time I had my degree, I knew I wanted to coach and teach physical education. I pursued my master's degree at Tennessee and continued my competitive running. When I finished my degree I taught for a year in a Knoxville high school and had my first hands-on coaching with student-athletes in a fledging program. (Our track was the perimeter of the parking lot.)

In 1973 the University of Tennessee invited me to teach and spearhead its new women's track program. Nancy Ley, the women's athletic director, had just hired Pat Summitt (see chapter 12) as a graduate student to coach the basketball team, and the university was making a commitment to include women in its athletic program. I was in the right place at the right time, thanks to people who believed in me despite my lack of a solid background. I stayed at Tennessee for 11 years, during which time our team won a national championship. The key ingredient in our success was attracting some great athletes to the program in the early stages, which put us on the map in the late 1970s and '80s.

In 1984 I went to the University of Texas to work for Donna Lopiano, who wanted me to build a perennial champion. I looked forward to the opportunity to work with her since she was one of the dynamic movers in women's athletics at the time. We won five national championships at Texas. We had the advantage of being in a first-rate athletic department with an aggressive and innovative staff and administration. And again, we were able to recruit the best athletes from around the country.

In 1992 the opportunity to come to Cal Poly as the head coach for both men men put a new—and enticing, because it was a new challenge—twist career. The Division II program there created a very different athletic atmosphere than what I had been accustomed to at Tennessee and Texas. It was more moderate and less financially endowed, which forced me to change my recruiting strategies.

Recipe for Coaching Success

A typical cliché you hear in college sports is "Recruiting is the name of the game." But recruiting is only one aspect of a successful program. When you put the following three ingredients together and stir them up, you have a great recipe for success.

First, a head coach has to have the administrative and leadership ability to guide and organize people. (A great deal of material is available on leadership training and personnel management if you feel you need to improve in this area.) Second, she has to have solid methodology and technical knowledge of the sport; she cannot afford to land a great athlete and then not be able to help her improve. Nothing gets as much discussion in coaching circles as programs that don't help athletes continue to develop; great recruiters whose prize athletes stagnate once they are on campus will find their programs doomed.

The final ingredient is the coach's ability to relate to young athletes, their parents, and other coaches, and sell them her abilities, program, and school. To do that effectively, she must believe in what she is selling. Those who have passion for the job, program, and school will find that their enthusiasm is contagious and draws athletes to them. My passion for track and field and recruiting has been the key to my success as a recruiter.

> As a coach, you must believe in what you are selling. Those who have passion for the job, program, and school will find that their enthusiasm is contagious and draws athletes to them.

Fine-Tuning the Recruiting Process

I have always watched people like a hawk as a way to improve my coaching skills. I've benefited from having good mentors throughout my career, but I also observe the opposition's coaching staff. I watch how they recruit, how they teach technique, how they interact with their athletes. There is an understanding in track and field: Watch and steal from everybody. Don't try to come up with your own stuff. See what everybody else is doing and then adapt it to fit your needs, be it a workout, coaching or recruiting strategy, or play.

In our women's track-and-field community, we are trying to do a better job of inspiring young coaches to network. I think it is hard for female coaches to network like male coaches do. They've got to be willing to pick someone's brain, observe, and try to do things like other people do.

Just like being successful as a coach has many aspects, so does being successful as a recruiter. As with any complex endeavor, you must develop a strategy, plan your attack, and then work hard to bring the pieces together.

Develop a Strategy. Coaches have to be realistic in evaluating their program's needs, setting goals for their athletes individually and as a team, and understanding what their administrators view as success. That's the foundation of a recruiting philosophy.

Being realistic means developing a plan that will improve your program. Every year you will need to tweak that plan based on your personnel, coaching strategy, or the team's success. If your team doubles its point production at the conference meet but still finishes in the bottom of the standings, you should set the bar a little higher for the next year, but don't immediately start knocking on the same recruits' doors as the five-time league champion does. If you win a national championship, reevaluate your program to figure out how and what it will take to win another one.

As I mentioned, I have changed my strategy drastically in the three positions I've had as a coach. All were enjoyable and interesting, yet each program differed in the way I structured its recruiting policy and the strategy I developed to help it reach its recruiting potential within the overall philosophy.

Define the Recruiting Pool. Be astute about analyzing what your program has to offer and what your recruiting territory should be in order to attract athletes who can help your program be successful. It would be ridiculous for me to take Pat Summitt's recruiting strategy at Tennessee and try to put it into place at a smaller school like Cal Poly. We are more regional in terms of the athletes we attract; we don't have the budget to fly assistant coaches to Europe or Jamaica to see athletes.

One of the things I enjoy about Cal Poly is that we recruit in-state. We are fortunate to have a great recruiting base for track and field. I have to keep up with only California athletes from the time they are sophomores and starting to compete in a yearly track season and advance to the state meets. At Tennessee and Texas I had a national recruiting program, which is more complicated and overwhelming as you try to keep up with results from around the country. Such programs require a much more complex, detailed recruiting plan in terms of involving assistants and evaluating talent.

The point is that you have to know where you want to recruit and who you are recruiting. If you are going after the top three athletes in the nation, you focus on events that are set up to showcase elite athletes, such as the Nike basketball camps and Junior Olympic track-and-field meets. If you aren't among the few coaches with the luxury of being so selective, you start observing athletes early in their high school careers. How soon you start to track an athlete depends on your recruiting strategy.

Execute the Plan. Over the years I have developed a formula that helps me fine-tune my plan and set my recruiting budget. For every scholarship athlete I had to replace, I planned on recruiting a minimum of four individuals. I would look at least that deep in the state or national charts to see who those top four people were in a particular event. I would then research them to see if they fit into my recruiting profile in terms of academics, where they were from, the kind of atmosphere they might be expecting, the quality of coaching they'd received in their careers, the type of teammate they were—any information that would help me determine how those athletes would fit into my program. I would then use that formula to develop my recruiting budget, determining how many home visits I'd need to make, how many meets I'd have to attend, and how many official visits I needed to schedule.

When I am recruiting an athlete I research her background, looking for three primary character traits that I consider of utmost importance. I find that I am best served when I don't let myself take to an athlete who doesn't embody each trait.

There are three character traits to look for when recruiting an athlete: athletic talent, coachability, and honesty.

First, and most obvious, the person needs to have real talent and natural ability. She should have athletic tools and an athletic persona that fits in with the level and attitude of your team. Tempting as it may be, signing an athlete who is head and shoulders above the rest may not be the best move.

Second, the athlete needs to be coachable, and this is where your research will pay off. Ask the recruit and her parents how she feels about taking correction, and pay attention not only to what they say but how they say it. Talk with her current and past coaches. Observe her interaction with coaches at meets. A great athlete who does not believe she needs any instruction to get better probably won't reach her potential.

Third, the athlete should be honest and sincere, which ensures quality interaction with her coaches and teammates. It also improves the chances that she will be forthcoming about problems or changes in her life. She might return to school her sophomore year with different ambitions and tell you, "College athletics is not for me any more. I'm not going to try to wimp along and hold onto my scholarship. I am going to try to go out and seek my happiness and interests in another way."

If an athlete has those three ingredients, a good coach can relate to her and help her develop and continue her success. A person with those qualities will be a solid contributor to your program because of her value system and honesty.

Be Flexible. A recruiting strategy, even though you want to follow it for the year, needs to have some flexibility. A year ago we signed one of the top high jumpers in the country, obviously a full-scholarship athlete, who placed second in the California state meet. High jumping in track and field is unique in that the athlete focuses on that event only. We felt we had a potential All-American and NCAA scorer who could fill that slot on the team for the next four years. The next year, the young lady who had beaten our athlete during her junior and senior years of high school was interested in visiting our campus. We included her in an early recruiting visit, knowing that she would require a serious scholarship allotment should she choose our school. She did, and I had to decide whether to make another significant investment in an athlete in the same event area.

It was a dilemma, but as a result of my research and getting to know her, I felt she was such a high-caliber athlete and had such a great background (both of her parents were athletes) that I took the gamble. The athlete ended up as the number one high jumper in the nation in her freshman year. The national exposure we got by signing this person—a dark horse to make the 2004 Olympic team—was huge. I rolled the dice by deviating from the plan instead of sticking with it when a great opportunity presented itself.

Sometimes team-sport coaches can get too narrow in their focus, too. Coaches might fluff over a great athlete merely because she plays a position they aren't specifically recruiting for. You always need wiggle room in your recruiting strategy to make exceptions if they can benefit the program down the road.

The top programs may be able to sign four great recruits and be finished, but that works for them because they get four world-class athletes. Everyone else has to realize which level their program is in, and be realistic. Don't follow another model simply because it is successful for your favorite coach or mentor.

Obtaining Team Feedback

During an official recruiting visit we focus on letting the recruit and our team members connect and spend time together. I tell our athletes that if we ask a recruit to come and visit, as coaches we have done our homework and have decided that this person is an appropriate candidate for our team based on what our needs are and the kind of talent we are looking for. The experience offers the recruit the chance to develop good chemistry with our team and helps our players learn whether they feel comfortable with her.

Since the focus of the official visit is for recruits to spend time with the team, I tell parents that our goal is not to wine and dine them but to provide them with as realistic an experience on our campus and in our community as possible. We have them stay with our athletes in the dorm, go to class, and join the team in social settings. If I get a negative response from our athletes about how a particular recruit reacted to them or about her attitude and behavior, then I will research those things more closely. The team's feedback has a definite impact on my continued interest in that athlete.

Communicating With Recruits, Parents, and Coaches

The recruitment of high school athletes has changed drastically during my career to the point where it is almost an obsessive-compulsive behavior. In some cases the approach that parents and high school coaches take to get an athlete into a college program is way over the top. This behavior occurs at all levels. Doing some recruitment is good, but doing too much of it is bad. Opportunities in women's athletic programs have progressed from a scarce, poorly-funded few to the present well-funded abundance. Today a much higher level of athlete is being promoted. But with these improvements comes the responsibility on all sides to be truthful, honest, and thoughtful in making the most of those opportunities.

Encourage Research. I like to tell high school coaches, club coaches, and parents to get educated about the process of recruitment. Parents of aspiring college athletes should find out what the standards of competition are in college athletics and then be realistic about where their children fit in. Then they should pursue the opportunities that fit into that reality instead of adopting the parental attitude that says, "My daughter deserves everything because she is the best person on her team." I also ask that coaches not oversell their athletes. Coaches and parents do athletes a great disservice by overselling their abilities, possibly setting them up for failure.

I advise coaches, athletes, and parents to do their homework and start looking at schools and options early. Instead of using the recruiting process as a joy ride, athletes should be practical and methodical in evaluating their desires for themselves and their families. They need to ask themselves from a financial and emotional standpoint how far away from home they can comfortably be, the kind of coach they'd like to work with, and which programs can meet their needs. They should investigate the degree options, academic reputation, and standards of the school to make sure they get a quality education.

Be Truthful About the Atmosphere. Years ago there was talk about cutting back scholarships and, in certain sports, starting athletes on tuition-only scholarships. At the time, I felt that was a terrible idea; now, as my wisdom has grown, I think that limiting scholarships would be wonderful. Because the recruiting process is so competitive now, some coaches paint a false picture of their programs, making it sound almost like they are offering someone a full scholarship to live at a resort and be handed a college degree after four years. The athletes get a very unrealistic picture of the expectations that will be placed on them; some even think that someone has given them a present to enjoy for the next four years simply because they were successful in high school.

Be Realistic About Expectations. Coaches must clearly communicate what they want from an athlete, what to expect from being a part of their team, and any side roads they may take. I don't give a recruit a full scholarship with the idea that she will definitely be an All-American, but it should signify to her that you expect her to be successful. An athlete who expects a full scholarship should aspire to be as successful as possible and plan to make the necessary sacrifices to do so. The more scholarship money offered, the higher the expectations. I talk to recruits seriously about the expectations in our program. A head coach from a Big 12 school recently told me that he frequently tells young athletes and their parents that they don't want a full scholarship in the first year because the expectations could be too overwhelming. Putting that thought in their heads is a good way to make them start to examine what this process is all about.

Essentially, recruits go through a job search. They find positions for themselves based on their credentials, therefore their goal must be to live up to their employer's expectations. The recruitment process is not too early to offer that perspective to freshman athletes. Hopefully they come to college to prepare themselves for a career. Their athletic path through college can be one of their best experiences in learning responsibility, accountability, and how to meet the expectations of their supervisor. It's one of the best lessons you can help a recruit grasp, whether she is the best athlete in the nation, an average talent who you hope to develop to a higher level, or a walk-on.

Coaches must clearly communicate what they want from an athlete, what to expect from being a part of their team, and any side roads they may take. An athlete who expects a full scholarship should aspire to be as successful as possible and plan to make the necessary sacrifices to do so.

Less than 5 percent of student-athletes will be able to make a living from their athletics, and the sooner you talk about that, the better. The key is not to be so hard-nosed that you turn an athlete and her family off, but to be honest and realistic, neither overselling nor scaring them.

The process has become so competitive that it feels like you have to tell athletes that the scholarship is theirs for four years as long as they are good citizens. However, very few coaches or administrators are comfortable with teams full of scholarship athletes who don't contribute to the success of the program. I am relieved that in my position I can start an athlete on a smaller scholarship and find out who she is and how she will be able to contribute to my program before I commit a great deal of scholarship money to her.

Recruiting Challenges

One of the biggest challenges in recruiting (and greatest opportunities) is that incoming athletes are in transition, not only from high school sports to college sports but in their whole lives—personally, socially, and academically. During that entire freshman year, you can't say about an athlete, "Oh, wow, I got a lemon!" because you don't know yet. You've got to allow that person to grow so you can see who she becomes, and then find out how she is going to adjust into that person she is becoming. Making that adjustment smoothly and sensibly is largely up to the athlete, which is why I say that even in a best-case scenario, recruiting is still a crapshoot.

Changes in Young Women. The element of chance is heightened when you recruit women. Coaching female athletes presents some unique challenges because who they are at 17 and who they become at 19 or 20 can be significantly different. Although men typically continue to gain strength and aggressiveness as their skill levels improve with maturity and a commitment to training, a young woman may start to change her perception of herself in a social setting, what her life's goals are, and how she manages her academic and athletic lives. Physiologically a 15- or 16-year-old girl's body can drastically change and affect her athletic ability up until age 19, which can affect her psychologically in how she feels about herself. Add to that the complications of society's view of females, their roles, and the expectations placed on them, and you continue to roll the dice.

For example, let's say you recruit a young woman who is the number one thrower in your state and you expect great things from her—NCAA qualifier, potential All-American—but she meets the love of her life her freshman year. The young man doesn't want to see her get bulkier by adding more muscle, which you have to do to become a world-class thrower. That becomes a struggle for that athlete.

Early Commitments. Early commitments are becoming more and more popular for a couple of reasons. One is to minimize the sensationalism of the recruiting process, since athletes realize they can be overwhelmed and inundated throughout the process. Making an early verbal commitment has become more attractive, especially to the top athletes whose credentials are well established by the time they enter their senior year of high school. For college coaches who have the opportunity to recruit that top athlete, an early signing gives them a clearer picture of who will be joining the team and who else to focus on. With that player in hand, they may be able to start building their recruiting list for the next year. This practical approach allows coaches to be more organized and keeps the recruiting process from being so frantic.

Asking an athlete to commit as a junior can be risky, though, especially with certain types of sports. Offering a team-sport athlete a full scholarship may be different. However, much can change in a young person's life, affecting her priorities, values, and goals.

Getting commitments earlier is an example of how rampant and wild this whole recruiting process has become. I don't think it is the best thing for an athlete to do, although it may work for the 2 to 3 percent of the athletes around the country who have truly established their credentials. For example, if someone like Chamique Holdsclaw commits, getting her into your program, whether or not she becomes an All-American, will enhance its profile.

I am not in favor of trying to get athletes to commit in June after their junior year. However, if they have started the process early, their parents are involved, and their coaches are helpful in the research and dialoguing with college coaches, by November of their senior year most athletes understand their options and the impact of their decision better. And having that decision made early in their last year of high school can be a great relief for recruits.

I encourage juniors who perform well in their season to get aggressive about the recruiting process during the summer. Hopefully they started their research during their junior year so that by the time they finished that school year and were in a position to be contacted by coaches, they had narrowed down their list to approximately five schools. I advocate this approach to parents and coaches as well.

Watching talent evolve during an athlete's senior year can be advantageous. Some sports lend themselves to that more than others; track-and-field athletes, in particular, can have drastically improved marks at the end of their senior year compared to their junior year. I never commit all of my scholarship money in early signings. I always try to reserve a pool of money for emerging athletes or entice them by saying, "At this time we only have this scholarship amount left, but we'll increase it next year if you show a certain amount of improvement." I think coaches of sports that are equivalent to track and field are always wise to hold back a little money.

International Student-Athletes. I have mixed feelings about recruiting student-athletes from other countries. I have found that they bring a new and different dimension to a team, often positive, and in many cases they are more mature since their educational systems usually keep them in a secondary-school environment longer than the United States does. They also tend to be more realistic in terms of why they are accepting a scholarship—they know that being on scholarship makes coming into a program more like a job. However, the primary reason why coaches recruit athletes from other countries is because they are more accomplished than the U.S. athletes in their recruiting pool.

I've worked with some outstanding international athletes who have been passionate about team goals and willing to contribute in any way that was asked of them. They have been very positive people, adding to team leadership and camaraderie and enhancing my program.

However, some political ramifications concern me, and I don't agree with the programs that primarily seek athletes from across the ponds. College programs are, in most cases, the farm teams that help develop athletes for our Olympic teams. I'd like to think that as many of our U.S. athletes as possible are getting those opportunities.

Negative Recruiting. Anything that is competitive in our world tends to have a negative side to it. If you look at political campaigns or who is going to get invited into a sorority or fraternity, a negative spin is always put on those who are trying to get an edge. As long as people have an opportunity to lose something, the negative-recruiting aspect can come into play. Positive recruiting has to do with coaches' integrity and how they manage their own strategies. I have never felt like negative recruiting, or criticizing other programs, was an advantage to my program or that those who did it against me gained anything. (You can counteract negative recruiting by taking a sincere approach with athletes and their parents.) I think the majority of coaches don't get involved in it; those who do, however, are hurting their future.

Over the years I have learned to be realistic and come up with an effective plan so that my recruiting doesn't take the frantic, all-consuming approach it did when I was a young coach. One of my former athletes who coaches now told me, "I lost everybody I went after in the fall and I have to start all over again." My immediate thought was, "Wouldn't it have been better to start with a more moderate plan instead of having to start over with a backup plan?"

Over the years, going through so much rejection—which is, in part, what recruiting is—can be difficult to take. I have had many sleepless nights and frustrated moments trying to figure out why an athlete didn't come to my school. It is a huge blow to a coach's ego. Through experience you develop a tougher skin and a resiliency that allows you to let go of that recruiting connection with an athlete as soon as she declines your offer. Instead, you can see it as an opportunity to make your program better by going after somebody else. Maintaining a positive outlook, a never-give-up attitude, and accepting it when an athlete chooses another program works in the end.

Sometimes I track athletes I have lost; watching them fail to live up to the goals you would have had for them can offer some consolation. You think, "Maybe I'm lucky I didn't get that athlete." That happens to me as often as an All-American getting away does. That kind of balance helps keep a coach sane as she deals with the challenges of recruiting.

Relationship Building and Promotionl Activities

16

Coach–Athlete Relations

Connecting with athletes throughout their careers

Kim Kincer

Iloved my job as a club professional and manager of a municipal golf course in Lexington, Kentucky, and was perfectly happy—or so I thought. I had been in that position for almost eight years when I received a phone call from my former college golf coach, Carol Johnson, who had heard of a golf coach's position that was open at a small private college in Fayetteville, North Carolina. I was not looking for a job; however, a few drawbacks at work were just enough to pique my curiosity about the coaching position.

Although I had never had any formal coaching experience, I felt I was qualified because of my experience as a golf professional. I coached men, women, and children when I gave golf lessons, and I also coached course employees, teams, and family and friends on a regular basis, especially when they were preparing for a golf tournament. To me, teaching and coaching go hand in hand. I also believe that in order to be a good manager you must be a good coach.

When I got the job as the head women's golf coach and assistant director of professional golf management at Methodist College, a small liberal arts school, I knew I was walking into a program that had been incredibly successful. What I didn't know was that I was going to be the third coach for some of the players on the team. A coaching transition is never easy; the players have to get used to a new system, a new set of rules, and a new personality.

I started the job mid-season, which was hard for the team. They had not expected their former coach to leave—then in walked in a new coach halfway through the year, changing the rules, the practice schedule, and the disciplinary action. But what could have been a terrible transition turned out to be one great year. We won the NCAA Division II/III national championship in 1998, which was the beginning of one of the greatest rides of my life. After that, the Lady Monarchs won four more NCAA national championships—five in a row during my tenure as coach. Our team's success was such an enjoyable aspect of coaching for me; however, obstacles arose along the way. One was the number of players on the team. Sixteen golfers were on the women's team; most Division I schools have a maximum of eight players. Although I was stretched thin, I tried to develop an individual relationship with each player. A well-defined relationship between the coach and athletes is essential in order for a large team to understand the group's dynamics.

Individual Meetings

Individual as well as team meetings were important in developing player–coach relationships. We had three official team meetings and two individual meetings each semester, and others as needed. I usually held individual meetings in my office; at other venues we always seemed to get off task, so a more formal setting worked best. Getting out from behind the desk to sit face to face with the student eliminates the barrier between you. Of the two yearly individual meetings, one's purpose was to establish individual, team, and academic goals; the other's was to check on the player's progress. Establishing a coach–athlete relationship means involving yourself in students' lives both on and off the course. In assessing a player's progress our coaching staff evaluates her scoring average and statistic sheet, which includes her shot making, practice habits, attitude, and grades. We would also revisit her individual goals to make sure they were on track.

During the first individual meeting with each freshman, I would spend time getting to know her. Coaches need to reach out to every player and understand who she is, where she is from, and what type of environment she grew up. Players need to know that you are interested in them as people, not just as athletes. I always let my athletes know that I had an open-door policy and they could come to me about anything at any time—golf, academics, boyfriends, family issues, or homesickness—and they did. Many of them were far from home, and they knew they could call on me in times of need, even in the evenings or in the middle of the night. Each coach has her own definition of an open-door policy; she has to figure out what works best for her and the team.

I tried to achieve five elements—trust, respect, communication, commitment, and discipline—that build successful relationships. I knew that if we achieved each of these we would continue the Methodist College tradition of producing a great team.

Trust

Players have to be able to completely trust their coaches. My players had to trust that I was going to make the right decision for them on the golf course and that I would help them make positive changes to their golf swings. They had to trust that I would get them to and from a golf tournament safely driving a school van, and they had to trust that they could talk to me about anything, at any time. Almost everything we do in athletics is about building relationships. It is a coach's responsibility to nurture her relationship with each player. A team member must have trust in me when I ask her to hit a six iron instead of the seven iron she *wants* to hit on the tee of a par three in the national championship tournament—then she will do as I ask, realizing that it's for the good of the team. I must develop a level of trust with each player so that she never questions my motives.

I gained that level of trust with one golfer early in her collegiate career. Michelle Meadows was a long way from home when she received her first speeding ticket in Fayetteville. A quiet, soft-spoken young lady from Lubbock, Texas, Michelle came into my office one afternoon to let me know she would miss class because she had to go to court. After discussing the details I asked her if she wanted me to go with her. Her eyes brightened and a big smile flashed across her face. Michelle knew from that day forward she could trust me and that I cared about her. Sometimes all a coach needs to do is offer the personal support that a parent or older sibling might. Building trust often requires time and energy, but is worth the lifetime bonds that result.

On the other hand, it took me quite a bit longer to gain the trust of another player. Hope Thomas walked into my office the summer before her first year at Methodist. She tapped on my door, plopped down in the nearest chair, and began to talk so fast with her thick Boston accent that I couldn't understand a word. I did figure out that she wanted to try out for the women's golf team. I told her a little about the team and the tryout procedure before she bounced out of my office as abruptly as she bounced in. My memories of that conversation are that it was one-sided. I listened to what Hope had to say, and when she left I didn't think I would ever see her again. She was 34 years old, married, and the mother of a young son. She did, however, decide to come to Methodist College, so as a 38-year-old coach I had a 34-year-old freshman on the team. It took Hope a year and a half to completely trust me. In the beginning she always balked when I chose which club she should hit. She did not trust the swing changes I asked her to make, and she always thought I would leave her behind because of something she might say or do. In golf, the decision making is black and white when choosing the five players for the traveling team: Those who play the best make the cut. Hope was and is a very good golfer, but she thought she would be sitting at home if she made the slightest mistake. Finally, after many one-on-one conversations, Hope was having success with the swing changes we made, increasing her ability to make the traveling team, and she slowly began to trust me. I quizzed her about why she wouldn't trust my advice and discovered that her self-doubt made her question herself. We also spent a lot of time on the driving range working on drills in which she saw success, which helped her understand that I was not going to steer her wrong. It wasn't until her sophomore year that she finally trusted me, but we have developed a relationship that will last a lifetime.

> Building trust often requires time and energy, but it is worth the lifetime bonds that result.

Just as my players must trust me, I have to be able to trust my players. If we have agreed on a plan for how they should play a particular hole on the golf course, I have to know that they will do so even when I am not with them. I continually emphasize how important it is that all members of the team follow the game plan for the day. I would not stand on the sidelines like many other coaches, so we had to decide in advance how we would play a particular golf course or hole. I might not be there to make adjustments during the round, but I would see them all several times while they were playing and help in whatever way I could. The whole point of a practice round is for us to play the course so that we know how best to approach the tournament rounds. Although we are not concerned with the score during a practice round, we are aware of how we should play each hole and we trust each team member to do her part.

I also have to feel confident that the players will be honest with me about all team-related issues, especially regarding rules, which is one of the reasons why we build a solid relationship from the beginning. We all make mistakes, but being dishonest about it does not sit well with me. I tried to show enough compassion for the players so that they would feel comfortable confiding in me. And getting to know each player personally is imperative. Coaches must take a true interest in the student-athlete, identifying her strengths and weaknesses as a golfer as well as her outside interests. Team get-togethers during the season offer players the chance to get to know a coach and build trust. Although I did not socialize with students outside of team activities, I did participate in campus activities in which the students would see me in a completely different arena. At those non-sport-related events, player and coach can strengthen their bond through shared enjoyment of the same kind of activity.

Respect

My parents taught me to respect my elders and respect authority. I respected my parents so much that I would not dare embarrass them by being disrespectful to others. I expected the women on the team to do the same; they had to respect me and any other authority figures.

Coaches can begin to determine a prospective student-athlete's level of respect for authority at the first recruiting visit. Observing how a student responds to questions or to their parents during the recruiting visit tells you what to expect from them in the future. If a student responded to my questions with a "Yeah" or a "Nope," I knew I would have some work to do if she came to Methodist College. Another indication of their level of respect is how they respond to their parents during their visit. If they don't respect their parents, they probably won't respect a coach. Trust and respect both have to be earned, but respect for authority figures in general should be an ingrained trait by the time players are of recruitment age.

The women on the golf team had to know what to expect from me, and I had to deliver time and again before they learned to trust and respect me. However, there will always be a few players whose respect you never gain. As much as it bothered me at first, I quickly realized I couldn't make everybody happy and that one or two players would always disagree with me. You can't help all those who need help, and you may never gain respect from a select few over the years.

How do you begin to earn respect from your team? I was taught to lead by example, so I did just that. If the players were aware of my respect for Methodist College, my boss, our golf team, and others, they would hopefully follow my lead. As a coach, you are responsible for talking to your players about what it means to be a member of the team. Make it clear that you expect them to realize that their actions reflect on more than who they are. When they put on that team uniform, my players represented not only themselves but also the college, their families, and each other.

Occasionally some players on the team would completely disrespect each other. If one player was causing the problem, I would bring her into the office to discuss her actions. I would ask her how she would feel if she were the one being treated unfairly, let her know how I expected her to treat the other player, and notate our conversation in her file. I would also explain that disciplinary action would follow any further incidents. If both players were culprits I would talk with each of them individually before bringing them into my office together to hash out the details. Often, getting the players together helped solve other underlying issues.

Communication

I have learned not to underestimate the importance of communication in coaching. As a leader you must be an effective communicator, but you are also responsible for teaching the team members the importance of communication. I would emphasize that in both individual and team meetings, because I wanted the women on the Lady Monarchs golf team never to hesitate to come to me about any team or personal issue, and I wanted them to be approachable for each other.

The first thing I would do to build the relationship between myself and a team member was to spend time getting to know her. Equally important is that the team members get to know one another and realize that they are all from different environments and have different experiences. If practice was delayed or canceled, we would meet as a group to talk about team-related issues and do get-acquainted exercises that would allow both coaches and team members to get to know each other on a more personal level. One fun activity is to provide each team member with an index card and have her write down something about herself that no one in the room knows. Then collect the cards, put them in a hat, and have a team member pull one out and read it aloud. (The cards shouldn't have names on them, and a team member can read her own card if she draws it.) Then the team has to guess whose card has been read. The winner is the person who is hardest to identify.

Another get-acquainted exercise is an interview. Provide questions for players to ask each other and have them come up with questions of their own, then pair them up with someone they do not normally socialize with. After completing the interview the players introduce each other to the group.

After learning about the athletes, coaches have to learn how to communicate in many different ways. For instance, some players require a lot of attention at practice while others are comfortable working on a few key things you've discussed. Practice posed a few challenges for me in my first year as a coach. I was coaching 16 women in what is generally viewed as an individual sport, and they all wanted my undivided attention. When practice lasted two and a half hours, I could spend about nine minutes with each player, which is not enough time to work effectively. Private lessons with golf professionals usually last one hour, so I knew I had to evaluate how to structure practice more effectively.

I solicited the help of our team captains to come up with creative solutions to difficult communication problems. Asking them for ideas brings you closer to the captains and to the team. We tossed around several ideas and came up with one that would make practice more efficient. We split the team up into two groups, each led by one captain who took over some routine functions, and developed practice plans that gave me more hands-on time with each player. If a player felt like she needed help beyond what we could accomplish in practice, she could set up a private lesson with me. Some players took individual lessons on a regular basis; others never did. However, I would require the players to take one or two individual lessons during the season whenever the team dynamics indicated a need.

Different personalities require different avenues of communication. Some players need to be scolded or fussed at about how they're playing while others needed to be stroked and encouraged. I probably lost two good years with one player because I wasn't hard enough on her. It's not my nature to be hard on players, but once this young lady started traveling on a regular basis I realized I had made a big mistake. Jessie Hunter was confident but not arrogant; she knew what she stood for, was excited about being a part of the Methodist College tradition, and wanted to be a leader. She qualified for the first tournament in her freshman year, which was unusual at the time.

Jessie did not make another trip until her junior year, when I learned that she didn't mind me getting in her face while she was playing. On that trip Jessie couldn't seem to get it going. I was on the tee at a par three when she came through to play that hole. She commented about how she was playing and I thought she seemed a bit blasé about it. Before we talked about how she would play that particular hole, I fussed at her about how she was play-ing and about her attitude, telling her to get her head screwed on properly and play golf. I told her that there was no excuse for her to be playing poorly because she had been playing so well lately. Then I gave her a few pointers and a word of encouragement before she teed off. She proceeded to birdie the next two holes and finished with a respectable round. Later she told me that my fussing at her got her pumped up. Had I done my homework earlier, she might have been a regular contributor all four years. She did end up being a two-time NGCA All-American and a member of two NCAA national championship teams. Jessie is another player whom I know I will have a relationship with for years to come.

Figuring out how to communicate with a player can take time. If you get to know your players and are a good judge of people, you should be able to adapt your communication style to meet their needs. I changed my tactics with each player in an attempt to get them to maximize their potential. Of course I made mistakes; my first year at Methodist a gal was in tears because my approach was not in line with her personality. However, other coaches may have different approaches. Some rant and rave; others want nothing to do with confrontation. Each coach has to figure out what works best for her.

Effective communication is simple: Talk to each other. We verbalized our team goals, and everyone had to understand them and believe in them. The quality of the players' relationships with each other often influences a coach's relationships with team members. Emphasize that they must talk to each other to get to know and understand each other, cheer for each other, and hold each other accountable to the team goals. Communication can make or break a team; we chose to use it to our advantage.

Commitment

An athlete's commitment to herself and the team depends on her relationship with the coach. My relationship with each athlete began at those individual meetings at the beginning of each year, to which the players brought their team, individual, and academic goals. Together we evaluated them to make sure they were realistic. If we determined that a goal was unattainable, we would change it to make it more realistic. One year a sophomore's goal sheet stated that she wanted to be an All-American, play on the NCAA national championship team, win an individual title at a collegiate tournament, and make an A in every class. These seemed like lofty goals for a young lady who had traveled only a time or two as a freshman. Certainly she had the potential to reach those goals, but not in her second year. We rewrote her goals so that she could be successful that year; although she would have to work hard to attain them, they were realistic for her.

As a leader, a coach is responsible for defining each player's role on the team. Young players need to realize that they are not expected to be number one on the team. Even an athlete who made our traveling team in her first year needed to understand her role as the number four or five player. With so many women on the team, a young player did not always rise to the top quickly; often it took a couple of years to make the traveling team. The players from number one down to number sixteen each had to understand the dynamics of their role on the team. As the players gained more experience and matured, their roles changed, so I talked to each one about a four-year plan for them. I emphasized that although they might play a minor role on the team initially, their role would become more significant as they improved. I explained that the effort they put into improving their game as well as their performance was the key to how quickly their roles would change. Some athletes were determined to work as hard as they could to improve so that they could play a key role on the team; others were satisfied with working hard in practice but not going above and beyond to reach the next level. The individual meetings afforded me a good opportunity to emphasize the importance of the team and to define roles, but it was an equally important time for me to *listen* to each player. I allowed them to express their concerns, ask questions, and talk to me about whatever was on their minds. Listening to what they said was important in reading who they were and identifying their concerns.

> As a leader, a coach is responsible for defining each player's role on the team.

One of my goals for the individual meetings was to have the player leave the meeting feeling excited about being a part of a great team. I wanted them to understand the incredible opportunity they had to be a part of the tradition at Methodist College. Each young lady on our women's golf team had the potential to be an All-Scholar Athlete, an All-American, and a member of an NCAA national championship team. Defining a player's role, letting her look at a couple of NCAA national championship rings, and explaining that she too could have a plaque on our All-American wall was usually enough to get her excited.

The players also had to know that I was committed to each of them. I needed to spend time with all of them because they would most likely become a part of the traveling team eventually. Regardless of whether they would become national champions, each needed my time. And each student-athlete understood that she had to be completely committed to the team throughout the season; I too had to show my commitment by being at practice on time and using the time wisely. Hopefully my commitment to the team would have a trickle-down effect on the players.

Discipline

The commitment each player makes to a team helps her strive for excellence. I used my close relationships with the players to talk with them, both individually and collectively, about striving to be the best they could be in all that they did. If we settle for simply being good athletes, we will not achieve all of our goals. Putting our best foot forward every time increases the chance of a positive result.

Discipline was one of the greatest keys to our success. One of my favorite quotes from Coach Mike Krzyzewski is, "You develop a team to achieve what one person cannot accomplish alone. All of us alone are weaker, by far, than

199

all of us are together." We never would have built a women's golf program so rich with tradition with only individual winners year in and year out. It took a team of five women playing their hearts out to win 16 out of 18 national championship titles. More important, it took a team of 12 to 16 women to field a traveling team of 5. Once the team members had expressed the desire to be committed to our golf program, it was time to take their commitment one step further by helping them develop a training regimen .

Our practices were very structured for a reason: We were coming together as a team to play an individual sport. Without that structure, it would be difficult for us to come together as a unit during a tournament. We had to know that someone "had our back" out there on the golf course if we weren't having a particularly good day. If we never worked as a team in practice, we likely would have played like five individuals on the golf course. What's wrong with that? My observation over the years is that the team that plays the best is exactly that—a *team*.

My players needed to know what being a part of a team means. First, we determined that hard work was the foundation of achievement. No, not everyone on the team had the same work ethic; that is unlikely on any team. However, we had a lot of young women who were willing to work hard to attain their goals. Those who took shortcuts realized that it was the reason that they rarely, if ever, traveled. If I could impress anything on young athletes it would be that there is no compromise to a work ethic. Second, during individual meetings I evaluated the extent to which each athlete was determined to work hard. I also had to get each player to understand that she must prepare herself for pressure. Any collegiate tournament was accompanied by pressure. We felt like we were the hardest-working NCAA Division III team in the nation. Were we? Who knows—what matters is that we believed it! We did work hard. We had a plan for practice, and we stuck to it. We worked hard on shots from 100 yards into the green, which were a huge weakness for us. We practiced in the rain. We qualified in the rain. We worked on our whole game. We worked on specific shots and didn't leave practice until everyone was able to hit them or make the putt. At the end of many practices we would do one of two exercises. I would choose a 3 or 4-foot putt, and everyone would have to make it before we left for the day. We would putt one at a time with everyone watching. If someone missed, the team would have to run a lap around the driving range. Then we would start over until all 16 players made the putt. We played a similar game from the first tee. The ball would have to land in the fairway or the team had to run. These exercises put pressure on the players, but they also gave them an opportunity to cheer for each other.

The time the athletes spent getting to know each other and my relationships with each of them made it easy for them to understand the value of working together as a team. I believe the players followed my lead because they *believed* in the plan. My relationships with them, individually and collectively, were secure enough for them to follow the plan I had laid out, which allowed us to compete successfully in NCAA Division III events.

I am a firm believer in developing solid relationships with each player on the team; they helped me become a better coach. If the NCAA championship was on the line and I was out on the golf course with the last player on the team, when she could make a difference in the score, I would know how she would respond to the pressure. I would fall back on the relationship I had developed with her over the years, a relationship that encompassed the five elements that were part of our team credo. The team members and I understood that applying each element—trust, respect, communication, commitment, and discipline—to our lives as a team would breed success. Coaches who develop caring relationships with players, with trust and respect at their pinnacle, enable their teams to reach their goals year after year.

17

Team Cohesion

*Unify athletes with
a common objective and identity*

Sharon Pfluger

Photo by Steve Smith

Team cohesion is the force that glues a team together—its bond and chemistry. A cohesive team demonstrates loyalty, respect, commitment, and dedication in all of its members. Any differences the players have are put aside for the good of the team.

Some of the primary ways to create team cohesion are through implementing an organized educational process, teaching the players to be respectful of their teammates and opponents, and to train themselves to become the finest people they can be. I am very strict about my expectations regarding athletes' behavior. Although I am flexible about many things, I have a no-tolerance policy for inappropriate behavior and I don't let our players treat themselves or others with disrespect.

I grew up in a house with my parents, sister, and grandparents; I felt like I had two sets of parents around me at all times. When our extended family got together about every other month in "family circles," we had so much fun. I am rearing my children the same way—friends are always welcome and there is always enough food, love, and warmth for everyone to feel fulfilled. Our home is a safe, secure place whether we are all just hanging out or if someone is in need of help.

I loved being a part of a team and having so many people around me while I was competing. Being around others who had developed the same passion for sports was great, like being part of an extended family. It reminded me of those family circles in my childhood. We all had our immediate families, but we also had common bonds: our coaches, passion for our sport, and a willingness to learn and work hard.

During my playing career I had two extremely dedicated, outstanding coaches. They ran their programs professionally yet still allowed their athletes to have fun. I have taken much of what I learned from them into my own coaching practice. Were it not for Deborah West, my field hockey, basketball, and softball coach at Pompton Lakes High School, I never would have gotten involved with athletics. At least five of her students within a three-year period became health and physical education instructors because of her impact. And Melissa Magee, a member of the U.S. field hockey team and my field hockey and lacrosse coach at The College of New Jersey, was a dynamic educator as well as fun, intense, and hardworking. She excelled at breaking down skills and teaching strategies and concepts for each sport.

When I became a coach I transferred the passion and work ethic I had had as a player into my teams. The teams become so much a part of me that they are my extended family. I nurture them as such and I care for my girls like they are my own daughters or sisters. I push them hard because I care so much about them. The first thing I tell them at the beginning of the season is that although I am competitive on the field and, like any coach, I love to win, my primary focus is their happiness, and if they are happy, then the coaches are happy. I explain to them that we are all working together. There are no power struggles or adverse relationships. The coaches are beside the players every step of the way.

When the girls graduate from the College of New Jersey, I want them to face the world with self-esteem, confidence, and the empowered feeling that they can become whoever they choose. I want them to know how to find success from a challenge. I want them to be able to come through for a struggling friend or family member in need, and I want them to come through for themselves. To me, teaching team cohesion at the collegiate level is the stepping-stone for a young adult to learn so much about unity. It involves many skills that become useful in all facets of life.

Communication is a large part of team cohesion, and one way we facilitate good communication is with an open door policy—the players can stop by the office anytime. Sometimes we arrange specific times to talk; at other times we clear out the office and take care of whatever needs immediate attention. I want both the coaches and the players to feel as comfortable in the office as I would want them to feel in my home. In fact, I have no problem with our players stopping by my home to speak with me or to simply spend time with my family.

Team Is Family

A cohesive team looks like a family that works hard every day. Cohesiveness is seen in the team members' willingness to reach out to others and their ability to recognize challenges as well as resolve the issues that surround them. Such teams run like machines, each part needing the others, yet they are filled with enormous levels of emotion day in and day out. This cohesiveness plays out in every interaction between its members. Cohesiveness is at the core of what happens to a team. Without that bond, a team's goals are difficult to attain and it becomes vulnerable to falling apart during any challenge, on or off the field.

A team is a family: That is the basis for how I run my teams, how I speak to the players, and how I have developed and maintained team cohesion for the 23 years I have been coaching. I want the players to feel a great sense of loyalty to the program. Our athletes do not invest time every day simply to play a sport; they are putting effort into becoming part of a family. I tell them that every step they take on the field is like purchasing stock in a company. The harder they work, the more stock they own. The company—our program, our family—is theirs, and they will always be a part of it.

When a team is tight and connected, the players work hard not only for themselves but for everyone around them. They learn that their actions affect each other and that if they have developed respect, love, and loyalty for those in their new family, three things happen. First, their desire for excellence increases, because they want what is best for the family. Second, their will to do whatever it takes to achieve that excellence increases, because they do not want to let the family down. And perhaps most important, the support they feel from others increases, because everyone else understands the challenges, pressures, and joys that come with striving for excellence. That starts a positive snowball effect. The more encouraging the environment is, the harder the athletes will work and the more willing they will be to take risks to improve their performance. The extra effort leads to more success, which further validates the process and deepens the bonds between the players.

I work hard every day to create and maintain such a supportive atmosphere for my athletes. Coaches teach, through words and by example, things the athletes have been taught all their lives, but I consider part of my job to be helping them continue growing into the finest people they can be. That includes guiding them to make good decisions, reach out to others, respect each other, and be accountable for their actions.

The effort I put into each player is the foundation of the family atmosphere. I show them how much I care by investing a great deal of my time and energy—just like parents invest themselves in their children—and I emphasize the importance of reaching out to each other. I have high expectations for the athletes' conduct off the field as well as on it; I can be tough because they know I care about them. What is most important, however, is that they learn to have high expectations of themselves, to have faith in their own abilities and to keep everything in perspective.

> Team cohesion requires work, creativity, problem solving, and attentiveness in every area of coaching. From recruiting players to increasing the athletes' confidence as players, people, and teammates, a coach must be vigilant at every step.

A desire for team cohesion and actual team cohesion are two different things. Every coach would love a team on which there were no problems, spats, cliques, playing-time issues, or jealousies. But, like seamless play on the field, it usually doesn't just happen. It requires work, creativity, problem solving, and attentiveness in every area of coaching. From recruiting players to increasing the athletes' confidence as players, people, and teammates, a coach must be vigilant at every step.

Recruiting and Confidence Building

How do you create a cohesive team? The quality of the individuals on your team is a good place to start. The recruiting process is valuable in determining whether an athlete will add to or take away from the atmosphere you want surrounding your team. However, not every coach gets to choose her own players. Some may have to start a mini-grass-roots effort with a few key players and slowly build toward the positive environment they envision.

Even at the NCAA Division III level, where we cannot offer athletic scholarships, we interview 40 or 50 recruits each year to see if they would fit into our

Photo by Steve Smith

When there is strong team cohesion, sharing hard-earned, exhilarating moments with "family" makes a great feeling even better.

program in terms of talent, athleticism, and personality. I prefer it when their parents come with them so that I can observe their interaction and the bond they have with each other. If I enjoy the parents, I know that the recruit (and her family) is a great choice for our program. We also research each player by making contact with her high school and club team coaches, guidance counselors, and sometimes teachers and opposing coaches to get a good sense of what she is about on and off the field. Every piece of information and interaction is critical in determining whether that prospect would thrive in our program's environment.

Sometimes a prospect appears to have exceptional character and heart but may not have the physical level of talent or athleticism we need. Often we will reconsider such a player because of her potential to increase team unity; we'll review her tape to determine if we can raise her level of play sufficiently for her to succeed on our team. Many times we have to rely on a gut feeling.

In order to have a group who cares about and reaches out to one another, the individuals must be confident. Part of our jobs as coaches is to build confidence in the athletes. Their job is to function as a cohesive unit, but the confidence to do that is something that coaches must help build within each player. That process is a daily commitment. It starts with the coach making sure the athletes know she cares about them as people—that's the family part. You do that by speaking to them respectfully, being considerate of their beliefs, and interacting with them in a way and at a place that has nothing to do with the sport.

Once you have established that you regard them as more than athletes who can help pad your win–loss record, you can truly begin to teach and guide them. Let them know you believe in their abilities. During practice I will put some pressure on them by telling them what they are doing wrong and what they should be doing. But then I will tell them, "I know you can do this better." When I see them look into my eyes and know that they realize I am looking back, I feel like I am reaching deep inside them. I can feel them absorbing the information, confidence, and my belief in them. It is obviously easier to build confidence in some players than it is in others. Sometimes you have to use different tactics. With such players, I tell them about the potential that I believe they possess. Or I might start a conversation with them about other things, like classes, family, or something special they do off the field. I also try to bring positive attention to their opinions. For example, if a player is having a difficult time feeling confident with her performance, yet has been brave enough to speak up in the team huddle, I try to accentuate the details of her comment so she feels acknowledged and senses my belief in her observation. All of these methods can aid a struggling athlete to become more productive on the field.

College-age student-athletes vary quite a bit in their levels of maturity; some are ready for new challenges, but some are very young. Even though they love the game and are committed to it, they are more selfish and immature. Coaches need to bring those players to another level as people, as individual players, and as team players.

Athletes have to understand right from the start that the program and the team take priority over any individual. When they think about the team as "the family," then when someone has a crisis—concerns about playing time, family or school problems, or anything else—the rest of the family will help her through it. It all leads back to confidence, though. The more confident a player is, the more balanced she is. The more she has things in perspective, the greater is her ability to reach out to others.

Analyzing and Goal Setting

Another important part of the process of building a unified team is to teach players to analyze themselves after each drill, practice, or game. We begin evaluating each skill in the explanation and demonstration of the year's first practice. Analysis is an integral, daily part of our program.

Analysis helps the team's cohesiveness for several reasons. Training the players to identify points of emphasis is the initial step in teaching how to analyze, which is why I don't leave analyzing to the first loss of the season. Second, the process allows everyone the opportunity to speak and participate in finding ways for the team to improve. That level of mental investment leads to a greater level of physical and emotional investment in the team. Third, the players are learning how to identify and solve problems. Practicing those skills helps them learn to make the kind of in-game decisions that will lead the team to greater success. It also helps them recognize more readily the potential problems that can creep in and erode the team's cohesiveness.

Whether we are winning or losing, we are evaluating. It has gotten to be a big joke among some of our coaches and parents. They'll ask, "Sharon, what do you talk about for so long after a game you have won?" The post-game talk may be as long as 45 minutes, but I have found that it is the best time to coach. After a game, it is fresh on our minds. We can identify issues, the positive things that were done, and determine which aspects of our game we can improve. Then the next day at practice I do not have to spend time reevaluating; we have already identified our areas of concern. Instead, I present my solution to the players and ask if they have any suggestions.

When we lose, the process is the same, except that we have to deal with a different level of emotion. If we have lost two or three games within a few days, the stress builds up among the players, so I try to regroup them and get them focused on simple things. If we lose I get upset, especially if I know our team could have performed much better. But if we played our best and the other team still performed at a higher level than us, I explain that we need to respect that and let it motivate us to improve. During those times, the evaluation process shifts to figuring out what the opposition did to beat us, why we did not play our best, and how to gain the advantage next time.

During both the smooth, winning times and the challenging stretches, we pick everything apart, which is important in keeping the team together. I do not let the players make excuses. We identify problems and figure out solutions so we do not dwell in the negative for too long. My goal is to constantly build strength and consistency in our performance.

We analyze on an individual basis as well. Teaching athletes to analyze talent, skill, and execution helps when they are concerned about their level of performance or amount of playing time. There is a huge payoff when athletes learn to evaluate themselves. The perfectionists—those who always put forth 100-percent effort and almost always play well, but generally undervalue themselves—gain a better understanding of their abilities when they are taught how to evaluate.

Evaluation also helps the players who feel they deserve or want more playing time. When an athlete questions her playing time, we sit down together to evaluate her areas of strength and what she needs to work on to improve her performance. That helps her realize that decisions about playing time are not personal, that we do have a rationale for who plays, and it also helps her to take ownership for her performance. We come up with a plan for her to improve and, hopefully, have changed an attitude of confusion or dissention into one that will help the team. I'm not running a democracy, and the players understand that. But the more input I expect from them, the more they learn to think about the game for themselves, and the more they think about it, the more they understand and become invested in it.

Sometimes players don't know how to identify areas in themselves that need improvement. In order to attain goals, they must be taught how to analyze their own performance. If there are set goals without proper evaluation, only half the job is done—organization and focus are lacking. This creates a gap in the continuity of the process, and as a result, it becomes choppy.

The team mission is the ultimate goal, and the team goals help in achieving that mission. Our ultimate goal is to win a national championship every season. This is largely an unspoken goal; our daily focus is more on accomplishing short-range goals. Additionally, the players might be motivated by a theme—perhaps in the form of a quote or an idea—that helps them strive to achieve their goals and ultimately to realize our fundamental mission of winning the national championship. Some examples of these themes are "Fight to the finish," "Unfinished business," "It's a matter of pride," "On a mission," and "Rise to the challenge."

Team-Building Activities

Team-building activities have great value, and although some may seem elementary, they bring out the kid in all of us. Anything dealing with food is always fun. Dinners and trips for ice cream are part of many of our team meetings. Other fun activities include a rope-climbing or trust course, camping, or a trip to the beach or movies. Each coach needs to determine how much time her players are capable of investing. For example, scheduling a time-consuming activity during the week prior to final exams would not be good planning, yet a quick dinner at a coach's house might relieve stress while providing a chance for the team to spend some off-the-field time together.

Because I coach two different sports, I have different time tables for getting the teams ready. In lacrosse I can ease my way into the season because we have a fall off-season and a couple of months in the spring before our first game. But during the fall in field hockey, we have only about 10 days to get the team ready to play its first game. Because everything happens so fast, I try to plan out a few activities with the team's seniors while we conduct preseason camp. We schedule only a few things at that time, usually team dinners (during which I try to filter myself around to the players as much as I can), because the team's focus is on preparing for the first game. I have learned never to assume that upperclassmen, especially the seniors, know how to lead. Some are naturals; others need a guide. At the beginning of the season, I speak with the seniors quite often to make sure they are initiating the team bonding.

In the spring, during the lacrosse season, we have more time to spend together prior to the first game. Fall ball practice, team workouts, individual workouts, and two months of practice help a team bond and offer many opportunities to reach out to each other. The seniors tend to guide the team early since they do not have to focus on preparing for the first game. Team dinners, formals (all of the college's athletes plan this in the winter), and the spring-break trip are a few of the things we do.

We have traditions in our program that were started by my college coach. Before every game for the past 27 years, in both programs, a player has done the Psych. The Psych may be a poem, a homemade gift for each player, or thoughts that the player shares, but games are never without one. The captains put together the Psych schedule at the beginning of the season so that each player knows when it is her turn. Two members are usually paired together. The Psych gives everyone a chance to share or do something special for the others. It draws the team around two different people for each game, helps the players get to know each other, and distributes the responsibility of getting the team ready for a game. It is a great tradition.

We also have a buddy system for two portions of the season. The first is during our spring-break trip, which kicks off our lacrosse season. The players are paired up for the week. I tell them that even though everyone should be helping to take care of everyone else, their buddy is someone special to watch out for during the trip. Long trips can be great bonding experiences, but they can also be difficult for some players. I want the players to feel comfortable with each other, and they will become increasingly so if they care about the result of their season. Once we get to postseason play, each player has a secret buddy for whom they make gifts, write notes, and leave little surprises. It seems so simple, but it is the little things in life that count. They learn who their buddies will be prior to the weekend of the national championship.

Because food is a great bonding tool, the players sometimes organize a pasta party to which they invite the assistant coaches, my children, and me. It is a chance for them to share some responsibility for entertaining their teammates. I am planning to invite each class of students over to my house for a meal during the season, starting with the seniors. I feel this will help me stay connected with the players. Early in my career, when I had no children, I spent more time in my office and the athletes would often drop by after practice and throughout the evening, making it easier to get to know them. These meals will present another way for me to bond with them, and it will help the players recognize my interest in them. This acknowledgment will strengthen my bond with them, which will enhance the overall cohesion of the team.

Also, as I have gotten older, I have realized something that sounds obvious but as a younger coach did not occur to me: As time moves on, we coaches get older and our lives change, yet the age of our athletes stays the same. Before having children of my own this didn't affect my relationships with our players since I often spent extra hours in my office. This was a time when the players and I always had ample opportunities to bond. However, after having children I significantly reduced the amount of extra hours I spent in the office. It was then that I realized I needed to make more of an effort to bond with the players during the time I had with them.

Most of the teams I have coached have been very close-knit, because that is a huge priority to me. I might tell the players to take a teammate they do not spend much time with to dinner. If I see cliques beginning to form, I make sure everyone understands that kind of behavior is not acceptable on my teams. Because this is made clear to everyone, we rarely have further problems with the issue. We go bowling periodically, and I know of teams that spend an afternoon playing paintball or going rock climbing. Any activity, no matter how big or small, that allows the players to interact outside of their sport can improve the chemistry of the team.

Team Disrupters

Regardless of the energy, thought, and time you put into creating and maintaining a positive atmosphere, you will not achieve 100-percent success in your efforts. However, if you have cultivated an environment in which the players and staff form a tight group that has each other's best interests at heart, identifying and dealing with the occasional disruption is a much less complex process.

I have learned to have a low-key attitude about certain things, how to delegate, and how to let some things go. When I let things go, the players see a more relaxed coach. When I am intense, they know I mean business. But certain things are very important to the team and me, and team cohesiveness is at the top of that list. If my teams are not cohesive, I know something is wrong, and I set about trying to figure it out.

> If you have cultivated an environment in which the players and staff form a tight group that has each other's best interests at heart, identifying and dealing with the occasional disruption is a much less complex process.

When a disruption occurs, I ask myself, "What is the problem? Where is it? Who isn't getting along? Why?" I investigate what the problem is and who is involved. When a player is being destructive to a team, something is wrong. In such cases, I speak to the athlete one on one, and to the rest of the coaches as well. Is she selfish or immature, or is there an underlying problem with her? "Can this individual grow before she destroys the team?" is a question I may raise to the coaching staff. A player who constantly draws attention to herself is harmful to the rest of the team.

My teams know I will not accept a player who stirs the pot in a negative way. Earlier in my career some of my players learned hard lessons by sitting out. Those decisions were tough for me because I was experiencing so many new things at once. Yet I always responded by doing what I felt would benefit the team in the long run. Sacrificing a strong player on the field to teach a lesson was a risk in competition, but necessary in the big picture. No win is worth sacrificing the family structure of a team. Now those decisions are easier for me. I have been coaching for a long time, and my players pass down some "words of wisdom" to the newcomers each year. They know that I am a fair coach who cares about them and that I believe that no single player will make our programs a success. We are a team, a family. I protect the players like I protect my own children, and I do not allow them to waste time hurting each other.

I will not hesitate to get involved in a situation when disruption affects the team. I speak with the captains and the seniors and hold individual meetings with the players involved, followed by joint meetings with the captains and those players. My bottom line is that no player will ever have enough control over the team to break the bonds of the family. No player or coach is bigger or more important than the program. That philosophy is the foundation we stand on every day throughout every season.

You cannot claim to value team cohesion over wins and losses and not back that up with actions that are consistent with that philosophy. Telling the players, "You can score 50 goals a year or save every shot as the goalie, but you are not going to destroy this team or this program," is easy. What is much more difficult is kicking that prolific scorer or your best defender off the squad because she has demonstrated that she cannot be a team player.

In my experience, the players who create disruption usually possess one or more of the following characteristics: insecurity, selfishness, or jealousy. They might have been able to get away with unacceptable behavior—or even had it catered to—previously at home or in high school. Some have had a traumatic experience that they have been unable to work through. I feel that my role is to try to help all of our players grow; I believe that a strong, caring leader can positively impact the world of a maturing young adult in many ways.

Role of Captains

A captain on my team is a working position, not just a person with a title. Captains are the glue between the coaches and the players. They have to be able to communicate with all the coaches, and they must have the respect of the players and coaches. I look for players who are loyal to the program and the coaches. I also like having captains who have a good perspective, the best interests of the team in mind, and the ability and desire to reach out to their teammates—and who are the hardest-working athletes on the field. The players like to choose someone who makes a presence on the field and spends time with them, especially the younger ones. Our captains' responsibilities include being a positive role model, making phone calls about changes in the schedule, meeting with me to discuss an issue, planning team events, and organizing fund-raising activities. Most important, their responsibility is to think of the team first and to comfortably communicate with and be loyal to the coaching staff as well as their team.

We have a team meeting at which the players help elect the captains, because I believe they should have a major part in the process. However, I do not allow the vote to turn into a popularity contest. First, I take the time to explain what a great leader is and describe the role, responsibilities, and honor of being a captain. I have everyone vote by writing in their candidates and explaining why they chose them. That feedback has been useful, and it assures me that they have put some thought into their decision. They can vote for themselves, but they also have to provide their insight into why they feel they can successfully lead the team. Because I expect a lot from the captains, I want the players to understand their importance and value to the team. I ask them players to seriously consider who is most capable of performing the duties we have discussed.

I do not have a set formula for how many captains I have on a team. Because each team's situation and needs are different, I let the number vary. Determining the right number and mix of captains requires creative thinking in order to accommodate unique situations.

Recently, I had eight seniors on the field hockey team, which is a large number. I presented the captain issue to them, and they wanted all eight to be captains because they were a tight group with diverse personalities that the other players felt would benefit the team. I've had as many as four or five seniors before, but eight was too many. At least one needs to be the nucleus. We followed the team vote and one player from each of the three off-campus houses was chosen. I explained to the rest of the seniors that at the beginning of each game when the officials call for the captains, all eight would meet with the opponent's captains and officials because they all were leaders, but that the three elected players would still fill the working positions as captains.

This past lacrosse season we had five seniors, and we did something completely different. One of our seniors had served as captain the previous year; she was steady, had good perspective and respect, and was a great role model. After quite a bit of thought I decided we would have one captain and four co-captains. We continued to follow the team vote since she, overwhelmingly, received the most votes, yet instead of having one other player split the responsibility with her, I felt the best team dynamic would be to have her fellow seniors assist her. They all felt like they had responsibility, but the one who truly stood out was then still able to accept the largest share of that responsibility. I normally don't do that because it is hard for one player to carry all that responsibility, particularly on a larger team, but this player was capable of it. Each situation is different, and when determining leaders, a coach must assess the individual strengths and weaknesses of each player as well as the needs of the team.

The culture of a group comes from the top. A coach can actively participate in creating that culture or through inattention go along with the culture being created by the group members. The team you coach is your extended family. I feel strongly about how I want the athletes to interact and represent themselves. I owe it to the parents of the players in the program to help our athletes become the best field hockey or lacrosse players they can be—that's my job—but I also intend to help them become the best people they can be. I believe that the "heart and soul" investment put forth by our coaching staff and players over the years has directly affected the overall success of the programs by creating that element essential to success: team cohesion.

18

Parent Relations

Establish trust and appropriate ground rules

Joan Powell

"My ultimate goal in life is to coach in an orphanage." That's how I begin my addresses to volleyball coaches at the clinics I conduct. A bit of silence followed by a burst of laughter is the audience's normal reaction. The statement is an obvious icebreaker, yet it intrigues all coaches because each one has war stories she would love to share regarding parental involvement. If I can make my colleagues laugh, they attain a sense of bonding with fellow sufferers and the healing can begin. Please understand that there are many fabulous, selfless parents who volunteer endless hours for their daughters and their teammates and coaches. But without exception, every coaches' group I have addressed has a dire need to validate feelings about parental issues that have made their lives uncomfortable—sometimes miserable. And they hope to find some answers that will allow them to avoid repeating certain incidents. Being challenged about one's ability or decisions or confronted face to face (most of the time without warning) is discomforting, but it can also be emotionally disruptive. Confrontations with parents usually rock a coach's core, causing sleepless nights and even hours spent in her administrator's office; some of my colleagues have quit the profession because dealing with parental interference became too difficult and took the joy out of coaching. Differences in philosophy and lack of communication are the two primary sources of tension between parents and coaches. I will address the issues that cause controversy and suggest strategies to help alleviate problems before they swell.

My early years as a naive rookie coach shaped the way I have dealt with athletes and parents throughout my career. Fresh out of college I landed my first coaching position at the high school I had attended and played volleyball for in the late 1960s. (As a student, I had tried out for cheerleading all four years, to no avail. My mother was supportive and hurt inwardly for me, but she never challenged the judges or the school!) Just off the collegiate court, I had to learn how to separate the roles of athlete and coach. I had the utmost respect for my college coach—she was a great teacher, very knowledge-able, and passionate about the sport. She appeared somewhat aloof but was revered by her teams. I owe a great deal to her for surreptitiously mentoring me. As a young coach, I assumed a similar demeanor, thinking it important to separate myself from my players, but I appeared unapproachable to parents (which was not necessarily a bad thing!). I considered myself competitive, a good teacher, professional, fair, consistent, and caring—and I had passion. In the early years the parents and administrators knew little about volleyball; they were happy to have a positive female role model, so parental pressure did not exist.

During my third season, my athletic director called me into his office and asked me if I enjoyed coaching. When I replied, "Why, I love coaching," he suggested that I let the kids in on it. He enabled me to look at myself and realize that my coaching style was not my own. From that day forward, I took strengths from my collegiate coach but developed a style that was more true to my personality (which is a bit more extroverted, to say the least).

> Differences in philosophy and lack of communication are the two primary sources of tension between parents and coaches.

Coaches must develop their own styles and philosophies, not be content with borrowing from others and forever trying to "find themselves." They must feel comfortable, and then develop and mature naturally. The last thing they need is inner strife while dealing with an external struggle. With that said, let's look at some issues regarding parents and explore helpful hints and possibly some solutions. Prevention is key, but even though you may feel that you have established a great program, a sound philosophy, and fair expectations, the time will come when a parent causes you to doubt yourself about an issue you have not addressed or have not had to deal with in previous years. I have encountered new issues every year.

Tryouts and Playing Time

Except at the Division I level, tryouts are a staple; although necessary, they can be the most unpleasant time of the season. With my experience in coaching, I could easily conduct tryouts and make cuts in one day; however, I would not have a leg to stand on with parents or my administration if I conducted them in that fashion. Instead, I provide a battery of physical tests, including agility, jumping, and cardiovascular endurance, followed by skills testing in which the scores are doubled. Each participant is tested twice, then the results are compiled on a spreadsheet and posted. The players understand that since some people are better testers than others, subjective evaluation of their actual playing is included in the final evaluation. I communicate to the parents that they are invited to any practice, but not to tryouts. My doors had been open during tryouts in the past, but I found that there was enough pressure on the players without the added anxiety from doting parents.

I preempted controversy from players, parents, and administrators years ago when I established this documented method for tryouts, yet I still get parents and players who will question a cut from the team or a placement level. The dispute is resolved quickly when documentation is provided. Cutting is stressful enough; the last thing a coach needs is to have a conference with a parent or administrator and have them ask where the documentation is for tryouts. As a coach, you must talk to each player that you cut. It is too easy to post a list. It took courage for them to try out, so you have to have the professionalism to speak to each player who took the risk. It continues to be the toughest day of the season for me; no one likes to make anyone feel unworthy.

Communication with players and parents prior to tryouts helps alleviate some potential problems. A flier sent during the summer or off-season regarding dates, times, and expectations solidifies your tryout mission. High school coaches may want to publish the information in the last school newsletter before summer and leave some fliers or calendars with the registrar or counselors in case there are new enrollees during the summer. Club coaches will want to establish tryout dates early and get them into the players' and parents' hands.

Playing time is most likely the toughest issue to handle with parents. This subject must be dealt with in an upfront manner at a parent/player meeting. Set the stage early, be firm in your convictions, and be able to live with your philosophy and expectations. Although this book includes a chapter dedicated to philosophy, I must reiterate the importance of not only establishing a philosophy of coaching but sharing it with players, parents, and administrators. Because of youth sports and the middle school concept, high school and club coaches have suffered the backlash of the "everybody plays, everyone gets a medal and a snack" philosophy. With diminishing budgets, school districts have been forced to implement an athletic fee. Many were quick to change the name from "participation fee" to "sport fee" when parents began demanding playing time because they were under the impression that they paid for participation. Many clubs have reasonable fees, others astronomical ones, and parents question the benefits of their financial commitment. I have heard some coaches tell parents that the money is for equal practice time, not equal playing time. A successful coaching colleague of mine, whose teams have won 10 state championships, was at practice one day when it was disrupted by loud clanking in the pushed-in bleachers. Unbeknownst to anyone, a player's mother had come in the back door with a video camera to film practice, and she stumbled. She was concerned about lack of playing time but was also out to prove that her daughter was not receiving quality practice time. How embarrassed was her daughter?

Another difficult subject regarding tryouts and playing time is nepotism. When I first began coaching at my former high school, my sister was a sophomore and a very good player. She was a deserving starter. I learned early that nepotism could be a red flag for those looking for an excuse. It was a valuable lesson that I had to pull out of the archives when I coached my daughter 20 years later. In retrospect I was harder on my sister and my daughter than on the other players, just in case anyone was looking to accuse me of favoritism.

The perception of nepotism or favoritism is difficult to prevent. If a player feels she is being treated unfairly or parents sense that their daughter is being overlooked, it is natural to accuse the coach of preferential treatment. Since I have experience in dealing with this dilemma, other coaches sometimes ask me for guidance. I suggest taking the matter head on by addressing the situation at the parent/player meeting. Humor is always a nice icebreaker. One basketball coach told the parents, "I know exactly what you parents want. You want me to identify the best four players and your daughter." It is a clever way of introducing the subject. Follow up with what you anticipate, and leave the door open to the idea that lineups can change throughout the year.

Coach-Parent Communication

Following tryouts, we introduce some team building; each year we plan an overnight camping experience that involves the team in the planning process. All three levels (C Squad, Junior Varsity, and Varsity) take part. During the first evening, prior to the class skits, the seniors speak about the team rules, policies, and expectations. The coaches could very easily do this, but there is something to be said about the buy-in factor from the players. The seniors talk about everything from appropriate dress, to court and classroom behavior, to substance use, to hickies on the neck! The week after our camping trip, we have a mandatory player/parent meeting, when the seniors once again relay the team rules: "It is a privilege to play volleyball at our school; because we are rich with tradition, drugs and alcohol have no place in our program. There is no warning; you will be excused." Everyone understands these rules. Your club, school district, conference, or league may have policies in place, and you may or may not be able to implement stricter policies.

Courtesy of Joan Powell

Communication with players and parents both prior to tryouts and after the team is selected helps alleviate potential problems.

Then the coaches speak about playing time. At our younger level (C Squad), we tell the parents that the coach will platoon and will play the best combination of players in the deciding game. At the junior varsity level, we are more competitive and cannot guarantee that everyone will get in every game. At the varsity level, we are playing to win, and I look for the best players with the best chemistry. We explain that skill and attitude are high priorities and that the parents have no idea what kind of contribution their daughter makes day in and day out on the practice court.

A few years ago at our player/parent meeting we conducted a mini practice so that the parents could see the types of things we do. They were given a handout titled "Observation of a Practice." The question asked is, "What does your daughter bring to a drill, to a practice?"

Coronado Volleyball Player/Parent Meeting

Observation of a Practice

What does your daughter bring to a drill? To a practice?

Things to look for in skill acquisition and drill performance:

1. Does she have good athletic ready position/anticipatory reaction? (Or is she surprised when reacting to the ball?)
2. Does she execute the skill properly with concerted effort to do so?
3. Does she "better the ball"? (Does the ball go to the desired target? If she receives an errant ball, does she improve its course?)
4. Does she "finish her move"? (Does she reach, make a token effort, or continue to move after contact?)
5. Does she move in a drill when not playing the ball? (Or does she spectate with an upright posture, back on her heels with locked knees?)
6. Does she possess a demeanor indicative of intensity and give an all-out effort?
7. If corrected, does she respond positively with body language and follow up with an effort to change technique?
8. Does she facilitate the drill by encouraging others, shagging balls, being emotionally involved?
9. Does she show frustration after mistakes and solicit attention to herself? (Does she often say, "My fault," "My bad," or "I'm sorry"?)
10. Does she handle pressure situations? (Or is she a rally killer?)
11. Does she take her practice self into competition? (Driller versus gamer?)

We have a few ground rules regarding how and when to address a coach that we share at the parent/player meeting:

- Timing is crucial. The time before or after a match is off limits for a player or parent. The 24-hour rule is a good one; emotions are less volatile after some cool-down time.
- After practice, a player can start a conversation advantageously by asking, "What can I do to improve? To start?" Or "Where do you see me? What is my role?"
- Parents need to call for an appointment, and the player should attend the meeting. (On rare occasions parents have requested meetings without their daughters.)
- E-mail regarding playing time will not be answered. (Technology is terrific, but we tend to be braver on the Internet than we are in person.)

Sometimes frustrated parents, instead of going to the coach who could explain the reasoning for something, go to the athletic director. At the player/parent meeting, I use the analogy that going to the athletic director or principal first is like having an employee who is disgruntled with a co-worker go directly to their boss instead of discussing the problem with the other employee. I encourage unhappy parents to discuss the problem with me first, because going to my athletic director will not automatically get their daughter a position or more playing time. Once a complaint is lodged with the athletic director, it is a no-win situation for the coach. It wastes time and energy, and many times the player gets hurt. The coach feels as if she is under a magnifying glass and that every substitution is being scrutinized. If the athlete in question plays, the perception is that you have given in, and if she does not play, you are being unfair and the problem could escalate. One incident can destroy a team because rumors spread quickly and players and parents begin taking sides. If this happens, you will need support, but avoid sharing information with your team, captains, or other parents. It may come back to haunt you later.

A suggested deterrent to potential parent problems is that coaches be direct in assessing talent and assigning roles. A depth-chart concept is ideal, along with the understanding that things may change due to circumstances like injuries, elevation in play due to practice, or illness. You must be straightforward with your players: "Right now you are the third middle blocker," or "You are our backup setter," or "You are our defensive specialist with so-and-so coming in the front row for you." Follow up with, "Do you understand your role? Do you accept your role?" I have found that the players accept their roles, but that fact does not always get relayed to their parents, or else the parents find it difficult to accept the position.

Unfortunately, parents get overly involved when they feel their daughter's role on the team is unacceptable. After observing some unfavorable antics in the stands by one player's mother, I had a meeting with her. Due to her obstinate behavior, I finally had to communicate that she had three choices: 1) take her daughter out of the program; 2) accept her role on the team; 3) don't attend her matches. My favorite parental comment is, "But she was the starting number one outside hitter for her club team and has never played opposite before." It is so hard to refrain from being critical sometimes; the parent simply does not understand the needs of *this* team. You must communicate with your players, especially when changes are made. A coach does not have to explain every decision (sometimes she'll have a gut feeling about a move and has to go with it), but communication with the players is a must.

Problem Players

One year I was to acquire an exceptional athlete from one of our feeder schools. My observations of her prior to her entrance into high school gave me a negative opinion of her—attitudinally she would be a project. Her middle school coach confirmed my opinion, along with a few of my rival high school coaches and some referees. I thought long and hard about how best to tackle this situation until finally, with tryouts right around the corner, I decided to arrange a meeting with the family. I asked if my assistant coach and I could meet with them in their home (a more comfortable environment for them), and they were very amiable. I was ill at ease to say the least; no one likes to tell parents that their daughter is a potential disrupter.

After the necessary introductions I spoke directly to the youngster, explaining that she was a very good athlete but that her behavior on the court was not favorable and would not be tolerated. It was obvious by her expression that no one had talked to her about this, nor had her coaches tried to curb the behavior by sitting her out; she was too good and it was easier to ignore her behavior. After her initial shock at my frankness, she offered the typical teenage reason for her intensity level: "I just get mad sometimes." I told her that the coaching staff was willing to help her change the reputation she had created but that we all needed to be in agreement regarding a plan. Together we decided that if she "copped an attitude," she would be released to the locker room. If the behavior continued, she would be suspended from competition or possibly released from the team.

Coaching this athlete was like training a horse. She simply needed to know what was expected of her and what the consequences of her actions would be. Her parents were grateful. She was a varsity starter her first year and was sent to the locker room only twice in her high school career. As a senior, she was still rough around the edges and sometimes an irritant to her teammates, so I could not consider her for captain even though she was our obvious impact player. In preseason I asked her how not being a captain affected her. She told me that it about killed her because it was something she had always wanted, plus not being captain was difficult to explain to her non-volleyball classmates. I explained that her leadership skills were suspect and that she appeared to be self-centered. I also told her that making her a captain would send the wrong message to her teammates and the younger players. She understood.

From that day forward, I saw the most dramatic change in her, and I eventually made her co-captain. She was our MVP and a state champion 14 years ago; she went on to play four years at the Division I level and is now married and has two daughters. She reminds me often that I had the most impact on her life. I could have excused or ignored her behavior as her coaches had done in the past, but I believe coaching is about more than the wins and losses. I had a responsibility to help her become a better volleyball player and, more importantly, a better person. Had I not made the initial contact and had her parents' support, the scenario would have been completely different.

Scholarships

In circles of pedigree dog owners, many owners think their dog is the best. Their blinders prevent them from seeing other qualified dogs, and of course, they think their dog should be the winner. Due to the "kennel blindness" of many parents as dollar signs and prestige take over sensibility and reality, coaches face continual pressures. Coaches do have a responsibility to assist their athletes to the next level of play. Place a trusted parent in charge of filming your matches. At the player/parent meeting, let the students know that if they receive recruiting inquiries and would like a letter of recommendation, phone call, or video you will be willing to help them. Stay abreast of the NCAA Clearinghouse regulations, and obtain updated information about recruiting from NCAA, NAIA (National Association of Intercollegiate Athletics), and the NJCAA (National Junior College Athletic Association). Returning all phone calls from inquiring colleges in a timely manner is important. Rather than filling out numerous postcards and letters of inquiry for each athlete, I help my athletes draft a letter of information that includes all the pertinent details: year in school, GPA, rank in class, test scores, possible career interests, sports played, positions, height, reach, jump, and so on. This letter can accompany a videotape of introduction, followed by skill and game footage; remember to include the jersey number. The player should keep a master copy so that a tape is always available. A more technologically-minded player could even create a CD, DVD, or a Web site.

Coaches are not responsible for securing scholarships for their players; they are merely facilitators. Yet some parents think that the coach's sole job is to get their daughter a ride. Some will argue over statistical information because they believe it is the most important factor in getting a good scholarship. One year we were playing a team that had beaten us rather handily. After the match, while my players were showering and getting ready for the bus trip home, I noticed that a parent and his daughter were in a heated discussion with the opposing coach. I asked the opposing assistant to tell the coach that

I needed her in the locker room. I thought that because the match went so quickly, the coach could not get players in fast enough and that this father was not happy because his daughter did not get into the game.

Thinking that there may have been an injury or theft, the coach came immediately. I told her that I had wanted to get her out of the situation that seemed to be brewing. She thanked me and explained that the father was upset because they were setting the middle too much and his daughter, who played outside the entire match, did not get enough sets! According to him, "With her ensuing scholarship, these stats are very important." Any college coach will tell you that statistical information is not that important. I explain that myth at the player/parent meeting and tell them that we report stats to the local paper and use them for coaching purposes. I choose not to post them because it causes too much consternation. I have heard horror stories of parental interference with statistical information given to college coaches or the media.

Another time, early in my career, a troubled dad called because his senior daughter had lost her spot to a sophomore. I explained that the varsity court is classless. He argued that she had been loyal for three years and that I owed her another chance. I do not believe I owe anyone anything, and loyalty is not a prerequisite for playing. I told him that if two players were comparable the younger player would get the nod; the senior needs to beat her out. Then I mentioned that the sophomore happened to have better stats. The father said, "Well, it looks like I need to start keeping my own stats." I shared this with my athletic director, who said, "You should have said, 'That's a great idea; we'll have all the dads take stats and have a weekly meeting on Wednesdays to determine the starting lineup.'"

After the phone conversation with that father, I made it a policy that parents needed to make an appointment to talk to me; I would not discuss problems over the telephone. There will be times when you may want to ward off aggressive parents and set up a meeting to discuss the future of their daughter. I have found that if you keep abreast of the local players' advancements, you are able to compare more readily. For instance, if your league's or conference's best player from the previous year goes to a local Division II school, help the parents compare their daughter with last year's standout. Many athletes receive many letters from colleges; most of the time they are feelers. The assessment process for college coaches is difficult, as is the waiting game for the athletes and parents. Be there for your athletes, run interference, and help them cope with the stresses that surround the recruitment process. Keep the athletes' best interest in mind. It may be better for them to play at a lower level than to sit for four years at the higher level. However, you must understand that the parents of this generation have a vested interest and active role in the achievement, performance, and outcome of their children. The money they invest in camps, club sports, and national scouting services is substantial, and many parents become obsessed with getting a return on their investment.

In such cases, offering an honest assessment and doing what you believe is right for the athlete may create conflict with the parents.

Diverse Family Dynamics

Being in tune with your players' backgrounds is imperative and can help you understand why the player or parent acts the way they do. It also allows you to be sensitive to issues that may arise. I have had players from wealthy homes and impoverished homes and players from diverse backgrounds; some were being raised by a single parent, some were raising themselves, some were under joint custody, and others were adopted. Some players suffer from internal sibling rivalries; others are victims of incest, have little support because the parent or parents work two jobs to survive, or have a "helicopter" parent (who continually hovers over the child), whose support borders on encroachment. Granted, those coaches who do not work in an educational setting do not have access to counselors or social workers to inquire about their players. I am fortunate that where I coach, the information is readily available. Get to know your players by asking questions on a road trip, or ask school authorities. Your team is a great resource, but the players need to feel safe sharing information about their teammates' personal lives; they need to be assured that you are interested in everyone's welfare, not merely being nosy. You need to be subtle but inquisitive. The player mentioned earlier who was a potential behavioral problem had a complex step-family, and her biological father had abused her mother, was involved in drugs, and was in jail. And we would get mad when she misbehaved! Family dynamics do influence the behavior of your players. A tough upbringing does not exclude a player from being responsible for her behavior, but knowing about that background helps the coach understand the player better.

> Being in tune with your players' backgrounds is imperative and can help you understand why the player or parent acts the way they do. It also allows you to be sensitive to issues that may arise.

Communication is crucial. Be aware of any financial implications a team outing or article of clothing might have on a family's budget. Do not assume that once the season is underway families no longer face a financial burden. The purchase of a team sweatshirt or shoes may have major financial implications. Make it your business to know which students are on reduced lunch or receive financial aid. Common courtesy needs to be a high priority for every coach; no athlete should be made to feel embarrassed because of her family's financial restrictions.

A sure way to anger parents is to announce practice end time and then not abide by it; be considerate of their needs. Some middle and high school athletes have to catch an activity bus. Many parents are coming from work to pick up their daughters; some car pool or have other children they need to attend to; others have multiple commitments or work at night. If you say your practice is over at 5:30 p.m., parents can expect that their child will gather her belongings and be out the door shortly thereafter. Activities such as putting away equipment, making lengthy announcements, conducting a team meeting, deciding which uniform to wear, or discussing the itinerary for tomorrow's contest need to be attended to within the practice time. Remember, you expect your players to be on time and most likely impose a consequence if they are not. Courtesy goes both ways.

In our technological whirlwind of a world, the cell phone has become a necessary evil. Many of my athletes are attached to them like they are to a CD player. When I took my team to an out-of-state camp one year, I gave the parents my cell phone number and asked if I had their permission to take their child's cell phone for the duration of the trip since the parents had access to their children through me. This camp experience was so important as a team builder that I did not want to have any distractions. The parents were overwhelmingly in favor. Many expressed concern about how much time their daughter spent on the phone. One dad had already taken his daughter's phone away from her due to an exorbitant bill. The strategy worked; we reaped the benefits as a team, but asking permission was essential.

Academic Eligibility

Coaches are responsible for staying abreast of their student-athletes' academic progress. Be aware of your school, district, or state rules governing eligibility to participate in sports. If you believe they are too lenient, find out if you are allowed to initiate stricter regulations. However, you must exercise caution not to impose unreasonable standards; for instance, a no "D" policy. Such a policy could have a negative impact on an athlete who has a recognized learning disability that causes her to receive poor grades. As coach, you need to be aware of any special situations that may warrant you to accommodate a player. College coaches are at a disadvantage because of the Privacy Act. This law protects students by not allowing parents or coaches to view grades without the student's written permission. Coaches often are the last to know about academic probation or ineligibility. Parents of collegiate athletes may also be in the dark if progress reports or grades are not divulged.

Eligibility rules may test your ethics. If you are informed that your athlete is ineligible on the day of an important contest, do not take matters in your own hands by determining the consequences and the time line. Ask your athletic director what the consequences of being ineligible are, and familiarize yourself with policies and procedures governing ineligibility. We all know of unethical coaches who bend rules and plead innocence afterwards.

Your involvement in your athletes' academic success, such as inquiring about tutoring, a remediation plan, or a study table, is appropriate and necessary. Keep abreast of their progress. At the middle and high school levels, coaches should inform the parents if the school has not done so. The one thing a coach does not need is the overzealous parent who invokes consequences for unrealistic expectations, like insisting that his child have straight As. Address this subject in your player/parent meeting and suggest alternatives for parents to consider, such as taking away their child's cell phone instead.

Self-Defeating Behaviors

Young adults are bombarded by information about their physical appearance and popularity. Self-worth is a monumental issue in their everyday lives. The problems surrounding self-defeating behaviors can be destructive and become routine in adult life. Drug experimentation, eating disorders, depression, self-mutilation, attempted suicide, or promiscuous sexual activity are prevalent among adolescents and young adults, and they do impact the athletic world. However, unless you are a certified psychologist or counselor, understand that you cannot solve any of these issues.

If a player engages in anorexic or bulimic behavior, realize that the problem is not food; it is about control and deeper issues that you are probably unaware of. The choice to overindulge, starve, or binge and purge is an attempt to fill a void. Once you have recognized the signs or a teammate has shared information with you, sit down with the athlete and assure her that you are interested in her well-being. Then you may want to involve the parents and seek professional assistance. Denial is a huge factor; you may feel as though you are not getting anywhere with the athlete. Keep an eye on her, and keep your ears open. Above all, do not expect an overnight change in behavior.

In my experience with athletes who exhibit self-defeating behaviors, all except one have accepted help. I was told that this player was exercising a great deal—getting up at 4:00 a.m. to run, sneaking back into bed in time for her mom to wake her up for school, running after practice, and throwing up after lunch. When I spoke to her, she confessed to overexercising but saw no harm in it, and she denied the accusation of vomiting. I felt obligated to call her mother, who was in total denial. I turned it over to a counselor, and the next thing I knew the mother had transferred her daughter to another school.

Self-destructive behavior is a sensitive subject; no one wants to make false accusations or get parents involved on the basis of hearsay. However, coaches cannot afford to take the risk that ignoring an allegation could harm an athlete, so be on the safe side by dealing with the issue head on. As coaches, we are in a position of trust and are responsible for the safety and welfare of our players; situations will arise when we need to solicit help from professionals like school counselors or administrators regarding the physical and emotional stability of our players. The first thing you need to relay is that you are interested in the player's welfare and you want to help. One of my former players began engaging in bulimic behavior during basketball season her senior year but did not seek help until she was in college. I ran into her after about 10 years. She was a nurse, married with two children. We talked about her eating disorder during high school, and she told me that she and her mother had been in denial. But finally she sought help and is under control today. Unfortunately, some players are very good at hiding these behaviors, and the consequences of these actions have devastating implications as they enter adulthood.

A successful athletic program includes parents in positive roles. For years, I did everything myself, then I realized that parents are hungry to help and I learned to delegate. A few years ago, I had a father in my program, a great guy who wanted to be involved. Thanks to him, my program has evolved into a partnership with parents; he left a documented legacy. At our end-of-the-year banquet, the senior parents pass a baton, along with a three-ring binder filled with information for the new season, to the junior parents. Each summer I meet with the senior parents. We follow the book and assign parents to different tasks. They have taken ownership of our annual tournament, transportation, programs, picture buttons, and the banquet. At the conclusion of my agenda at the initial player/parent meeting, the parents take over; they have the necessary sign-up sheets for all the future events. And I get to coach!

I continue to have my share of disgruntled parents, but the partnership has allowed most parents to feel like an integral part of the program. Although they may not always agree, they are more accepting of their daughter's role in the program. Parents want their daughters to be involved in the program because of the intangible benefits of being a member of a team. They know that their daughters receive more than great training and the highest level of competitiveness; they know that all players are treated fairly and consistently, and that the life skills their daughters learn will follow them into adulthood.

19

Marketing and Media

Promote the program enthusiastically, frequently, and effectively

Sarah Patterson

Ialways knew I wanted to coach. What I didn't know was that a degree in marketing would have made my coaching career much easier.

In 1974 I made my decision to attend Slippery Rock State Teacher's College in Pennsylvania. I chose to pursue a teaching degree in physical education because, as everyone knows, successful coaches are at their core successful teachers. If I had it to do all over again I would still become a coach, but my educational credentials would have included a marketing degree and an MBA. (A psychology degree would have helped as well!)

I received an offer to become the head gymnastics coach at the University of Alabama a month or so before my graduation from Slippery Rock. At age 22, I was in charge of a Division I collegiate program, and my athletic director was none other than the legendary Paul "Bear" Bryant. Ann Marie Lawler was the women's athletic director during my first year at the Capstone, and over the next few years I learned a great deal from her. Her support and advice would prove invaluable. I was young and enthusiastic, and I had a vision that one day thousands of people would enjoy the excitement of collegiate gymnastics and cheer our team on to a national championship. Ann Marie Lawler encouraged me on every level.

The university had 10 national titles in football in 1978. As the youngest member of the Alabama coaching staff, it seemed logical to me that another sport could also achieve this level of success. After all, a championship tradition was already in place. I had dreams, and I wasn't satisfied to leave them unfulfilled. Turning a program that, before my arrival, hadn't had a winning season in any of its first four years into a winner would take plenty of hard work. Strong recruiting and coaching would be the key factors in pushing our program to a championship level. We had the ingredients to become a winning program, but for me that wasn't enough. I wanted to win and I wanted to fill the stands. I knew that would take some real work.

I have served under nine different athletic directors during my time at Alabama, but it was the third, Cecil "Hootie" Ingram, who really helped me see the clear picture of collegiate athletics today and how I could best make my mark in the sport world. It was Hootie, along with several prominent newspaper editors, who convinced me that if my team were to receive the kind of funding, attention, and media coverage I so desperately desired, I would have to do two things: win, and put fans (paying fans) in the stands on a consistent basis.

Winning came easier than putting people in the stands, but it was a necessary first step. Once we started winning, though, things started to progress rather quickly. One of my rival coaches, the University of Utah's Greg Marsden, told me I could increase my attendance by winning or hosting a national championship. We won our first NCAA title in 1988, and he was right—attendance did surge. From there, I set out to host an NCAA championship and win it as well. Greg was right again: We experienced another surge in attendance after hosting and winning the 1991 NCAA title.

Winning, even winning national titles at home, hasn't been the only key to our success in the arena of fan support. It also has required rolling up my sleeves and doing the hard work, from the glamorous jobs to the monotonous ones, and sticking with it over the long haul. When you make it a goal to have excellent fan support, you must be willing to put in the long hours yourself, whether you have that degree in marketing or not. I learned along the way, taking things from other successful programs, learning from those around me, and never giving up when others said what I wanted to do was impossible. Perseverance, I have learned, is an incredible marketing tool.

One of my favorite coaches is Pat Summitt, head coach of the University of Tennessee women's basketball program for the past 30 years. I admire her greatly, not because she has won six national titles and is one of the nation's most prominent women's coaches, but because she saw the importance of marketing and media exposure long before others did. Pat worked as hard at promoting her program as she did at coaching and recruiting. She once made the statement to the *Birmingham News* that if you weren't committed to marketing your program yourself, you didn't deserve to play in front of supportive crowds.

For 25-plus years, I feel I have worked as hard at marketing and promoting our gymnastics program as I have worked at coaching. Sometimes, depending on the time of the year, I wonder whether my job title is coach or marketing director!

Developing a Successful Marketing Plan

A successful marketing plan comprises five components. The first three steps are research oriented in determining your market and what draws them to events. The last two phases involve implementing what you learned from your research:

1. Identify the current and possible fan base.
2. Study the competition for your target market.
3. Determine what your program has to offer that audience.
4. Tailor your events to those spectators.
5. Decide how to best reach your audience through various marketing, advertising, and media efforts.

The first step to marketing your program is to identify the target audience, both that which already exists and that which you want to attract. The key to effective promotion of your program is knowing whom you are promoting it to. What base of fans already is interested in your sport or team? Do you get lots of student support? Is your audience filled with family members of all ages? Do you see entire teams of young girls wearing their own team's uniform? Do you have a large senior citizen fan base?

Brainstorm about whom else you believe you can attract to your program. Study the demographics of your existing fans for ideas about how to expand the audience. If you've noticed dads bringing their girls to the games, you may be able to reach even more dads looking for ways to spend time with their daughters. The presence of a few young teams in uniform could foretell an opportunity to fill the stands by hosting a "Wear Your Uniform to the Game" night. A community with a strong base of participants in your sport could be a group you can tap into. You may believe that a group such as the Girl Scouts, fans of a different but similar sport, or community organizations would connect with your program if given the opportunity. A member of your team may be associated with certain groups, such as clubs on campus, or a parent may belong to a business association. The ideas are endless, but it is ineffective to launch marketing efforts without a clear picture of whom you are targeting.

Next you need to determine who your competition is for that audience. Who or what else is trying to attract the same spectators' time, money, and allegiance? Is your competition other sport teams? Civic or cultural events? Much like scouting your opponent before a contest to determine how to beat them, identifying the competition for your target audience enables you to develop unique ideas about how to reach that group and make your program stand out in the crowd.

The third phase in marketing your program is to establish the draw of your program. Determine what your event has to offer the general public and sell it that way. Do your events have an exciting atmosphere? Do they highlight top-notch competition? Do they provide a chance to interact with great role models? Do they feature inexpensive entertainment? Why should spectators come to *your* event instead of the many others vying for their attention?

Fourth, after determining the market, competition, and draw of your program, consider what you can do to tailor the event to that market without sacrificing the integrity of the competition and your athletes' experience. Consider the expectations and needs of that audience as much as possible when making decisions about your event, such as their day and time, structure, price for parking and admission, promotional activities, and programs or handouts.

For example, in the early 1990s, I thought we needed to make some changes and add a new dimension to our events. I had seen professional athletes introduced in spotlights and always enjoyed the light shows surrounding professional figure-skating events. I decided to take a chance and rent four large theatrical spotlights and a large disco ball. In 15 minutes we transformed our competitive arena into a stage-show production that brought an overwhelming response from the crowd. By the time the athletes were all highlighted and introduced, the coliseum was rocking. In a matter of minutes, we created an atmosphere that became a hot topic of conversation among our community. A friend of mine leaned over to the athletic director as the fans were working themselves into a frenzy and asked my boss what he thought of my new production. He calmly answered, "It worked," and from that point I knew we were in business.

I failed to mention that I created this production without administrative approval for fear that my ideas would be derailed by others before they even got started. This promotional project was something I believed in and accepted full responsibility for regardless of the outcome. Needless to say, I was thrilled with the results, and eventually the university purchased an expensive "Quick Light" system, enabling our basketball teams to create a similar atmosphere for their competitions. Perseverance and willingness to take a chance definitely paid great dividends in the production and promotion of our events.

The final component is the one that most people identify as marketing: promoting your program. Getting the word out doesn't just mean mailing flyers to your existing fan base or putting an advertisement in the local newspaper. It means brainstorming about new distribution methods and patterns, such as e-mailing an invitation to your school's faculty or leaving schedule cards at community businesses. It means out-of-the-box thinking, such as challenging the media to a friendly competition or handing out flyers at the local mall after a skills demonstration. It means working hard to host a regional competition to attract more attention to the sport and get new fans to your facility. It means being willing to make appearances around town and support causes in your community, such as speaking to the Rotary Club or participating in a read-to-children program.

> Getting the word out doesn't just mean mailing flyers to your existing fan base or putting an advertisement in the local newspaper. It means brainstorming about new distribution methods and patterns, thinking outside of the box, working hard to host a regional competition, and being willing to make appearances around town and support causes in your community.

At the University of Alabama, we have identified our target market as families, so we promote our events as family entertainment. Our competitions are shorter than most movies and definitely less expensive for a family of four. We have done everything we can to make our events family friendly, such as adjusting our competition schedule and the type of music we play in the arena.

We have paid particular attention to the start time of our competitions and experimented with holding meets on different days of the weekend, trying to identify the one night where we can capitalize on attendance. We determined that Friday nights are our best opportunity to draw large crowds, and we chose the slogan "Fun Family Fridays" to help us captivate our market's attention. We tell the community, as many different ways as we can, to "start the weekend spending time with your family and share in the excitement of Alabama Gymnastics!"

Marketing Ideas

- Distribute schedule cards and posters at local businesses.
- Hold a friendly competition event against high-profile members of the media as a fund-raising event for a local charity.
- Conduct clinics for youth and adults to teach the skills and strategies of your sport.
- Promote your program at other well-attended athletic events at your school or university.
- Market to senior citizens in the area.
- Pay attention to marketing tactics used by other schools or organizations, and try the ones that seem especially effective.
- Have a local celebrity—a star athlete, the mayor—attend your event.
- To increase understanding of your sport, distribute spectator guides that include rules and strategies of the sport.
- Develop a student-run audio broadcast of your competitions using donated equipment and hosted on a school Web site or donated Web site.
- Remember that your first priority is to coach your team so that they improve and enjoy themselves. That in itself generates excitement and a strong fan base.

Advertising With a Limited Budget

Most coaches are limited by budget constraints. Advertising in newspapers and on radio or television is expensive, so a full-scale advertising campaign is unrealistic. However, there are ways to advertise that are cost effective and do the job of getting the word out.

One way to get the most out of your advertising dollars is to focus your efforts on one or two of your best events. Perhaps you are hosting the league championship, or your have special promotions planned for a certain game. Purchase advertisements for that event only. If you have an exciting double-header with the boys' team, pool money from both budgets to promote both games.

Another possibility is getting your advertising paid for or donated by local businesses that have an interest in your program. This can be in the form of advertisements in the media or printed pieces such as schedules and posters. We have had great success in asking local businesses to allow us to use or share their advertising time to help promote our events. Businesses have designated funding for advertising, and convincing just a few to allow you to use their advertising dollars can be beneficial for both your program and the local business. You must be aware of the fiscal calendar that they follow, however, so that you can approach them with plenty of time to fit the donation into their annual budget plans.

Get involved with a local charity or fund-raising event. The least of the benefits is the possibility that you will receive free advertising in the form of media exposure based on your event's community value. More important, it helps a worthwhile event and teaches your players the importance of giving back to the community and making a difference in the world.

At Alabama, we encourage our student-athletes to be active in the community and to be, to the best of their abilities, role models for young girls. Crimson Tide gymnasts are involved in a variety of annual projects. We participate in a food drive, hold a bake sale to raise funds to buy Christmas presents for children whose parents are in prison, and host receptions for children with cancer. Our student-athletes have built a rapport with the community, which has been rewarded with outstanding attendance at our events. David Patterson, my husband and co-head coach, and I also are highly involved in the community, serving on boards and as chairs of various organizations, among other projects.

Before you secure advertising or use your players in advertisements, make sure you check with your sport's league, conference, or national governing bodies about rules concerning such activities. The NCAA prohibits businesses from using athletes to promote products or services, and other associations also have regulations in place that oversee issues such as eligibility and amateurism of athletes. A little free exposure is not worth ruining the future athletic career of an athlete.

Working With the Media

Local media coverage is probably the most effective marketing and advertising tool because it is free and it reaches a large number of people. Sports reporters from newspapers, radio and television stations, Web sites, and magazines are constantly on the lookout for new information about teams and athletes in their community to fill their pages and airways. Granted, the bulk of the coverage goes to local professional sports and college football and basketball teams, and it seems the media is more focused on negative stories. But, regardless of whether your team is at the club, junior high, high school, college, or professional level, you can gain positive exposure by being personable, polished, respectful, and proactive.

It's certainly not a right for your program to be covered by the media. It is a privilege, one that most of us have to work at to enjoy. I am as personable and accommodating as possible with our media, which has had an extremely positive impact on our coverage. Get to know the media reporters and editors. They are much more likely to cover someone they have had personal contact with than someone who is merely a name in a press release or media guide. Some of my most cherished professional relationships have come through getting to know various members of the media.

Not all members of the media are looking to expose harmful stories about your program, but few will ignore them. Learn to focus on the positive and not vent to or around the media. Choose your words carefully. Realize that few if any conversations are truly off the record. Don't degrade a player or opponent during an interview or in casual conversation that the media could overhear. Practice speaking out loud in front of friends, family, or a mirror to improve your presence in front of a camera. Have a speech, communications, or media expert conduct a clinic for your team on how to talk to the media. Provide insight to the team and interesting, meaningful quotes rather than a stream of clichés. The media can help get the word out about your team, but make sure you project the image you want the public to see.

> It's certainly not a right for your program to be covered by the media. It is a privilege, one that most of us have to work at to enjoy.

Your media coverage depends in large part on your sport's impact in your particular area. The nature of media coverage is that an extremely popular team will get more coverage than one that has a smaller following, and a very successful team will gain more media attention than a mediocre one. Being understanding and respectful about the media's time and resources doesn't mean you shouldn't work to increase your coverage, but it does mean you are familiar with their business and don't let unrealistic expectations sour the relationship. You may not agree with their allocation of space or time, just as they may not agree with your game-day tactics. But it is your job to make them want to cover you, not demand that they do so. A difficult or demanding personality will likely get you the undesirable result. Also remember that it is not the reporter's fault that she is charged with covering 10 local teams by herself. Her editor makes most decisions about what events the reporter covers. But if you develop an understanding relationship with that reporter, she might lobby in your favor with the editor when given the chance.

Familiarity and respect aren't enough to generate media interest. You have to give them a reason to cover you. At Alabama, we set out to do two things that we thought would force the media to cover us. First, we began winning conference and national championships as well as the majority of our regular-season meets. Second, we proved that people—lots of people—cared about our team. An average of more than 9,000 fans per meet over the past several years certainly confirmed that point. Those two accomplishments made all the difference. We went from having no coverage at all to holding weekly teleconferences to accommodate all 11 daily newspapers in the state. We have a weekly television program called "The Sarah Patterson Show"; have been covered by local, regional, and national magazines; make regular appearances on the Crimson Tide's weekly radio program; and perform several times a year before national television audiences on CBS, ESPN, and Fox Sports.

Courtesy of Sarah Patterson

Get to know media reporters and editors. They are much more likely to cover someone they have had personal contact with than merely a name in a press release or media guide.

Improving Media Exposure

In the humble beginnings of building your dynasty, you have to make it easy for the media to cover you. This can be done both in regular communication with and reporting to the media, and as special events or information warrants.

Make a list of the local media you'd like to have cover your team. Call the outlets and get the name and phone number of the sports editor. Find out the best way to report results after a competition. Some media sources prefer a phone call, others an e-mail or fax.

Between two and four weeks before the season begins, send each sports editor information about your team, such your schedule, roster, and best time and method to reach you. You may also write short biographies about each player and coach that include athletic, academic, and personal tidbits. An athlete's family may be hosting a foreign exchange student. A player may be a returning all-state performer or have won scholastic awards. Make the information concise, easy to read, and accurate.

Before a competition, send an e-mail or fax reminding the media of your event. Include any pertinent facts about the competition, such as the date, time, and place; information about your opponent; special significance of the event (perhaps a win will clinch the city championship or break the school record for consecutive victories); and any special plans for the event (a raffle give-away at halftime or a star athlete from another team will be in attendance).

You may have media relations specialists at your school, but if not, be prepared to host any members of the media that attend the event. Provide them with a press pass and parking pass, especially if either require payment. Set up a special place for them to sit, with easy access to an electrical outlet and phone line if possible. Provide refreshments such as sodas and snacks before or during the competition to make them feel welcome and appreciated. Make yourself and your athletes available after the competition to provide quotes.

As soon after the event as possible, be very diligent about reporting the results to the media, regardless of the outcome. Be prepared to share the score, top performers, and key points in the contest. Reporters may not always be able to include the extra information, but they certainly won't if you don't tell them. Your goal is to get the media in the habit of expecting your results, so you must be reliable about reporting them. A dependable student manager, assistant coach, or parent may be able to help you with the reporting. Reporters operate under tight deadlines, so the sooner you inform them of the results, the more likely it is they will be able to include them. If your event ends at 2 p.m., don't wait until 9 p.m. to call in.

Throughout the season there are numerous ways to keep your program on the media's radar. Invite them to watch a practice or accompany you on an away competition. Their time with the team will give them a better sense for your program's goals, challenges, and personality. Share any human-interest stories that come up. Let them know of upcoming clinics, camps, special events, or community appearances. Write your own stories about an event, the season, or a special player and submit them. Invite them into the locker room for the pre- or postcompetition talk with the team.

Expanding Your Concept of the Media

When most people think of media, the local newspaper and television stations are what come to mind. But you can use many other forms of media to get your program's name in front of the public. The initial impact may not seem as significant, but a grassroots effort to publicize your team will pay dividends in the long run.

Don't overlook your local radio stations. Their on-air personalities can mention your team on the air, host a special event for you, or conduct a remote broadcast from one of your competitions to attract attention. Provide them with giveaways such as team T-shirts, posters, or miniballs.

Local radio talk shows are a great way to increase exposure. Have supporters call in to talk about your team. The more calls the radio stations get about your program, the more others hear about it. The more they hear about it, the more perceived interest in it. The more perceived interest in it, the greater the likelihood that the radio station will invite you to be an in-studio guest, which generates more interest. It's an upward spiral if you can get it started. I have done many live broadcasts in the early hours of the morning just to promote one of our athletic events, but the opportunities available are certainly worth any effort or inconvenience incurred.

Many communities have free publications about local events in their area, and the staff will be willing to include your schedule, team photo, or story. Regional newspapers may also cover your team, especially if a member of your team or your team's main rival is from their area. Specialty sports publications, magazines, or community calendars are another possibility for getting your schedule in front of possible fans, as are school or university newsletters, newspapers, and alumni magazines.

The Internet also is a valuable tool for keeping current fans informed and reaching out to new support bases. Information about the Crimson Tide gymnastics team can be found on the official university Web site as well as our own booster club Web site. Make sure the Web site address gets to as many people as possible, and keep the information updated. Post the season's schedule, results, statistics, and special events. Write season updates or behind-the-scenes reports about competitions or road trips. Have players write diaries about the season from their points of view. Include question-and-answer stories from coaches and players. Fans like to feel a part of the team, and having the inside information will make them more loyal followers.

Getting Others Involved

Most colleges have marketing and media relations personnel with whom you should work to publicize your program. Those at larger schools will be able to take on more of the workload, whereas smaller schools may not have any or enough bodies to help as much as they'd like. In that case, you may be able to tap into local marketing or advertising specialists to help as a gift in kind.

If you do have to spearhead most of your publicity, marketing, and media efforts, careful planning and selective recruiting will save you time and reap more widespread rewards than if you haphazardly tried to do it all yourself. By putting forth a focused effort and expressing genuine appreciation, you can find several groups that could be eager to help you carry the torch.

Involve your student-athletes as walking, talking billboards for your event. Encourage them to invite their family, friends, and—most important—other students to make your sporting event a social gathering. You will find that your student-athletes are a tremendous marketing tool and will be well received within your community.

Support from the student body also can be beneficial to your program, so market to them and make them feel special. We currently have a new student organization called the Ten Troupe that receives 150 of the most prime seats in our arena. Although thousands of students have attended our events over the years, these special students receive five different T-shirts, dinner, and front-row seats for the price of $15 per season. Few college students can turn down T-shirts, free food, and the opportunity to support their university from the best seats in the house. High school students also can enjoy this type of entertainment as well, and you can usually find a local sponsor interested in helping defray the cost of implementing such a program.

Don't forget to reward your student support groups for their participation. We have received donations from local businesses willing to donate items such as DVD players, mountain bikes, and video systems, which we give away in drawings during the competition. This creates an atmosphere of excitement and can reinforce the connection you have made with your student support group. Student groups bring a fun and energetic dynamic to your event and bring a different dimension to sport entertainment.

Extend a special invitation to the faculty and staff at your school or university, either by having the student-athletes themselves personally invite them or creating a special flyer for them. The effort can help bridge a gap that sometimes exists between academics and athletics. Relations with the administration and faculty often are greatly improved when they see the dedication and effort the student-athletes are making in their sport.

Create a booster club to support your program. These groups can consist of parents of current or former athletes, interested community or business leaders, or friends who want to be involved. A well-organized group can provide support in a number of ways. They can help brainstorm about new ideas, lend an adult perspective to a situation, spearhead fund-raising and marketing efforts, and provide emotional support for you and the players. Regular meetings will make your special events run more efficiently. All they ask for in return is appreciation and a feeling of being part of your program.

Get children involved by forming a club especially for them to join for a small fee. You may use them as ball kids, have them form a tunnel through which your team runs before or after the competition, or invite them to a special clinic where they can interact with the players. Give each child a

T-shirt, make them feel special, and then sit back and watch them bring their parents back time and again.

Building exposure for your team is difficult, but the rewards are well worth the effort. Generally, an athlete's experience with your program will be enhanced if competitions take place before a crowd and there is ample community interest. Exposure also increases awareness of your athletes' hard work and could increase their chances of earning honors or attracting the attention of a higher-level team, such as a college or professional coach or scout. Increased support leads to extra revenue that can be used for special events such as banquets, an out-of-state competition, or new equipment that might not be affordable without supplementing your the budget.

Remember that your first priority is to help your athletes and team improve their performances and enjoy their time on the team, but realize also that increasing awareness of your program will go a long way toward improving their experience.

20

Networking

*Make yourself known,
and trust that the true you
will be perceived positively*

Amy Ruley

As a kid I frequently organized our neighborhood games. I went door to door, recruiting as many people as I could to come out to play. I loved to put the teams together, design the plays, and direct the action. In a sense those were my first efforts at coaching. My interest in sports continued from playground sports to organized athletics.

I participated in every sport offered for girls at Lowell High School in Indiana and went on to play basketball and field hockey at Purdue. However, in 1974, my freshman year, Purdue did not sponsor women's intercollegiate sports through the athletic department. That was a privilege reserved for male athletes. It was two years after Title IX legislation had been passed, but athletic opportunities for women were limited and organized through the co-recreation office. My first networking experiences came when I met other female athletes on campus who wanted more organized and competitive experiences. Together we made telephone calls, wrote letters, administered petitions, and even organized a sit-in at the university president's office. Our big day came in October, when central administration decided that the university should sponsor the women's sports teams through the department of intercollegiate athletics. It was a strong demonstration of how networking—this time with other students, fellow student-athletes, parents, administrators, and supporters—was a positive way to accomplish a goal.

Women must become comfortable with networking; unfortunately, they have not embraced the concept as readily as men. Men traditionally have been better at it; the "good ole boys" method of networking has existed for years. Many people would describe women as more social than men, but networking has a reputation for being businesslike, structured, and a way to use others for personal gain (but ignoring them as people). Although at times networking can take on a self-serving air, we women may need to change our perception, understand its importance, and recognize what it looks like in practice. At its core, networking means developing meaningful relationships in our professional lives.

Reasons to Network

The reasons for networking are numerous. First, women coming into the profession of coaching need each other. We need to network with male coaches too, but athletics is such a competitive environment that women can benefit greatly from the support of other women. We understand the career challenges that are unique to our gender. We can support each other, provide information, give advice, and offer friendship as a result of having had similar experiences.

Furthering your skills. Networking is a great way to increase your knowledge about your sport. When I was a college student-athlete, I met with many other people who shared my interests. I sought information from my talented coaches and networked with them to understand more about coaching. Deb Gebhardt, my first basketball coach in college, was a very good teacher of fundamental skills. Ruth Jones, my coach in my junior and senior years, was an outstanding tactician. Fred Schaus, the men's basketball coach at Purdue at the time, allowed me to watch his team's practices. In addition, I attended the AAHPERD conventions and as many coaching clinics as I could fit into my schedule. I have always admired former Boilermaker and all-time coaching great John Wooden, whom I had the pleasure of meeting. I have read many books and articles by him or about him and his method of coaching, and I've listened to his presentations at various clinics. At the time I was preparing for a coaching career, there were few female coaches available to serve as role models. Today, however, many successful female coaches populate the world of sports.

> Networking is a great way to increase your knowledge about your sport. Meet with other people who share your interests, and seek information from many talented coaches and networked with them to understand more about coaching.

Hiring and getting hired. Networking is an important part of the search for a coaching position. Prior relationships with other coaches, whether as a player, assistant, or peer, can be a big asset in securing a job. The Women's Basketball Coaches Association (WBCA) convention provides a great opportunity to learn more about women's basketball, get to know other coaches, and look for jobs. As a young coach, you have to sell yourself and let other coaches know that you have the skills, interest, and enthusiasm to do the job. Most coaches who are hiring will call other coaches, explain what type of person they are looking for, and ask if they can recommend anyone.

Mentoring. A number of my former players have chosen to coach after college, and they keep in touch with me over the years. Some call for advice concerning challenges in their jobs—perhaps they are looking for an offense that will fit their personnel, or they may be struggling with a parent who challenges their decisions. Sometimes they are excited about something that has happened and want to share their enthusiasm with someone who will understand and appreciate how they feel. So, in a sense, mentoring is a networking activity as well.

An important part of mentoring is encouraging players and younger coaches to network and offering suggestions about ways to do it. They may have a natural talent for it or they may have to work at it. Either way, learning to network will help them learn and achieve in their careers. Our former and current players help us with our summer camps, which is a great opportunity for them to be around other coaches. They also spend time with our boosters and fans, which can lead to possible job opportunities. Generally, women need to be exposed to these types of socializing and networking opportunities.

Promoting your team. Networking can be a positive tool to promote your program and athletes. The time you spend in conversation with other coaches makes them more aware of what your program has accomplished and the quality of your athletes. Many times coaches in professional organizations are involved in selecting athletes for honors or awards, and they need to make educated decisions. Your athletes may have the opportunity to be recognized if those coaches know you and your program well.

Recruiting. Recruiting at summer tournaments provides a major networking opportunity for everyone involved. Players have a chance to interact with players they do not normally compete against; high school and Amateur Athletic Union (AAU) coaches can meet coaches from other parts of the nation. College coaches can enjoy each other's company in a less competitive environment than during the season. This may be thought of as socializing, but it is a form of networking. Our coaching staff makes sure to wear our North Dakota State University apparel so that people know we are there. However, responsibility goes along with the visibility. We cannot be loud, obnoxious, and undisciplined. Instead, we must be friendly, take time to communicate with different people, sell our program, and tell our story. We never know when we will get a phone call from someone we met who knows a prospective student-athlete, assistant coach, or donor.

Fund-raising. Fund-raising is another important reason to network. It is an area in which many women need to improve, from both the asking and giving perspectives. Asking for money is not comfortable for many coaches, but it is an important responsibility of the job in most cases. Improved opportunities and experiences for your players may depend on fund-raising. Donating to your program gives boosters an opportunity to help and allows them to get involved. Encouraging former athletes who have had positive experiences to give back to the program is becoming as common a practice for women as it has been with men. The history of women as participants in organized scholastic or collegiate sports is not as long as that of men. We are only now building a strong, deep pool of women who not only competed but were well supported while doing so. Programs with full-time coaches, full scholarships, significant budgets for team travel and equipment, and facilities in which to practice and play are now the rule as opposed to the exception. The first athletes and coaches who enjoyed the benefits of improved support after the passing of Title IX are now emerging with the wherewithal to give back to their sport and school. More and more of these women realize that they have that responsibility and are stepping forward.

Our former players have been very generous in creating the Amy Ruley Endowment, which is an athletic fund. With alumnae sending in several thousand dollars a year, it has grown to be a significant fund. Networking

Courtesy of Amy Ruley

Be a role model to players by stressing the importance of networking and demonstrating the ways to network. Learning to network will help them learn and achieve in their careers.

with our alumni keeps the bond strong and provides an avenue to encourage them to give: "OK, gals, you had opportunities and enjoyed scholarships. We need you to help us continue in that direction."

I work with our assistant athletic director in charge of development in any way I can to help him in his job, including accompanying him to meet potential donors. Fund-raising in general is a challenging job. Those who are successful at it are able to convey a genuine interest in the potential donor while conveying commitment to their cause.

Sometimes financial support comes from unexpected places. For example, the elderly mother of an alumnus of the university was interested in our program. Her son shared her story with me, and over the years she and I developed a bond. During certain times, such as in our pregame radio show, I would acknowledge her on her birthday or other special occasions. All of her elderly friends thought that was great and asked how she had made that connection. It made her feel so good! When she passed away, her son came in with a $25,000 gift, based on the relationship I had developed with his mother and how important it was to her. He has continued to donate to that fund, which has grown significantly.

How to Network

Many activities of everyday life as a coach involve networking. The simple communication with audiences and individuals that occurs on a daily basis is a form of networking. I try to take time each day to send congratulatory, thank-you, or general notes. I may speak at a local service group or have lunch with an interest group. In addition, I speak to our athletics booster group once a week during the basketball season. I read and return e-mail correspondence and telephone calls. The Internet is a great tool for keeping in touch and networking with coaches across the country. Whenever I notice a colleague has had a great weekend, I e-mail a note to her congratulating her on the win and asking about various aspects of the game.

Opportunities abound for coaches to get involved in their sport and network. The following are a few of the opportunities I have enjoyed during my tenure at North Dakota State University.

Professional organizations. I got involved with the professional organizations as soon as I started coaching. I remember when the Women's Basketball Coaches Association was first getting started. The WBCA is now a solid organization and the major voice for women's basketball. My first involvement with the WBCA other than as a member was as a representative. Later I served as the executive committee secretary. My 13 years on the board allowed me to get to know a variety of people. Through the NCAA I also participated on the Women's Basketball Rules Committee, which enabled me to get to know more coaches in the women's game as well as in the men's game.

Getting involved with USA Basketball was also a great networking experience for me. I got to know college coaches outside of NCAA Division II, with whom I normally would not have had much contact. Committees that are composed of a variety of coaches offer opportunities as well. I was fortunate to serve on one that selected athletes to compete on summer teams. I also worked with USA Basketball as an assistant coach in 1995. Even though you must commit four or five weeks during what would have been your down time, the experience is incredible.

Clinics and camps. At the start of my coaching career, I worked at various summer camps in Minnesota and directed our camps at NDSU. It was a big time commitment, but it augmented my salary and gave me a chance to interact with others in the profession. Coaching clinics, where you can network with coaches at all levels who are presenting and attending, are a great avenue to meet new people and make new contacts. Coaches need to be involved with other coaches at all levels, not only those in their own circle of competition. College coaches can learn from high school c oaches; club coaches can learn from middle school coaches.

Coaching clinics, where you can network with coaches at all levels who are presenting and attending, are a great avenue to meet new people and make new contacts.

Other coaches. Many college coaches find it invaluable to let high school and club coaches know about their programs, priorities, and methods of coaching. With that information they can provide meaningful feedback to and about female student-athletes in their area who are potential collegiate athletes. This also works in the other direction for those of you who are high school and club coaches. Developing a rapport with coaches of college programs at all levels gives you a foot in the door when you are trying to help an athlete to continue her athletic career in college. College coaches who are familiar with your program, respect the way you coach, and know what you expect from your players are more likely to seriously consider your recommendations.

Assistant coaches often are better at networking than head coaches. They are apt to be friendlier with each other, more relaxed, and appear to appreciate each other's company and conversion. They also seem less paranoid than head coaches, who may be more nervous about sharing trade secrets.

You can also network with coaches of men's teams. I had that opportunity while working on a NCAA committee; Roy Williams chaired the men's basketball rules committee while I chaired the women's committee. I had the pleasure of visiting informally and sharing dinner and stories with the members of the men's committee. That was a great experience! You may not realize how many opportunities like that exist unless you are interested and willing to put the time into them.

Alumnae. Keeping in touch with former players is a huge part of my job. I have been at NDSU for 25 years, and the program has a very active alumni group. We have an alumni event every year in conjunction with the game against our rival. The alumni play against each other in uniform before our game and are introduced at our game's halftime. Afterward, we have a social at the campus Alumni Center. In addition we have an alumni weekend at my lake house in August. Former players leave their husbands, kids, pets, and worries behind and enjoy their friends for the weekend. Those two weekend events strengthen the bonds between current and former players and staff. Many of the women who have become good friends through those alumni games and weekends at the lake now form a terrific support group for our program.

The alumni in general, not only our former athletes, are an important group with whom to foster a positive relationship. I attend their meetings as often as possible, whether they are local or across the country. These people can be great resources about potential student-athletes around the country.

Media. Media personalities are also important people in your network. I stay connected with our television affiliates, especially the one that airs our basketball show on Sundays. I receive much information from them, and I provide them with insight and information about our team that will help them promote us. I also try to keep the sportswriters at the *Fargo Forum,* a daily newspaper, informed. Radio personalities are also a part of our networking circle. With the broadcast of our games and our weekly radio show, the community is kept informed about our women's basketball program. The more we educate these broadcasters about our players and our program, the better job they will do in telling our team's story. Coaches must see to it that members of the media receive the necessary information. This is easier to do when your team is winning and not as easy when you're losing. However, coaches have a responsibility, regardless of wins or losses, to take time consistently with the media if they want the media to give them time and endorsement in return.

Much has changed since my first years as a coach. In the early days, I wore many different hats as a coach—statistician, trainer, classroom teacher, and marketer, to name a few. Although the job has not slowed much since then, it has changed. Now, I'm surrounded by professionals who handle many of the jobs I previously tackled. I focus more attention on actual coaching and have more time for the team. Networking is the one area that has grown in terms of time spent, but I enjoy the contact and the camaraderie that go with it. I encourage young coaches to get involved with professional organizations and to work at networking to improve their career development.

Index

A

academic eligibility 228-229
academics 171-172
accountability, player 33
achieving commitment 95-96
activities, off-season 141
activities, team-building 212-213
advertising 236-237
AFCA (American Football Coaches
      Association) 16
aggressive parents 225-226
alcohol consumption 23
alumnae 251-252
American Football Coaches Association
      (AFCA) 16
Amy Ruley Endowment 246
anorexic behavior 229
assistant coaches
    empowering 160-161
    ethical behavior of 22-23
    focus 104-105
    qualities of 156-159
    responsibilities 159-161
athlete. *See* player

B

Barmore, Leon 65, 67-68
Barnes, Rita 128
behavior
    players 8-9
    self-defeating 229-230
    unethical 14-15
Bennis, Warren 38
Bergen, Paul 114
Berry, Ceal 65
bias 76
Big Ten Conference win 65
Blair, Gary 65

bonding 211
booster activity 18
booster clubs 242
Bragel, Tannie 52
Brand, Myles 14
Brennan, Frankie 160
Brennan, Frank Jr. 156, 162
Brown, Warren 65
Bryant, Paul "Bear" 230
buddy system 211
bulimic behavior 227

C

Caldwell, Nikki 140
CBS 237
cell phones 226. *See also* phones
changing focus 108-110
chronic fatigue syndrome 115-116
coaches as used-car dealers 91
coaching challenges 114-115
coaching clinics 248
Coaching Code of Ethics (USOC) 16
coaching skills, effective 65-66
coaching stress 116
coaching tasks, daily 130-132
coach-parent communication 221-224
coach-player interaction 67-68
coach-player relationship 65-66
code of ethics, AFCA 16
code of rules and ethics, NCAA 17
college preparation 171-172
commitment 95-99, 199-200
commitments to recruitment 186
commitment to training 93-94
communication
    avenues of 144-146
    coach-parent 221-224
    discipline and 83-84

communication *(continued)*
    to establish team focus 109-110
    as a leadership tool 48-50
    methods of 174-176
    with parents 175
    program management 170-171
    in recruitment 183-184
    with staff 144-145
    teaching team members 196-198
    for team motivation 68-72
    uniform method of 10
compassion 174
competition, healthy 9
competition schedule development 168
competitiveness 57-58
competitive players 52-54
compliance office 19
conflict resolution 146
conflict-resolution skills 159
connecting with players 58
Conradt, Jody 64, 115, 119
consequences 83-85
consistency 4
conviction 5
courtesy 226
Covey, Sean 135
Cruz, Aury 53

D

Darsch, Nancy 65
Davis, Rochelle 128
DeBoer, Kathy 52, 54
decision making 77-79
decision making, teaching 10
decision making process 75
delegating tasks 128-129
depth-chart concept 223
DeSensi, Joy Theresa 15
Dewey, Carol 52
discipline
    external 89-91
    external to internal transition 92-93
    as a key to success 200-201
    player 24-26
    the web theory 56
disruptors, team 214-215
documentation 169
Dorrance, Anson 127
dressing for success 32
drills, need for variety in 144

E

Edwards, Teresa 69

effective coaching skills 65-66
effective communication 197-198
elements of a great teacher 74
eligibility, academic 228-229
elite athletes 180
e-mail 176
encouraging competitiveness 57-58
energy signature 89
Epstein-Barr virus 115-116
Erwin, John 108
ESPN 67, 237
ethics
    assistant coaches 22-23
    college recruiting 18-19
    definition of 15
    game coaching 20
    overselling 21
    recruitment 20-21
    reporting violations 19
    team 21-24
Ethics in Sport Management(DeSensi;
        Rosenberg) 15
evaluating staff 147-151
events and scheduling 167-169
expectations 83-85
external discipline 89-91
external to internal discipline transition
        92-93

F

family dynamics 227-228
Fargo Forum 252
favoritism 220
fear as motivation 71
feedback 111, 151
field hockey team, Old Dominion University
        11
financial support 248-249
Finding the Winning Edge (Walsh) 40-41
flexibility in recruiting 182-183
Florida State softball team rules 24
focus
    changing 108-110
    definition of 102
    game 110-111
    hole in the dam theory 103
    teaching 104-105
followers, characteristics of 8
food as a bonding tool 213
Fox Sports 239
Franklin, Benjamin 85
freshman eligibility rules 171-172
fund-raising efforts 169, 246

G

Gamble, Gil 74
game coaching, unethical 20
game focus 110-111
game objectives and strategies 131
game preparation 11-12
Gearin, Nadine 138
Gebhardt, Deb 245
Gender and Competition (DeBoer) 54
gender differences in sports 54-56
get-acquainted exercises 196
Gilles, Tom 104
goals
    communicating 48
        team 45-46
goal setting 88-89, 106-108, 134, 210-212
Gokberk, Aycan 56
graduate assistants 140-141

H

halftime talks 70
harassment, sexual 20
head coach promotion 162-163
hiring process 138-141
Holdsclaw, Chamique 186
home competition management 168
Hoosiers (movie) *110*
Howard, Gwen 176
Hunter, Jessie 198

I

illegal booster activity 18
Ingram, Cecil "Hootie" 232
"inner circle" 45-48
international student-athletes 187

J

Johnson, Carol 192
Jones, Ruth 247
Josephson Institute of Ethics 26-27

K

Kearney, Bev 117
Krzyzewski, Mike 200

L

Landsberger, Joe 75
Lawler, Ann Marie 232
"Law of the Lid" 42-43
leaders
    characteristics of 8
    locker room 46-48
leadership
    definition of 38-39
    player 33

Leadership Moment (Useem) 50
Ley, Nancy 178
Lindsey, Shelly 104
locker room leaders 46-48
Lockwood, Dean 140
long-term goal setting 134
Lopiano, Donna 132, 178
loyalty 140, 158
Luckenbill, Kristen 46
Luft, Tina 127

M

Magee, Melissa 204
managers 140-141, 141-142
managing stress 116-119
Manz, Jenny 53, 57
marketing ideas 236
marketing personnel 241
marketing plan development 233-236
Marsden, Greg 232
maturity 186
Maxwell, John C. 15, 26, 42, 45
Meadows, Michelle 193-194
media
    coverage 237-239
    exposure 239-240
    networking 252
media relations specialists 240, 241
media representatives 35-36
meetings 175, 192-193
mentoring 152-153, 247-248
Moore, Billie 152
moral algebra 85
motivating role players 68
motivational quotations 68-70

N

NABC (National Association of Basketball
        Coaches) 14
National Association of Basketball Coaches
        (NABC) 14
National Collegiate Athletic Association
        (NCAA)
    code of rules and ethics 17
    compliance office 22
    The Summit 117
    unethical behavior of coaches 14
National High School Athletic Coaches
        Association 126
National Soccer Coaches Association of
        America 126
National Soccer Coach of the Year 126
NCAA. *See* National Collegiate Athletic
        Association (NCAA)

NCAA compliance office 22
NCAA News 22
negative recruiting 187
negative self-talk 95
nepotism 220
networking 246-252
NICAA Division II national tournament 107
nonverbal behavior 59
notebooks 176

O

Observation of a Practice 222
Office of Civil Rights 34
off-season activities 141
On Becoming a Leader (Bennis) 38
organization 126-127
organizational chart, staff 138-139
Overbeck, Carla 40

P

parent communication 175
parent/player meeting 223-224
parents, aggressive 225-226
parents as coaches 19-20
Perry, Tonya 106
perspective 4-5, 9
phones 176, 226
physiological changes 186-187
player
    accountability 33
    behaviors 8-9
    commitment to training 93-94
    discipline 24-26
    early commitment 186-187
    level of dedication 67-68
    managing stress 120-121
    off-court development 172-173
    personalities 198
    physiological changes 186-187
    role on the team 58
    statistical information 226
    time management 134-135
players
    building self-confidence in 58
    competitive 52-54
    connecting with 58
    evaluation of staff members 147-151
    focus 105-106
    positive talk for 58
player selection 81-87
player self-analysis 210-212
playing time 70-71, 219-220

postgame talks 70
practice, structured 200
practice scheduling 168
Predictive Index 145-146
pregame talks 70
preseason training 130-131
pride 7-8
Priestly, Joseph 85
problem players 224-225
problem solving, teaching 10
professionalism
    appearance and presentation 31-32
    definition of 28
    in recruiting 29-30
professionalism towards staff 34-35
professional organizations 250
program continuity 158-159
program promotion 30-32, 235-236
prudential algebra 85
Psych, the 212-213
punishment, player 25
Pyramid of Success 111

R

radio stations 241
radio talk shows 241
realistic goal setting 106-108
recognizing stress responses 115-116
recruit expectations 184-185
recruiting
    challenges 186-188
    coaches violation of rules 16-17
    communication 183-184
    negative 187
    professionalism in 29-30
    stress 116
    team feedback 183
recruiting pool 180
recruiting process 179-183
recruiting profile 181-182
Reese, Eddie 117
resource management 169-170
respect
    coach-athlete relations 195-196
    coaching philosophy of 9
    professionalism and 32
    for rules 173
responsibility 9
responsibility delegating 118
rewards as motivation 71-72
Riise, Hege 40, 41, 43
Roberts, Tiffany 43-45

role models 26, 84
role players, motivating 68
Rosenberg, Danny 15
roster building 41-42
rules and ethics, NCAA code of 17
rumors 30

S

Schaus, Fred 247
scholarships 184, 225-227
See You At The Top 110
self-communication 176
self-discipline 93-94, 95
self-doubt 194
self-talk, negative 95
setting expectations 143
sexual harassment 20
short-term goal setting 134
Simpson, Alice 52
Sinclair, Sue 104
skills, conflict-resolution 159
Smith, Dean 103
Smith, Katie 69
Snell, Eleanor 6
softball team rules, Florida State 24
Sports Illustrated 54, 142
staff diversity 140
staff duties 141-142
staff-evaluation questions 148-151
staff evaluations 147-151
staff guidelines 161-162
staff involvement 143-144
staff organizational chart 138-139
staff secretary 140
stress
     coaches control of 121
     player 120-121
     recognizing responses 115-116
stress in coaching 116
stress management 116-119
structured practice 200
student-athletes, high school recruitment
          of 19
student-athletes, international 187
student body support 240
Study Guides and Strategies 75
success, definition of 111
success, dressing for 32
Summitt, Pat 178, 231
support from the student body 240
support network 117-118
support personnel 138

Swoops, Sheryl 69

T

teaching focus 104-105
team
     budget 169
     building 130-131
     commitment 97-99
     ethics 21-24
     focus 106-108
     meetings 48, 120
     policies 173-174
     rules 24
team-building activities 212-213
team captains 215-216
team cohesion 207-210
team disrupters 214-215
team mission 172
team vision 39-41
Ten Troupe 242
Texas Excellence Award for Outstanding
          Teachers 126
The 7 Habits of Highly Effective Teens
          (Covey) 135
The 21 Irrefutable Laws of Leadership
          (Maxwell) 42
The Leadership Moment (Useem) 38
the Psych 210-211
There's No Such Thing As "Business" Ethics
          (Maxwell) 15, 26
"The Sarah Patterson Show" 237
Thomas, Hope 194
Thomas, Isiah 108
Thomas, Tom 108
20-hour-per-week rule, NCAA 17
time management 132-136
traditions 210-211
training
     player commitment to 93-94
     preseason 130-131
     program development 79-81
transition 92
travel plans 168
trust 193-195
tryouts 219-220

U

United States Olympic Committee (USOC)
          16
unity among coaches 161
University Inter-scholastic League 130
USA Basketball 65, 250

used-car dealer analogy 91
Useem, Michael 38, 50
USOC (United States Olympic Committee) 16

V

VanDerveer, Tara 65
variety in drills 144
video
    as a communication tool 49
    for player feedback 111

W

Walsh, Bill 40
Warlick, Holly 140
Watson, Marge 6

Web sites
    Josephson Institute of Ethics 26
    Study Guides and Strategies
        (Landsberger) 75
web theory 56
West, Deborah 204
Williams, Elizabeth (Libby) 6
Williams, Roy 249
Women's Basketball Coaches Association 250
Women's Basketball Rules Committee 250
Women's World Cup team 43-45
Wooden, John 111, 247
work ethic 201
Wynn, Katie 142

About the Editor

With more than 630 wins in 26 years of coaching collegiate volleyball, including 7 conference championships and 14 postseason appearances, **Dr. Cecile Reynaud** ranked in the top 9 in career victories among active Division I coaches when she retired from Florida State University after the 2001 season. Reynaud received the prestigious George J. Fischer Volleyball Leader Award from USA Volleyball in 1996 in recognition of her contributions to the sport. She is a former president of the American Volleyball Coaches Association and was a member of the Volleyball Hall of Fame selection committee. Reynaud served 12 years on the USA Volleyball board of directors and 3 years on its executive committee. She earned her PhD in 1998 and is a faculty member in the sport management program at Florida State University. She lives in Tallahassee, Florida.

About the Contributors

Beth Anders has led the Old Dominion University field hockey team to nine NCAA championships, posting a 430-64-7 (.865) record since 1980. She has served three stints as head coach of the U.S. field hockey team—1985, 1990-93, and 2003-04. Ten of her former players have earned spots on U.S., Dutch, and Argentine Olympic teams, and 10 more have played for the U.S. national team. As a player, Anders represented the United States in international play from 1970 to 1984, scoring an Olympic-record eight goals to help her team clinch the bronze medal in 1984.

Terry Crawford has coached 6 national championship teams, 12 Olympians, and more than 125 All-Americans since 1974. She has been director of track and field and cross country at California Polytechnic State University since 1997 after beginning as its women's head coach in 1993. She served as head coach of the 1988 Olympic team and was inducted into the USA Track and Field Coaches' Hall of Fame in 1996. Her national titles came while she was at the University of Tennessee, her alma mater, and the University of Texas. The latter remains the only program to win the Triple Crown, capturing the cross country, indoor, and outdoor track and field titles under her tutelage in 1986. She is currently president of the United States Track Coaches Association and is the chair for the Coaches Advisory Committee of the United States Track and Field Federation.

Photo by Walt Smith

Diane Davey has a career record of 408-121-56, and her teams rank in the top 5 in the nation. Under her guidance, the Plano Senior High Wildcats have won 4 UIL Texas State Soccer Championships, 16 district championships, and 8 regional championships. In addition to receiving the prestigious Plano Independent Secondary Teacher of the Year Award in 2002, she was named NSCAA National Coach of the Year in 1991 and 1997, as well as NHSACA National Coach of the Year in 1998. Davey was also a recipient of the Lillian B. Rhodes Award, presented by the Texas Exes (a University of Texas organization), as one of 12 outstanding teachers in the state of Texas in 2003.

Photo by David Gonzales

Lele Forood has been a Stanford University tennis coach for 8 of the program's 13 NCAA titles and all 16 Pac-10 Conference championships. Three national titles have come since her promotion to head coach in 2001, the rest in her 13-year tenure as an assistant and associate head coach. The 2004 Pac-10 Coach of the Year, 2003 Wilson/ITA National Coach of the Year, and 1997 ITA National Assistant Coach of the Year, Forood was the first female head coach to guide a team to an NCAA title. She was an All-American at Stanford in 1976, ranked as high as 30th on the women's professional tour, and was the 1975 national amateur singles and doubles champion.

Nell Fortner coached the U.S. basketball team to a gold medal in the 2000 Olympics after serving as a national team assistant in 1996 and national team coach from 1997 to 2000. She also led her team to win the 1998 World Championships. Fortner earned *Basketball Times'* National Coach of the Year award in 1997 after leading Purdue University to a share of the Big Ten title. She spent three years as head coach and general manager of the WNBA's Indiana Fever, which she led to its first playoff appearance in 2002. Before being named Auburn University's head coach, Fortner also worked as an ESPN studio analyst and commentator from 2001 to 2004 inducted into the Texas Sports Hall of Fame for her achievements on the basketball and volleyball courts while in high school and at the University of Texas.

Dorothy Gaters is the winningest coach in the history of Illinois high school sports, regardless of gender or sport. As head basketball coach at Chicago's Marshall High School since 1974, Gaters has amassed an overall record of 795-86 (.904). Her teams have won seven state titles and 23 city league championships. More than 20 of her athletes have gone on to have successful collegiate basketball careers. Gaters has earned Illinois Coach of the Year honors 7 times and District Coach of the Year 23 times, and she has been inducted into the WBCA Hall of Fame and four other city and state organizations' Halls of Fame. She also has coached in various USA Basketball competitions.

Dr. JoAnne Graf is the all-time winningest college softball coach in the nation, with a combined slow-pitch and fast-pitch record of 1,276-367-6 (.776). As head coach at Florida State University since 1979, she has posted winning seasons every year of her career. Her fast-pitch teams have advanced to the College World Series 7 times and the NCAA tournament 17 times, and they have won 10 Atlantic Coast Conference titles. Her slow-pitch teams won two national and three state championships before making the switch to fast-pitch in 1984. Graf, four-time NFCA Coach of the Year and six-time ACC Coach of the Year, was inducted into the NFCA Hall of Fame in 2003.

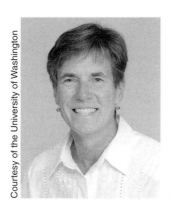

Courtesy of the University of Washington

Jan Harville's University of Washington crew dominated the NCAA team championships since their inauguration in 1997, winning three times and placing second twice. UW won 11 consecutive Pac-10 Conference titles, while Harville earned 9 Conference Coach of the Year honors. Retired after the 2003 season after more than 25 years at UW as a rower, assistant, and head coach, Harville has been named National Coach of the Year and USRowing Woman of the Year, and she was inducted into the National Rowing Hall of Fame. She was an assistant coach on the 1996 Olympic team after having been an Olympian herself in 1980 and 1984.

Kim Kincer led the Methodist College golf team to NCAA Division III championships in each of her five years as head coach from 1998 to 2002 after working several years as a golf professional. She was named the National Golf Coaches Association Division III National Coach of the Year in 2001 and was honored as *Golfweek Magazine*'s National Coach of the Year on four occasions. The Lady Monarchs won 13 tournament titles in Kincer's tenure, during which she produced 18 All-Americans, four NGCA Players of the Year, six academic All-Americans, and two individual national champions. She currently is associate director of Professional Golf Management and director of PGM education at Methodist College.

Courtesy of Northwestern University Media Services

Marcia McDermott parlayed her success as a soccer player for the University of North Carolina into success as a coach. In her second year at the helm of the Carolina Courage of the Women's United Soccer Association, her team captured the professional league's regular-season championship before winning the Founders Cup II in 2002. She also spent two years as the assistant general manager of the Courage. At the collegiate level, McDermott helped to build programs at the University of Maryland, the University of Arkansas, and Northwestern University. While at NU, she was named the NSCAA's Great Lakes Region Coach of the Year in 1996 and 1998. McDermott was an All-American, co-captain, and three-time national champion for the UNC Tarheels.

Sarah Patterson's University of Alabama gymnastics teams have won four NCAA team championships, finishing in the top three a total of 15 times in the past 19 years. The Crimson Tide's head coach since 1979, Patterson has a 333-73-4 (.817) record, including 19 NCAA regional titles and five Southeastern Conference championships. Her athletes have won 17 individual national titles and earned almost 200 All-America honors. Alabama has led the nation in attendance twice, both times averaging more than 10,000 fans per meet. Patterson has been named National Coach of the Year four times and SEC Coach of the Year three times. She also has been inducted into the Alabama Sports Hall of Fame.

Mary Jo Peppler is one of volleyball's all-time legends. She was named the sport's third most influential person of the 20th century and earned a spot on USA Volleyball's All-Great team. Her star-studded playing career spanned almost 40 years and included appearances in the Olympics and Pan American Games, on the USA Volleyball team, and on the professional circuit. Peppler also has coached more than 100 All-Americans and 12 national championship teams at the AAU, USAV, collegiate, and professional levels of play. Currently the director of coaching for the Coast Volleyball Club, she received the Founders Award from the American Volleyball Coaches Association and has been inducted into the USAVB, Women's Sports Foundation, AVCA, Volleyball, CBVA, and Cal State-Los Angeles Halls of Fame.

Photo by Steve Smith

Sharon Pfluger has guided the College of New Jersey lacrosse squad to nine NCAA championships and nine other top-three finishes. Heading the most successful Division III lacrosse program, Pfluger has an overall record of 275-19-1 (.934) in that sport. She also coaches the Lions field hockey team, which has won 7 national titles and 16 regional titles. Pfluger has a winning percentage of 89.8 and has compiled an overall record of 345-37-5 in the past 19 years as TCNJ's field hockey coach. In lacrosse, Pfluger was named National Coach of the Year twice and Regional Coach of the Year five times. In field hockey, she received the National Coach of the Year award twice and Regional Coach of the Year award three times. Pfluger earned the 1991 NCAA 10th Anniversary Outstanding Service Award and was inducted into the NFHCA Hall of Fame in 2004 and the New Jersey Lacrosse Hall of Fame's Charter Class in 1997. She is one of only two women featured in the NCAA Hall of Champions' Legends of the Game display.

Courtesy of Colorado Classic Images

Joan Powell has coached the Coronado (Colorado) High School volleyball team since 1976, leading the program to three state championships in 14 appearances in the playoffs. Coronado also has won 3 regional titles, 10 conference championships, and 12 district titles. Powell's overall record is 449-208. Twenty-nine of her athletes have gone on to play volleyball in college, and 15 of them became coaches. She was named Women's Sports Foundation Active Female Coach of the Year in 1989. She also was the YWCA Sportswoman of Colorado Coach of the Year in 1983 and was inducted into their Hall of Fame in 2003. In 2004, she was inducted into the Colorado Springs Sports Hall of Fame. Powell has also refereed three Division II NCAA championships and five Division I NCAA championships.

Lorene Ramsey served as head coach of the Illinois Central College basketball team from 1969 to 2003 and as head softball coach from 1970 to 1998, winning a total of 1,727 games. Her basketball program won five national and 21 regional championships, posting an 887-197 (.818) record along the way. The softball team won 2 national and 16 regional titles, accumulating an 840-309 (.731) mark. More than 250 of her players have advanced to the next level of play. The three-time National Coach of the Year was inducted into the Halls of Fame of the Women's Basketball Coaches Association and the National Fastpitch Softball Coaches Association, as well as the Amateur Softball Association Hall of Fame as a player.

Amy Ruley became the second active NCAA Division II women's basketball coach to reach 600 wins, all at North Dakota State University. Since 1979, her teams have won 5 national championships, advanced to 20 postseason tournaments, and compiled a 605-158 (.793) record. The Bison have won 10 conference titles, and more than 20 of Ruley's former players have joined the coaching ranks. She has been named Coach of the Year on more than 25 occasions at the state, regional, and national levels, including by the Women's Basketball Coaches Association. She earned the WBCA Carol Eckman Award and has been inducted into the Women's Basketball and North Dakota Halls of Fame. As a player, she scored the first points in the history of Purdue University women's basketball. Ruley was inducted into the Purdue Hall of Fame in 2004.

Jill Sterkel has led the University of Texas swimming and diving program to 11 top-10 finishes at the NCAA championships in her first 12 years as UT's head coach. She has guided the Longhorns to six consecutive Big 12 championships and coached six Olympians. In 1996, Texas captured the final Southwest Conference team championship, having won all 14. Sterkel was a part of 13 of the 14 as either a competitor or coach. One of the all-time great swimmers, Sterkel is a four-time Olympian with 2 gold medals, 2 bronze, and 16 national titles to her name. She has been recognized as the Big 12 Conference Women's Swimming Coach of the Year four times and named to the Southwest Conference All-Decade (1980) Women's Swimming Team.

Pat Summitt has won more NCAA basketball titles than any coach besides John Wooden and was the first women's coach to reach 800 victories. The head coach at the University of Tennessee since 1974, Summitt has a record of 852-167 (.836). The Lady Volunteers have won 6 NCAA championships in 11 title-game appearances, along with 15 regional titles and 10 Southeastern Conference championships. Thirty of her athletes have gone on to play at the national, international, or professional levels, and approximately 50 entered the coaching profession. She has been an Olympian as a player (1976), assistant coach (1980), and head coach (1984). Summitt has been named NCAA Coach of the Year six times, Naismith Coach of the Century, and SEC Coach of the Year five times. She was inducted into the Women's Basketball Hall of Fame in 1999 and into the Naismith Memorial Basketball Hall of Fame in 2000.

Mary Wise became the first woman to coach in the NCAA Division I championship game in 2003 when she led the University of Florida volleyball team to the title match, and she is the only woman to coach in more than one Final Four. The Gators have competed in the Final Four 7 times and have won all 13 Southeastern Conference championships since Wise arrived in 1991, during which she has racked up a 431-43 (.909) record. Wise has mentored eight players-turned-coaches, and nine of her athletes have gone on to play nationally, internationally, or professionally. She has been named National Coach of the Year twice, Regional Coach of the Year in 11 of 13 seasons, and SEC Coach of the Year 10 times.

Margie Wright was the first NCAA Division I softball coach to amass 1,000 career victories, more than 950 coming at Fresno State University. Her remarkable 1,126-397-3 (.739) record includes a national title, 6 more top-three finishes, 10 regional championships, and 16 conference titles. Wright also led the U.S. national team to a gold medal at the 1998 ISF world championships. Wright has coached 10 Olympians, and approximately 15 of her former players are coaching softball. She has been named National Coach of the Year, Regional Coach of the Year seven times, and West Coast Conference Coach of the Year eight times. Wright is a member of the NFCA Hall of Fame.